Hawaii, University, Honolulu.

THE DIMENSIONALITY OF NATIONS PROJECT

ATTRIBUTES OF NATIONS
AND
BEHAVIOR OF NATIONS DYADS

1950 - 1965

PRINCIPAL INVESTIGATOR:

RUDOLPH J. RUMMEL
UNIVERSITY OF HAWAII

FIRST ICPR EDITION, 1976

INTER-UNIVERSITY CONSORTIUM FOR POLITICAL RESEARCH
P.O. BOX 1248
ANN ARBOR, MICHIGAN 48106

LIBRARY OF CONGRESS CATALOG CARD NUMBER   75-40620
ISBN 0-89138-121-x

ACKNOWLEDGMENT OF ASSISTANCE

All manuscripts utilizing data made available through the Consortium should acknowledge that fact as well as identify the original collector of the data. The ICPR Council urges all users of ICPR data facilities to follow some adaptation of this statement with the parentheses indicating items to be filled in appropriately or deleted by the individual user.

> The data (and tabulations) utilized in this (publication) were made available (in part) by the Inter-university Consortium for Political Research. The data were originally collected by Rudolph Rummel, University of Hawaii. Neither the original collector of the data nor the Consortium bear any responsibility for the analyses or interpretations presented here.

In order to provide funding agencies with essential information about the use of Archival resources, and to facilitate the exchange of information about ICPR participants' research activities, each user of the ICPR data facilities is expected to send two copies of each completed manuscript to the Consortium. Please indicate in the cover letter which data were used.

TABLE OF CONTENTS

	Page Number
Study Description	i
Processing Information	ii

Section I: Attributes of Nations

Table of Contents	1
Variables	11
Appendix A: Data Format and Summary Statistics	107
Appendix B: Notes	120

Section II: Behavior of Nation Dyads

Table of Contents	145
Variables	151
Appendix A: Data Format and Summary Statistics	202
Appendix B: Notes	210

STUDY DESCRIPTION

These data were originally collected by the Dimensionality of Nations (DON) project, under the direction of Rudolph J. Rummel. The DON project staff wish to point out that because these data have been collected for a particular theory involving computations which are insensitive to some gross data error, minor systematic errors and frequent random errors, potential users must gauge whether the confidence they can place in the data is adequate to their uses.

This code book describes two distinct but related data sets.

Attributes of Nations

The first data set contains attributes of nations for the years 1950, 1955, 1960, 1963, and 1965. The criteria for nationhood was recognition within the family of nations as evidenced by exchange of ambassadors, a population greater than 750,000 and at least two years of sovereign independence. For 1965, 113 nations met these criteria. All 113 nations are included as cases for each of the time-points in the data set. Those nations which do not meet the criteria for nationhood any time prior to 1965 are coded as missing data on the variables pertaining to those earlier years.

The data set contains 90 national attributes measured at five different time-points and three nation identification codes; a total of 453 variables per case.

For further information see, The Dimensionality of Nations Project, "Research Report No. 65", Department of Political Science, University of Hawaii.

Behavior of Nation Dyads

The second data set contains behavioral data employed by DON to define the behavioral dimensions for a selected sample of nation dyads for the years 1950, 1955, 1960, 1963, and 1965.

These dyads represent all the paired relationships between fourteen nations. This sample of nations, out of which the dyads were formed, was chosen from major factors emerging from DON factor analyses of 236 variables for 82 nations and 94 variables for 82 nations.

The data set contains 39 behavioral variables and 16 conflict variables for the five time-points mentioned above, for each of the 182 nation dyads; a total of 275 variables per case.

The primary source of data was United Nations publications. Only when data were not easily available were other sources sought.

For further information see, The Dimensionality of Nations Project, "Research Report No. 67", The Department of Political Science, The University of Hawaii.

For further information on both of the above data sets see Rudolph J. Rummel, National Attributes and Behavior, Beverly Hills: Sage Publications, 1975.

PROCESSING INFORMATION

Attributes of Nations

The International Relations Archive standard nation identification code has been added to the DON attribute data. (See, Bruce Russett, J. David Singer, and Melvin Small, "National Political Units in the Twentieth Century: A Standardized List", The American Political Science Review, 62, 3, 935-950.) The data have been sorted into ascending order on this standard code. A three letter alphabetic code has been added. Numeric identification codes used by the DON project have been retained.

As the data were originally supplied to the IRA, all variables had a five column fieldwidth. The maximum possible value of any variable was 99,999. Variables 89 and 108 (the number killed in foreign violence, 1950 and the number killed in domestic violence, 1965, respectively) contained cases which had values surpassing this maximum. These two variables were expanded to a six-column fieldwidth to allow inclusion of these large numbers. In the card-image data set only, variables 88 and 109 have been narrowed to a four column fieldwidth to offset this expansion. These two variables have been narrowed with no loss of information.

The original variables did not include time-point specification in their variable names. The variable names have been slightly altered to conform to the reprocessed data by including a year reference.

The mnemonic OSIRIS variable names have been taken from the DON project variable codes. The OSIRIS variable names can be found in the appendix. The variable descriptions used in this code book have been taken, for the most part, from "Research Report No. 65".

Users should note that any changes in this data set from "Research Report No. 65" are the result of correspondence with the principal investigator.

Behavior of Nation Dyads

The original DON dyadic data set contained 55 variables for 5 years for 182 dyads. The variables were arranged by year and within year by dyad number. The new data set has been altered into a format of 275 variables for 182 dyads, 5 time-points by 55 variables.

The original variables did not include time-point specification in their variable names. The variable names have been slightly altered to conform to the reprocessed data set by including a year reference.

There are very few missing data in the DON dyadic data set. Wherever missing data occurred the DON staff attempted to assign a plausible estimate of the missing data value. Estimated values are always indicated by a footnote.

Users should note that any changes in this data set from "Research Report No. 67" are the result of correspondence with the principal investigator.

SECTION I

ATTRIBUTES OF NATIONS

ATTRIBUTES OF NATIONS

TABLE OF CONTENTS

VARIABLES

Variable Number	Variable Name	Page Number
1,3	Russett, Singer, Small Country Code	11
2,1	Country Code	11
3,2	Rummel Code	12
4	Telephone/Population 1950	15
5	Telephone/Population 1955	15
6	Telephone/Population 1960	15
7	Telephone/Population 1963	15
8	Telephone/Population 1965	15
9	Agricultural Population/Population 1950	16
10	Agricultural Population/Population 1955	16
11	Agricultural Population/Population 1960	16
12	Agricultural Population/Population 1963	16
13	Agricultural Population/Population 1965	17
14	Energy Consumption/Population 1950	17
15	Energy Consumption/Population 1955	17
16	Energy Consumption/Population 1960	17
17	Energy Consumption/Population 1963	17
18	Energy Consumption/Population 1965	18
19	Illiterates/Population 10 Years of Age or Older 1950	18
20	Illiterates/Population 10 Years of Age or Older 1955	18
21	Illiterates/Population 10 Years of Age or Older 1960	19
22	Illiterates/Population 10 Years of Age or Older 1963	19
23	Illiterates/Population 10 Years of Age or Older 1965	19
24	GNP/Population 1950	19
25	GNP/Population 1955	20
26	GNP/Population 1960	20
27	GNP/Population 1963	20
28	GNP/Population 1965	20
29	Population x Energy Production 1950	20
30	Population x Energy Production 1955	21
31	Population x Energy Production 1960	21
32	Population x Energy Production 1963	21
33	Population x Energy Production 1965	21
34	National Income 1950	21
35	National Income 1955	22
36	National Income 1960	22
37	National Income 1963	22
38	National Income 1965	22
39	Population 1950	23
40	Population 1955	23
41	Population 1960	23
42	Population 1963	23
43	Population 1965	23
44	UN Assessment/Total UN Assessment 1950	24
45	UN Assessment/Total UN Assessment 1955	24
46	UN Assessment/Total UN Assessment 1960	24

Variable Number	Variable Name	Page Number
47	UN Assessment/Total UN Assessment 1963	24
48	UN Assessment/Total UN Assessment 1965	24
49	Defense Expenditure 1950	25
50	Defense Expenditure 1955	25
51	Defense Expenditure 1960	25
52	Defense Expenditure 1963	25
53	Defense Expenditure 1965	26
54	English Titles Translated/Foreign Titles Translated 1950	26
55	English Titles Translated/Foreign Titles Tradslated 1955	26
56	English Titles Translated/Foreign Titles Translated 1960	26
57	English Titles Translated/Foreign Titles Translated 1963	26
58	English Titles Translated/Foreign Titles Translated 1965	27
59	Bloc Membership 1950	27
60	Bloc Membership 1955	27
61	Bloc Membership 1960	27
62	Bloc Membership 1963	27
63	Bloc Membership 1965	27
64	US Aid Received/USSR and US Aid Received 1950	28
65	US Aid Received/USSR and US Aid Received 1955	28
66	US Aid Received/USSR and US Aid Received 1960	28
67	US Aid Received/USSR and US Aid Received 1963	28
68	US Aid Received/USSR and US Aid Received 1965	29
69	Freedom of Opposition 1950	29
70	Freedom of Opposition 1955	29
71	Freedom of Opposition 1960	29
72	Freedom of Opposition 1963	29
73	Freedom of Opposition 1965	30
74	IFC and IBRD Subscription/$(GNP)^2_2$ Per Capita 1950	30
75	IFC and IBRD Subscription/$(GNP)^2_2$ Per Capita 1955	30
76	IFC and IBRD Subscription/$(GNP)^2_2$ Per Capita 1960	30
77	IFC and IBRD Subscription/$(GNP)^2_2$ Per Capita 1963	31
78	IFC and IBRD Subscription/$(GNP)^2$ Per Capita 1965	31
79	Threats 1950	31
80	Threats 1955	31
81	Threats 1960	31
82	Threats 1963	31
83	Threats 1965	32
84	Accusations 1950	32
85	Accusations 1955	32
86	Accusations 1960	32
87	Accusations 1963	32
88	Accusations 1965	32
89	Killed In Foreign Violence 1950	33
90	Killed In Foreign Violence 1955	33
91	Killed In Foreign Violence 1960	33
92	Killed In Foreign Violence 1963	33
93	Killed In Foreign Violence 1965	33
94	Military Action or Not 1950	34
95	Military Action or Not 1955	34
96	Military Action or Not 1960	34
97	Military Action or Not 1963	34
98	Military Action or Not 1965	34
99	Protests 1950	35

Variable Number	Variable Name	Page Number
100	Protests 1955	35
101	Protests 1960	35
102	Protests 1963	35
103	Protests 1965	35
104	Killed In Domestic Violence 1950	36
105	Killed In Domestic Violence 1955	36
106	Killed In Domestic Violence 1960	36
107	Killed In Domestic Violence 1963	36
108	Killed In Domestic Violence 1965	36
109	General Strikes 1950	37
110	General Strikes 1955	37
111	General Strikes 1960	37
112	General Strikes 1963	37
113	General Strikes 1965	37
114	Riots 1950	38
115	Riots 1955	38
116	Riots 1960	38
117	Riots 1963	38
118	Riots 1965	38
119	Purges 1950	39
120	Purges 1955	39
121	Purges 1960	39
122	Purges 1963	39
123	Purges 1965	39
124	Demonstrations 1950	40
125	Demonstrations 1955	40
126	Demonstrations 1960	40
127	Demonstrations 1963	40
128	Demonstrations 1965	40
129	Roman Catholics/Population 1950	41
130	Roman Catholics/Population 1955	41
131	Roman Catholics/Population 1960	41
132	Roman Catholics/Population 1963	41
133	Roman Catholics/Population 1965	41
134	Air Distance From US 1950	42
135	Air Distance From US 1955	42
136	Air Distance From US 1960	42
137	Air Distance From US 1963	42
138	Air Distance From US 1965	42
139	Medicine NGO/NGO 1950	43
140	Medicine NGO/NGO 1955	43
141	Medicine NGO/NGO 1960	43
142	Medicine NGO/NGO 1963	43
143	Medicine NGO/NGO 1965	43
144	Diplomat Expelled or Recalled 1950	44
145	Diplomat Expelled or Recalled 1955	44
146	Diplomat Expelled or Recalled 1960	44
147	Diplomat Expelled or Recalled 1963	44
148	Diplomat Expelled or Recalled 1965	44
149	Divorces/Marriages 1950	45
150	Divorces/Marriages 1955	45

Variable Number	Variable Name	Page Number
151	Divorces/Marriages 1960	45
152	Divorces/Marriages 1963	45
153	Divorces/Marriages 1965	45
154	Population/National Land Area 1950	46
155	Population/National Land Area 1955	46
156	Population/National Land Area 1960	46
157	Population/National Land Area 1963	46
158	Population/National Land Area 1965	46
199	Arable Land/Total Land Area 1950	47
160	Arable Land/Total Land Area 1955	47
161	Arable Land/Total Land Area 1960	47
162	Arable Land/Total Land Area 1963	47
163	Arable Land/Total Land Area 1965	47
164	National Area 1950	48
165	National Area 1955	48
166	National Area 1960	48
167	National Area 1963	48
168	National Area 1965	48
169	Road Length/National Area 1950	49
170	Road Length/National Area 1955	49
171	Road Length/National Area 1950	49
172	Road Length/National Area 1963	49
173	Road Length/National Area 1965	49
174	Railroad Length/National Area 1950	50
175	Railread Length/National Area 1955	50
176	Railroad Length/National Area 1960	50
177	Railroad Lenght/National Area 1963	50
178	Railroad Length/National Area 1965	50
179	Religions 1950	51
180	Religions 1955	51
181	Religions 1960	51
182	Religions 1963	51
183	Religions 1965	51
184	Immigrants/Migrants 1950	52
185	Immigrants/Migrants 1955	52
186	Immigrants/Migrants 1960	52
187	Immigrants/Migrants 1963	52
188	Immigrants/Migrants 1965	52
189	Average Rainfall 1950	53
190	Average Rainfall 1955	53
191	Average Rainfall 1960	53
192	Average Rainfall 1963	53
193	Average Rainfall 1965	53
194	Membership of Largest Religion/Population 1950	54
195	Membership of Largest Religion/Population 1955	54
196	Membership of Largest Religion/Population 1960	54
197	Membership of Largest Religion/Population 1963	54
198	Membership of Largest Religion/Population 1965	54
199	Dwellings with Running Water/Dwellings 1950	55
200	Dwellings with Running Water/Dwellings 1955	55
201	Dwellings with Running Water/Dwellings 1960	55
202	Dwellings with Running Water/Dwellings 1963	55

Variable Number	Variable Name	Page Number
203	Dwellings with Running Water/Dwellings 1965	55
204	Foreign College Students/College Students 1950	56
205	Foreign College Students/College Students 1955	56
206	Foreign College Students/College Students 1960	56
207	Foreign College Students/College Students 1963	56
208	Foreign College Students/College Students 1965	56
209	Membership in Neutral Bloc 1950	57
210	Membership in Neutral Bloc 1955	57
211	Membership in Neutral Bloc 1960	57
212	Membership in Neutral Bloc 1963	57
213	Membership in Neutral Bloc 1965	57
214	Age of Country 1950	58
215	Age of Country 1955	58
216	Age of Country 1960	58
217	Age of Country 1963	58
218	Age of Country 1965	58
219	Religious Titles Published/Book Titles 1950	59
220	Religious Titles Published/Book Titles 1955	59
221	Religious Titles Published/Book Titles 1960	59
222	Religious Titles Published/Book Titles 1963	59
223	Religious Titles Published/Book Titles 1965	59
224	Emigrants/Population 1950	60
225	Emigrants/Population 1955	60
226	Emigrants/Population 1960	60
227	Emigrants/Population 1963	60
228	Emigrants/Population 1965	60
229	Seaborne Goods/GNP 1950	61
230	Seaborne Goods/GNP 1955	61
231	Seaborne Goods/GNP 1960	61
232	Seaborne Goods/GNP 1963	61
233	Seaborne Goods/GNP 1965	61
234	Law NGO's/NGO's 1950	62
235	Law NGO's/NGO's 1955	62
236	Law NGO's/NGO's 1960	62
237	Law NGO's/NGO's 1963	62
238	Law NGO's/NGO's 1965	62
239	Unemployed/Economically Active Population 1950	63
240	Unemployed/Economically Active Population 1955	63
241	Unemployed/Economically Active Population 1960	63
242	Unemployed/Economically Active Population 1963	63
243	Unemployed/Economically Active Population 1965	63
244	Leading Export/Exports 1950	64
245	Leading Export/Exports 1955	64
246	Leading Export/Exports 1960	64
247	Leading Export/Exports 1963	64
248	Leading Export/Exports 1965	64
249	Languages 1950	65
250	Languages 1955	65
251	Languages 1960	65
252	Languages 1963	65
253	Languages 1965	65

Variable Number	Variable Name	Page Number
254	Membership of Largest Language Group/Population 1950	66
255	Membership of Largest Language Group/Population 1955	66
256	Membership of Largest Language Group/Population 1960	66
257	Membership of Largest Language Group/Population 1963	66
258	Membership of Largest Language Group/Population 1965	66
259	Ethnic Groups 1950	67
260	Ethnic Groups 1955	67
261	Ethnic Groups 1960	67
262	Ethnic Groups 1963	67
263	Ethnic Groups 1965	67
264	Economic Aid Received 1950	68
265	Economic Aid Received 1955	68
266	Economic Aid Received 1960	68
267	Economic Aid Received 1963	68
248	Economic Aid Received 1965	69
269	Technical Assistance Received 1950	69
270	Technical Assistance Received 1955	69
271	Technical Assistance Received 1960	69
272	Technical Assistance Received 1963	69
273	Technical Assistance Received 1965	70
274	Government Education Expenditures/ Government Expenditures 1950	70
275	Government Education Expenditures/ Government Expenditures 1955	70
276	Government Education Expenditures/ Government Expenditures 1960	70
277	Government Education Expenditures/ Government Expenditures 1963	70
278	Government Education Expenditures/ Government Expenditures 1965	71
279	Female Workers/Economically Active 1950	71
280	Female Workers/Economically Active 1955	71
281	Female Workers/Economically Active 1960	71
282	Female Workers/Economically Active 1963	71
283	Female Workers/Economically Active 1965	72
284	Exports/GNP 1950	72
285	Exports/GNP 1955	72
286	Exports/GNP 1960	72
287	Exports/GNP 1963	72
288	Exports/GNP 1965	72
289	Foreign Mail Sent/Foreign Mail 1950	73
290	Foreign Mail Sent/Foreign Mail 1955	73
291	Foreign Mail Sent/Foreign Mail 1960	73
292	Foreign Mail Sent/Foreign Mail 1963	73
293	Foreign Mail Sent/Foreign Mail 1965	73
294	Imports/Trade 1950	74
295	Imports/Trade 1955	74
296	Imports/Trade 1960	74
297	Imports/Trade 1963	74
298	Imports/Trade 1965	74
299	Calories Consumed Minus Calories Required/ Calories Required 1950	75

Variable Number	Variable Name	Page Number
300	Calories Consumed Minus Calories Required/Calories Required 1955.	75
301	Calories Consumed Minus Calories Required/Calories Required 1960.	75
302	Calories Consumed Minus Calories Required/Calories Required 1963.	75
303	Calories Consumed Minus Calories Required/Calories Required 1965.	75
304	Proteins/Calories 1950.	76
305	Proteins/Calories 1955.	76
306	Proteins/Calories 1960.	76
307	Proteins/Calories 1963.	76
308	Proteins/Calories 1965.	76
309	Russian Titles Translated/Foreign Titles Translated 1950.	77
310	Russian Titles Translated/Foreign Titles Translated 1955.	77
311	Russian Titles Translated/Foreign Titles Translated 1960.	77
312	Russian Titles Translated/Foreign Titles Translated 1963.	77
313	Russian Titles Translated/Foreign Titles Translated 1965.	77
314	Military Personnel/Population 1950.	78
315	Military Personnel/Population 1955.	78
316	Military Personnel/Population 1960.	78
317	Military Personnel/Population 1963.	78
318	Military Personnel/Population 1965.	78
319	Balance of Investments/Gold Stock 1950.	79
320	Balance of Investments/Gold Stock 1955.	79
321	Balance of Investments/Gold Stock 1960.	79
322	Balance of Investments/Gold Stock 1963.	79
323	Balance of Investments/Gold Stock 1965.	79
324	Political Parties 1950.	80
325	Political Parties 1955.	80
326	Political Partice 1960.	80
327	Political Partice 1963.	80
328	Political Parties 1965.	81
329	Arts and Culture NGO/NGO 1950	81
330	Arts and Culture NGO/NGO 1955	81
331	Arts and Culture NGO/NGO 1960	81
332	Arts and Culture NGO/NGO 1963	81
333	Arts and Culture NGO/NGO 1965	81
334	Communist Party Membership/Population 1950.	82
335	Communist Party Membership/Population 1955.	82
336	Communist Party Membership/Population 1960.	82
337	Communist Party Membership/Population 1963.	82
338	Communist Party Membership/Population 1965.	82
339	Government Expenditure/GNP 1950	83
340	Government Expenditure/GNP 1955	83
341	Government Expenditure/GNP 1960	83
342	Government Expenditure/GNP 1963	83
343	Governemnt Expenditure/GNP 1965	83
344	Monarchy or Not 1950.	84
345	Monarchy or Not 1955.	84
346	Monarchy or Not 1960.	84
347	Monarchy or Not 1963.	84

Variable Number	Variable Name	Page Number
348	Monarchy or Not 1965	84
349	Pupils in Primary School/Primary School Teachers 1950	85
350	Pupils in Primary School/Primary School Teachers 1955	85
351	Pupils in Primary School/Primary School Teachers 1960	85
352	Pupils in Primary School/Primary School Teachers 1963	85
353	Pupils in Primary School/Primary School Teachers 1965	85
354	Legality of Government Change 1950	86
355	Legality of Governmnet Change 1955	86
356	Legality of Government Change 1960	86
357	Legality of Government Change 1963	86
358	Legality of Government Change 1965	86
359	Legitimacy of Present Government 1950	87
360	Legitimacy of Present Government 1955	87
361	Legitimacy of Present Government 1960	87
362	Legitimacy of Present Government 1963	87
363	Legitimacy of Present Government 1965	87
364	Largest Ethnic Group Membership/Population 1950	88
365	Largest Ethnic Group Membership/Population 1955	88
366	Largest Ethnic Group Membership/Population 1960	88
367	Largest Ethnic Group Membership/Population 1963	88
368	Largest Ethnic Group Membership/Population 1965	88
369	Assassinations 1950	89
370	Assassinations 1955	89
371	Assassinations 1960	89
372	Assassinations 1963	89
373	Assassinations 1965	89
374	Major Government Crisis 1950	90
375	Major Government Crisis 1955	90
376	Major Government Crisis 1960	90
377	Major Government Crisis 1963	90
378	Major Government Crisis 1965	90
379	UN Payment Delinquencies/Assessments 1950	91
380	UN Payment Delinquencies/Assessments 1955	91
381	UN Payment Delinquencies/Assessments 1960	91
382	UN Payment Delinquencies/Assessments 1963	91
383	UN Payment Delinquencies/Assessments 1965	91
384	Balance of Payments/Gold Stock 1950	92
385	Balance of Payments/Gold Stock 1955	92
386	Balance of Payments/Gold Stock 1960	92
387	Balance of Payments/Gold Stock 1963	92
388	Balance of Payments/Gold Stock 1965	92
389	Balance of Investments 1950	93
390	Balance of Investments 1955	93
391	Balance of Investments 1960	93
392	Balance of Investments 1963	93
393	Balance of Investments 1965	93
394	System Style 1950	94
395	System Style 1955	94
396	System Style 1960	94
397	System Style 1963	94
398	System Style 1965	94

Variable Number	Variable Name	Page Number
399	Constitutional 1950	95
400	Constitutional 1955	95
401	Constitutional 1960	95
402	Constitutional 1963	95
403	Constitutional 1965	95
404	Electoral System 1950	96
405	Electoral System 1955	96
406	Electoral System 1960	96
407	Electoral System 1963	96
408	Electoral System 1965	96
409	Non-Communist Regime 1950	97
410	Non-Communist Regime 1955	97
411	Non-Communist Regime 1960	97
412	Non-Communist Regime 1963	97
413	Non-Communist Regime 1965	97
414	Political Leadership 1950	98
415	Political Leadership 1955	98
416	Political Leadership 1960	98
417	Political Leadership 1963	98
418	Political Leadership 1965	98
419	Horizontal Power Distribution 1950	99
420	Horizontal Power Distribution 1955	99
421	Horizontal Power Distribution 1960	99
422	Horizontal Power Distribution 1963	99
423	Horizontal Power Distribution 1965	99
424	Military Participation 1950	100
425	Military Participation 1955	100
426	Military Participation 1960	100
427	Military Participation 1963	100
428	Military Participation 1965	100
429	Bureaucracy 1950	101
430	Bureaucracy 1955	101
431	Bureaucracy 1960	101
432	Bureaucracy 1963	101
433	Bureaucracy 1965	101
434	Censorship Score 1950	102
435	Censorship Score 1955	102
436	Censorship Score 1960	102
437	Censorship Score 1963	102
438	Censorship Score 1965	102
439	Geography - X 1950	103
440	Geography - X 1955	103
441	Geography - X 1960	103
442	Geography - X 1963	103
443	Geography - X 1965	103
444	Geography - Y 1950	104
445	Geography - Y 1955	104
446	Geography - Y 1960	104
447	Geography - Y 1963	104

Variable Number	Variable Name	Page Number
448	Geography - Y 1965	104
449	Geography - Z 1950	104
450	Geography - Z 1955	104
451	Geography - Z 1960	105
452	Geography - Z 1963	105
453	Geography - Z 1965	105

ATTRIBUTES OF NATIONS

Deck Number
Card: deck, all, col. 1-2

DEFINITION: The identification number of the data deck, found only in card-image data sets.

```
          Card-  OSIRIS
          Image  File
Variable    1      3      RUSSETT, SINGER, SMALL COUNTRY CODE
   OSIRIS: location 7  width 3        Card: deck all, col. 3-5
   Missing data code: none            Decimal place: none
```

DEFINITION: A three digit, numeric, nation identification code developed by Bruce M. Russett, J. David Singer, and Melvin Small.

This is the standard International Relations Archive nation identification code.

A complete list of the nations and identification codes can be found preceding Variable 4.

Sources: Russett, Bruce, J. David Singer and Melvin Small, "National Political Units in the Twentieth Century: A Standardized List," <u>American Political Science Review,</u> Vol. LXII, No. 3, September, 1968.

```
          Card-  OSIRIS
          Image  File
Variable    2      1      COUNTRY CODE
   OSIRIS: location 1  width 3        Card: deck 1, col. 6-8
   Missing data code: none            Decimal place: none
```

DEFINITION: A three character alphabetic nation identification code. The code used is that developed by Charles McClelland's World Event/Interaction Survey project. This code is identical to the alphabetic nation identification code used by the DON project except in the following cases:

Country	DON Code	WEIS Code
Burundi	BRN	BUI
Mauritania	MAT	MAU
Guinea	GUN	GUI
Malagasy (Madagascar)	MAD	MAG
Mongolia	OUT	MON

Variable 2 continued:

    United Arab Republic   EGP   UAR
    Union of South Africa   UNS   SAF

In order to update the WEIS code the IRA staff has changed Congo (Kinshasa, Leopoldville) coded as COP to Zaire, coded ZAI.

A complete list of nations and identification codes is found preceding Variable 4.

```
              Card- OSIRIS
          Image   File
Variable    3      2      RUMMEL CODE
OSIRIS: location 4  width 3       Card: deck 1, col. 9-11
Missing data code: none           Decimal place: none
```

DEFINITION: A three digit numeric nation identification code developed by the original collector of the data.

Nation	Alphabetic County Code	Rummel Numeric Code	RSS Numeric Code
Afghanistan	AFG	1	700
Albania	ALB	2	339
Algeria	ALG	106	615
Argentina	ARG	3	160
Australia	AUL	4	900
Austria	AUS	5	305
Belgium	BEL	6	211
Bolivia	BOL	7	145
Brazil	BRA	8	140
Bulgaria	BUL	9	355
Burma	BUR	10	775
Burundi	BUI	113	516
Cambodia	CAM	11	811
Cameroon	CAO	83	471
Canada	CAN	12	020
Central African Republic	CEN	84	482
Ceylon	CEY	13	780
Chad	CHA	85	483
Chile	CHL	14	155
China (People's Republic)	CHN	15	710
China (Taiwan)	CHT	16	713
Colombia	COL	17	100
Congo (Brazzaville)	CON	87	484
Zaire	ZAI	86	490
Costa Rica	COS	18	094

Variable 3 continued:

Country	Code		
Cuba	CUB	19	040
Czechoslovakia	CZE	20	315
Dahomey	DAH	88	434
Denmark	DEN	21	390
Dominican Republic	DOM	22	042
Ecuador	ECU	23	130
Egypt (United Arab Republic)	UAR	24	651
El Salvador	ELS	25	092
Ethiopia	ETH	26	530
Finland	FIN	27	375
France	FRN	29	220
Gabon	GAB	89	481
Germany (D.D.R.)	GME	29	265
Germany (Fed. Rep.)	GMW	30	255
Ghana	GHA	90	452
Greece	GRC	31	350
Guatemala	GUA	32	090
Guinea	GUI	91	438
Haiti	HAI	33	041
Honduras	HON	34	091
Hungary	HUN	35	310
India	IND	36	750
Indonesia	INS	37	850
Iran	IRN	38	630
Iraq	IRQ	39	645
Ireland	IRE	40	205
Israel	ISR	41	666
Italy	ITA	42	325
Ivory Coast	IVO	92	437
Jamaica	JAM	163	051
Japan	JAP	43	740
Jordan	JOR	44	663
Korea (Dem. Rep.)	KON	45	731
Korea (Rep. of)	KOS	46	732
Laos	LAO	80	812
Lebanon	LEB	47	660
Liberia	LBR	48	450
Libya	LBY	49	620
Madagascar (Malagasy)	MAG	93	580
Malaysia	MAL	94	820
Mali	MLI	95	432
Mauritania	MAU	96	435
Mexico	MEX	50	070
Morocco	MOR	97	600
Nepal	NEP	51	790
Netherlands	NTH	52	210
New Zealand	NEW	53	
Nicaragua	NIC	54	093
Niger	NIR	98	436
Nigeria	NIG	99	475

Variable 3 continued:

Norway	NOR	55	385
Outer Mongolia	MON	56	712
Pakistan	PAK	57	770
Panama	PAN	58	095
Paraguay	PAR	59	150
Peru	PER	60	135
Philippines	PHI	61	840
Poland	POL	62	290
Portugal	POR	63	235
Rumania	RUM	64	360
Rwanda	RWA	114	517
Saudi Arabia	SAU	65	670
Senegal	SEN	100	433
Sierra Leone	SIE	204	451
Somalia	SOM	101	520
Spain	SPN	66	230
Sudan	SUD	102	625
Sweden	SWD	67	380
Switzerland	SWZ	68	225
Syria	SYR	69	652
Tanzania	TAZ	109	510
Thailand	TAI	70	800
Togo	TOG	103	461
Trinidad	TRI	216	052
Tunisia	TUN	104	616
Turkey	TUR	71	640
Union of South Africa	SAF	72	560
USSR	USR	73	365
United Kingdom	UNK	74	200
USA	USA	75	002
Uganda	UGA	219	500
Upper Volta	UPP	105	439
Uruguay	URA	76	165
Venezuela	VEN	77	101
Vietnam (N)	VTN	81	816
Vietnam (S)	VTS	82	817
Yemen	YEM	78	678
Yugoslavia	YUG	79	345

-15-

Variable 4   TELEPHONE/POPULATION 1950

    OSIRIS: location 10 width 5   Card: deck 1, col. 12-16
    Missing data code: 99999   Decimal place: none
    N=72   Mean=345.79   Standard Deviation=631.32   Range=0-2846

    DEFINITION: Telephone refers to the number of public and private telephones installed which can be connected to a central exchange. Statistical Yearbook, UN. The units are telephones per 10,000 population.

    NOTES: Variables 4-8
    A. Estimates
    B. U.N. Statistical Yearbook, 1961
    C. The World's Telephones--1964, American Telephone & Telegraph Co.
    D. "Development Rank--A New Method of Rating National Development," Caplow and Finsterback, Table 1.

Variable 5   TELEPHONE/POPULATION 1955

    OSIRIS: location 15 width 5   Card: deck 1, col. 17-21
    Missing data code: 99999   Decimal place: none
    N=81   Mean=428.25   Standard Deviation=746.86   Range=0-3390

    DEFINITION: See Variable 4 for definition and note codes.

Variable 6   TELEPHONE/POPULATION 1960

    OSIRIS: location 20 width 5   Card: deck 1, col. 22-26
    Missing data code: 99999   Decimal place: none
    N=86   Mean=519.12   Standard Deviation=876.20   Range=0-4115

    DEFINITION: See Variable 4 for definition and note codes.

Variable 7   TELEPHONE/POPULATION 1963

    OSIRIS: location 25 width 5   Card: deck 1, col. 27-31
    Missing data code: 99999   Decimal place: none
    N=107   Mean=490.28   Standard Deviation=913.95   Range=2-4458

    DEFINITION: See Variable 4 for definition and note codes.

Variable 8   TELEPHONE/POPULATION 1965

    OSIRIS: location 30 width 5   Card: deck 1, col. 32-36
    Missing data code: 99999   Decimal place: none
    N=113   Mean=523.49   Standard Deviation=978.02   Range=3-4813

    DEFINITION: See Variable 4 for definition and note codes.

Variable 9   AGRICULTURAL POPULATION/POPULATION 1950

> OSIRIS: location 35 width 5   Card: deck 1, col. 37-41
> Missing data code: 99999   Decimal place: none
>
> N=61   Mean=49.738   Standard Deviation=24.133   Range=6-95
>
> DEFINITION: Agricultural population is defined as "all persons who depend upon agriculture for a livelihood, that is to say, persons actively engaged in agriculture and their non-working dependents." Yearbook of Food and Agricultural Statistics: Production.
>
> See Variables 39-43 for definitions and notes for the variable, Population.
>
> NOTES: Variables 9-13
> A. Estimates
> B. Moody's Municipal and Government Manual
> C. Oxford Economic Atlas of the World
> D. Worldmark Encyclopedia of the Nations
> E. International Politics, Karl W. Deutsch, p. 34
> F. U. N. Economic Survey of Latin America (1956), p. 167
> G. Yearbook of Labor Statistics 1967
> H. World Almanac (1964)
> I. Information Please Almanac (1964)
> J. Agricultural Development of African Nations, Vol. 1, S. C. Vora
> K. Readers' Digest World Almanac (1966)
> L. North Korea Today (1963)
> M. An Atlas of European Affairs (1964)
> N. Atlas of Economic Development

Variable 10   AGRICULTURAL POPULATION/POPULATION 1955

> OSIRIS: location 40 width 5   Card: deck 1, col. 42-46
> Missing data code: 99999   Decimal place: none
>
> N=69   Mean=49.188   Standard Deviation=24.343   Range=6-95
>
> DEFINITION: See Variable 9 for definition and note codes.

Variable 11   AGRICULTURAL POPULATION/POPULATION 1960

> OSIRIS: location 45 width 5   Card: deck 1, col. 47-51
> Missing data code: 99999   Decimal place: none
>
> N=84   Mean=47.738   Standard Deviation=23.704   Range=4-94
>
> DEFINITION: See Variable 9 for definition and note codes.

Variable 12   AGRICULTURAL POPULATION/POPULATION 1963

> OSIRIS: location 50 width 5   Card: deck 1, col. 52-56
> Missing data code: 99999   Decimal place: none
>
> N=105   Mean=56.057   Standard Deviation=26.051   Range=6-97
>
> DEFINITION: See Variable 9 for definition and note codes.

Variable 13   AGRICULTURAL POPULATION/POPULATION 1965

    OSIRIS: location 55 width 5   Card: deck 1, col. 57-61
    Missing data code: 99999   Decimal place: none

    N=113   Mean=54.142   Standard deviation=26.345   Range=4-95

    DEFINITION: See Variable 9 for definition and note codes.

Variable 14   ENERGY CONSUMPTION/POPULATION 1950

    OSIRIS: location 60 width 5   Card: deck 1, col. 62-66
    Missing data code: 99999   Decimal place: none

    N=68   Mean=975.87   Standard deviation=1533   Range=0-7543

    DEFINITION: Energy includes solid fuels, liquid fuels, natural and imported gas, and hydro and imported electricity. World Energy Supplies, UN.

    Units are kilograms per person. See Variables 39-43 for definitions and notes on the variable, Population.

    NOTES: Variables 14-18
    A. Estimates
    B. U. S. Department of State Research Memorandum REU-6, Sept. 15, 1961, "Indicators of Economic Strength of Western Europe, Canada, U. S. and the Soviet Bloc, 1960"

Variable 15   ENERGY CONSUMPTION/POPULATION 1955

    OSIRIS: location 65 width 5   Card: deck 1, col. 67-71
    Missing data code: 99999   Decimal place: none

    N=79   Mean=1068.3   Standard deviation=1491.7   Range=0-7745

    DEFINITION: See Variable 14 for definition and note codes.

Variable 16   ENERGY CONSUMPTION/POPULATION 1960

    OSIRIS: location 70 width 5   Card: deck 1, col. 72-76
    Missing data code: 99999   Decimal place: none

    N=84   Mean=1179.9   Standard deviation=1565.4   Range=4-8047

    DEFINITION: See Variable 14 for definition and note codes.

Variable 17   ENERGY CONSUMPTION/POPULATION 1963

    OSIRIS: location 75 width 5   Card: deck 2, col. 6-10
    Missing data code: 99999   Decimal place: none

    N=107   Mean=1086.6   Standard deviation=1638.1   Range=5-8508

    DEFINITION: See Variable 14 for definition and note codes.

Variable 18   ENERGY CONSUMPTION/POPULATION 1965

    OSIRIS: location 80   width 5   Card: deck 2, col. 11-15
    Missing data code: 99999   Decimal place: none

    N=111   Mean=1191.6   Standard deviation=1767.6   Range=0-9203

    DEFINITION: See Variable 14 for definition and note codes.

Variable 19   ILLITERATES/POPULATION 10 YEARS OF AGE OR OLDER 1950

    OSIRIS: location 85   width 5   Card: deck 2, col. 16-20
    Missing data code: 99999   Decimal place: none

    N=72   Mean 41.111   Standard deviation=31.765   Range=2-97

    DEFINITION: Literacy is defined as "the ability to read and write" (Demographic Yearbook, UN). For some countries, however, literacy includes those who can read or write. Demographic Yearbook, UN; Basic Facts and Figures, UNESCO: World Survey of Education, UNESCO; Norton Ginsburg, Atlas of Economic Development.

    The units are %.

    NOTES: Variables 19-23.
    A. Estimates
    B. Demographic Yearbook 1960
    C. Worldmark Encyclopedia of the Nations
    D. Basic Facts and Figures (1959)
    E. World Survey of Education: Handbook of Educational Organization and Statistics (1955)
    F. Atlas of Economic Development
    G. U. N. Statistical Yearbook 1965
    H. The Planning and Execution of Economic Development, L. J. Walinsky, pp. 190-199
    I. World Handbook of Political and Social Indicators
    J. Population, William Peterson, pp. 328-332
    K. Progress in the Asian Region: A Statistical Review, pp. 71-72
    L. World Illiteracy at Mid-Century, pp. 38-44
    M. New Nations of Africa (1963)

Variable 20   ILLITERATES/POPULATION 10 YEARS OF AGE OR OLDER 1955

    OSIRIS: location 90   width 5   Card: deck 2, col. 21-25
    Missing data code: 99999   Decimal place: none

    N=82   Mean=41.329   Standard deviation=32.200   Range=2-97

    DEFINITION: See Variable 19 for definition and note codes.

Variable 21   ILLITERATES/POPULATION 10 YEARS OR OLDER 1960

    OSIRIS: location 95   width 5   Card: deck 2, col. 26-30
    Missing data code: 99999   Decimal place: none

    N=87   Mean=36.874   Standard Deviation=31.603   Range=0-96

    DEFINITION: See Variable 19 for definition and note codes.

Variable 22   ILLITERATES/POPULATION 10 YEARS OR OLDER 1963

    OSIRIS: location 100   width 5   Card: deck 2, col. 31-35
    Missing data code: 99999   Decimal place: none

    N=106   Mean=43.981   Standard Deviation=35.528   Range=1-98

    DEFINITION: See Variable 19 for definition and note codes.

Variable 23   ILLITERATES/POPULATION 10 YEARS OR OLDER 1965

    OSIRIS: location 105   width 5   Card: deck 2, col. 36-40
    Missing data code: 99999   Decimal place: none

    N=113   Mean=46.310   Standard Deviation=35.531   Range=1-99

    DEFINITION: See Variable 19 for definition and note codes.

Variable 24   GNP/POPULATION 1950

    OSIRIS: location 110   width 5   Card: deck 2, col. 41-45
    Missing data code: 99999   Decimal place: none

    N=52   Mean=386.71   Standard Deviation=376.24   Range=43-1908

    DEFINITION: Gross national product is defined as the "total value of goods and services produced in a country in a year's time ..." The Role of Foreign Aid in the Development of Other Countries; Norton Ginsburg, Atlas of Economic Development. See Variable 39 for definition, year and sources of population data.

    The units are U. S. dollars per person. See Variable 39-43 for definition and notes for the variable, Population.

    NOTES: Variables 24-28
    A. Estimates
    B. U. N. Statistical Yearbook 1965
    C. Statistical Abstract of the U.S. (1961)
    D. U. S. Department of State Research Memorandum REU-6, Sept. 15, 1961, "Indicators of Economic Strength of Western Europe, Canada, U. S. and the Soviet Block, 1960"
    E. World Military Expenditures 1966-1967
    F. Communist China's Economic Growth and Foreign Trade, A. Eckstein, p. 121
    G. World Handbook of Political and Social Indicators

Variable 25   GNP/POPULATION 1955

    OSIRIS: location 115 width 5   Card: deck 2, col. 46-50
    Missing data code: 99999   Decimal place: none

    N=73   Mean=413.92   Standard Deviation=432.32   Range=45-2334

    DEFINITION: See Variable 24 for definition and note codes.

Variable 26   GNP/POPULATION 1960

    OSIRIS: location 120 width 5   Card: deck 2, col. 51-55
    Missing data code: 99999   Decimal place: none

    N=87   Mean=512.49   Standard Deviation=550.37   Range=45-2830

    DEFINITION: See Variable 24 for definition and note codes.

Variable 27   GNP/POPULATION 1963

    OSIRIS: location 125 width 5   Card: deck 2, col. 56-60
    Missing data code: 99999   Decimal place: none

    N=99   Mean=486.34   Standard Deviation=593.71   Range=40-3048

    DEFINITION: See Variable 24 for definition and note codes.

Variable 28   GNP/POPULATION 1965

    OSIRIS: location 130 width 5   Card: deck 2, col. 61-65
    Missing data code: 99999   Decimal place: none

    N=113   Mean=568.18   Standard Deviation=693.85   Range=39-3520

    DEFINITION: See Variable 24 for definition and note codes.

Variable 29   POPULATION x ENERGY PRODUCTION 1950

    OSIRIS: location 135 width 5   Card: deck 2, col. 66-70
    Missing data code: 99999   Decimal place: none

    N=57   Mean= 3994.8   Standard Deviation=324.26   Range=3883-6121

DEFINITION: The product of population x energy production has been used as a measure of the military strength of a nation. (Quincy Wright, The Study of International Relations, 1955, p. 599). See Variable 39 for definition, year and sources of the population data. Energy production includes the primary sources of energy: coal and lignite, crude petroleum, natural gas and hydro electricity. This data is expressed in the form (energy production standardized + 20) x (population standardized + 20). The units are this index times 10.

See Variables 39-43 for definitions and notes for the variable Population.

Variable 29 continued:

    NOTES: Variables 29-33
    A. Estimates
    B. U. S. Department of State Research Memorandum REU-6, Sept. 15, 1961, "Indicators of Economic Strength of Western Europe, Canada, U. S. and the Soviet Block, 1960"

Variable 30   POPULATION x ENERGY PRODUCTION 1955

    OSIRIS: location 140 width 5   Card: deck 2, col. 71-75
    Missing data code: 99999   Decimal place: none
    N=81   Mean=4004   Standard Deviation=332.6   Range=3879-6113

    DEFINITION: See Variable 29 for definition and note codes.

Variable 31   POPULATION x ENERGY PRODUCTION 1960

    OSIRIS: location 145 width 5   Card: deck 2, col. 76-80
    Missing data code: 99999   Decimal place: none
    N=82   Mean=4012.4   Standard Deviation=378.96   Range=3873-6065

    DEFINITION: See Variable 29 for definition and note codes.

Variable 32   POPULATION x ENERGY PRODUCTION 1963

    OSIRIS: location 150 width 5   Card: deck 3, col. 6-10
    Missing data code: 99999   Decimal place: none
    N=107   Mean=4004.1   Standard Deviation=358.33   Range=3883-6299

    DEFINITION: See Variable 29 for definition and note codes.

Variable 33   POPULATION x ENERGY PRODUCTION 1965

    OSIRIS: location 155 width 5   Card: deck 3, col. 11-15
    Missing data code: 99999   Decimal place: none
    N=113   Mean=4004.3   Standard Deviation=359.97   Range=3885-6335

    DEFINITION: See Variable 29 for definition and note codes.

Variable 34   NATIONAL INCOME 1950

    OSIRIS: location 160 width 5   Card: deck 3, col. 16-20
    Missing data code: 99999   Decimal place: none
    N=51   Mean=85.255   Standard Deviation=336.75   Range=1-2410

    DEFINITION: "National income is the sum of the incomes accruing within a year to the factors of production supplied by the normal residents of a country, before deduction of direct taxation, and equals the sum of compensation of employees, income from unincorporated

Variable 34 continued:

enterprises, rent, interest and dividends accruing to households, saving of corporations, direct taxes on corporations and general government income" (Statistical Yearbook UN, 1959, Table 166, pp. 447-448; 1961, Table 163, pp. 486-487.) National incomes given in domestic currencies were converted to U. S. dollars using exchange rate data. Since many countries give data on several kinds of exchange rates, if available, only the free rate (a rate that rises or falls to some extent in response to private purchases and sales) was used. If such data were not available, the following rates, in decreasing order of desirability, were used: selling or import rates, buying or export rates, official rate. Statistical Yearbook, UN, 1959, Table 171, pp. 464-473.

NOTES: Variables 34-38
A. Estimates
B. U. N. Statistical Yearbook 1959
C. Yearbook of National Accounts Statistics (1966)
D. "Indicators of Market Size for 88 Countries," Business International (1965)
E. The American Annual (1967)

Variable 35   NATIONAL INCOME 1955

OSIRIS: location 165 width 5   Card: deck 3, col. 21-25
Missing data code: 99999   Decimal place: none

N=67   Mean=111.03   Standard Deviation=408.84   Range=1-3302

DEFINITION: See Variable 34 for definition and note codes.

Variable 36   NATIONAL INCOME 1960

OSIRIS: location 170 width 5   Card: deck 3, col. 26-30
Missing data code: 99999   Decimal place: none

N=82   Mean=136.77   Standard Deviation=498.75   Range=1-4170

DEFINITION: See Variable 34 for definition and note codes.

Variable 37   NATIONAL INCOME 1963

OSIRIS: location 175 width 5   Card: deck 3, col. 31-35
Missing data code: 99999   Decimal place: none

N=88   Mean=157.94   Standard Deviation=551.24   Range=2-4750

DEFINITION: See Variable 34 for definition and note codes.

Variable 38   NATIONAL INCOME 1965

OSIRIS: location 180 width 5   Card: deck 3, col. 36-40
Missing data code: 99999   Decimal place: none

N=105   Mean=154.66   Standard Deviation=604.04   Range=1-5684

DEFINITION: See Variable 34 for definition and note codes.

-23-

Variable 39   POPULATION 1950

    OSIRIS: location 185 width 5   Card: deck 3, col. 41-45
    Missing data code: 99999   Decimal place: none
    N=72   Mean=2829.4   Standard Deviation=7256   Range=80-46350

    DEFINITION: Population figures--both census and estimates--are, insofar as possible, modified present-in-area counts. This means that they include data for jungle tribes, aborigines, nomadic peoples, displaced persons, and refugees, as well as national armed forces and diplomatic personnel stationed outside the territory, and that they exclude alien armed forces, alien diplomatic personnel, and enemy prisoners of war stationed inside the country. Demographic Yearbook, UN.

    The units are ten thousand (10^4) persons.

    NOTES: Variables 39-43
    A. Estimates
    C. U.N. Statistical Yearbook
    Q. The World Almanac

Variable 40   POPULATION 1955

    OSIRIS: location 190 width 5   Card: deck 3, col. 46-50
    Missing data code: 99999   Decimal place: none
    N=82   Mean=3075.1   Standard deviation=8312.6   Range=83-60819

    DEFINITION: See Variable 39 for definition and note codes.

Variable 41   POPULATION 1960

    OSIRIS: location 195 width 5   Card: deck 3, col. 51-55
    Missing data code: 99999   Decimal place: none
    N=87   Mean=3198.7   Standard deviation=8695   Range=94-65000

    DEFINITION: See Variable 39 for definition and note codes.

Variable 42   POPULATION 1963

    OSIRIS: location 200 width 5   Card: deck 3, col. 56-60
    Missing data code: 99999   Decimal place: none
    N=107   Mean=2875.3   Standard deviation=8336.8   Range=46-68000

    DEFINITION: See Variable 39 for definition and note codes.

Variable 43   POPULATION 1965

    OSIRIS: location 205 width 5   Card: deck 3, col. 61-65
    Missing data code: 99999   Decimal place: none
    N=113   Mean=2853.2   Standard deviation=8427.3   Range=46-70000

    DEFINITION: See Variable 39 for definition and note codes.

Variable 44   UN ASSESSMENT/TOTAL UN ASSESSMENT 1950

    OSIRIS: location 210   width 5   Card: deck 3, col. 66-70
    Missing data code: 99999   Decimal place: none

    N=72   Mean=130.43   Standard deviation=493.29   Range=0-3979

    DEFINITION: UN assessment refers to each country's U.N. assessment.
    Total U. N. assessment is the sum of all nations' assessments.
    Statesman's Yearbook.

    The units are percent times 100.

    NOTES: Variables 44-48
    B. U.S.S.R. assessment taken as sum of U.S.S.R., Byelorussian S.S.R and
        Ukrainian S.S.R.

Variable 45   UN ASSESSMENT/TOTAL UN ASSESSMENT 1955

    OSIRIS: location 215   width 5   Card: deck 3, col. 71-75
    Missing data code: 99999   Decimal place: none

    N=64   Mean=156.05   Standard deviation=480.47   Range=0-3333

    DEFINITION: See Variable 44 for definition and note codes.

Variable 46   UN ASSESSMENT/TOTAL UN ASSESSMENT 1960

    OSIRIS: location 220   width 5   Card: deck 3, col. 76-80
    Missing data code: 99999   Decimal place: none

    N=84   Mean=116.06   Standard deviation=395.57   Range=0-3251

    DEFINITION: See Variable 44 for definition and note codes.

Variable 47   UN ASSESSMENT/TOTAL UN ASSESSMENT 1963

    OSIRIS: location 225   width 5   Card: deck 4, col. 6-10
    Missing data code: 99999   Decimal place: none

    N=107   Mean=91.150   Standard deviation=352.21   Range=0-3202

    DEFINITION: See Variable 44 for definition and note codes.

Variable 48   UN ASSESSMENT/TOTAL UN ASSESSMENT 1965

    OSIRIS: location 230   width 5   Card: deck 4, col. 11-15
    Missing data code: 99999   Decimal place: none

    N=110   Mean=95.182   Standard deviation=351.62   Range=0-3191

    DEFINITION: See Variable 44 for definition and note codes.

Variable 49   DEFENSE EXPENDITURE 1950

   OSIRIS: location 235 width 5   Card: deck 4, col. 16-20
   Missing data code: 99999   Decimal place: none

   N=57   Mean=774.75   Standard deviation=3153.8   Range=1-20717

   DEFINITION: Defense expenditure includes total current and capital
   outlays found under the defense classification in the national account
   tables in the primary source: UN Statistical Yearbook.

   Since data are given in domestic currencies, exchange rate data were
   used to convert them to U. S. dollars. Since many countries give data
   on several kinds of rates, if available, only the free rate (a rate
   that rises or falls to some extent in response to private purchases
   and sales) was used. If such data were not available, the following
   rates, in decreasing order of desirability, were used: selling or
   import rates, buying or export rates, official rate. U.N. Statistical
   Yearbook; Statesman's Yearbook; Moody's Municipal and Government
   Manual.

   The units are millions (10^6) U.S. dollars.

   NOTES: Variables 49-53
   A. Estimates
   C. U.N. Statistical Yearbook
   D. Moody's Governments & Municipalities
   E. Statesman's Yearbook
   F. Warsaw Pact contributions

Variable 50   DEFENSE EXPENDITURE 1955

   OSIRIS: location 240 width 5   Card: deck 4, col. 21-25
   Missing data code: 99999   Decimal place: none

   N=58   Mean=1384.8   Standard deviation=6007.1   Range=2-44428

   DEFINITION: See Variable 49 for definition and note codes.

Variable 51   DEFENSE EXPENDITURE 1960

   OSIRIS: location 245 width 5   Card: deck 4, col. 26-30
   Missing data code: 99999   Decimal place: none

   N=48   Mean=1440   Standard deviation=6876.8   Range=2-47690

   DEFINITION: See Variable 49 for definition and note codes.

Variable 52   DEFENSE EXPENDITURE 1963

   OSIRIS: location 250 width 5   Card: deck 4, col. 31-35
   Missing data code: 99999   Decimal place: none

   N=104   Mean=1030.4   Standard deviation=5474.9   Range=0-53429

   DEFINITION: See Variable 49 for definition and note codes.

Variable 53   DEFENSE EXPENDITURE 1965

    OSIRIS: location 255 width 5   Card: deck 4, col. 36-40
    Missing data code: 99999   Decimal place: none

    N=113   Mean=1280.4   Standard deviation=6523.3   Range=0-51884

    DEFINITION: See Variable 49 for definition and note codes.

Variable 54   ENGLISH TITLES TRANSLATED/FOREIGN TITLES TRANSLATED 1950

    OSIRIS: location 260 width 5   Card: deck 4, col. 41-45
    Missing data code: 99999   Decimal place: none

    N=25   Mean=570.40   Standard deviation=854.41   Range=10-714

    DEFINITION: Book titles cover all non-periodical publications.
    UN Statistical Yearbook.

    The units are percent times one thousand (10^3).

    NOTES: Variables 54-58
    I. The Index Translationum (1965)
    J. English is the Local Language

Variable 55   ENGLISH TITLES TRANSLATED/FOREIGN TITLES TRANSLATED 1955

    OSIRIS: location 265 width 5   Card: deck 4, col. 46-50
    Missing data code: 99999   Decimal place: none

    N=27   Mean=379.56   Standard deviation=203.77   Range=30-692

    DEFINITION: See Variable 54 for definition and note codes.

Variable 56   ENGLISH TITLES TRANSLATED/FOREIGN TITLES TRANSLATED 1960

    OSIRIS: location 270 width 5   Card: deck 4, col. 51-55
    Missing data code: 99999   Decimal place: none

    N=40   Mean=456.25   Standard deviation=222.54   Range=33-933

    DEFINITION: See Variable 54 for definition and note codes.

Variable 57   ENGLISH TITLES TRANSLATED/FOREIGN TITLES TRANSLATED 1963

    OSIRIS: location 275 width 5   Card: deck 4, col. 56-60
    Missing data code: 99999   Decimal place: none

    N=51   Mean=355.39   Standard deviation=250.87   Range=0-827

    DEFINITION: See Variable 54 for definition and note codes.

Variable 58   ENGLISH TITLES TRANSLATED/FOREIGN TITLES TRANSLATED 1965

   OSIRIS: location 280 width 5   Card: deck 4, col. 61-65
   Missing data code: 99999   Decimal place: none
   N=61   Mean=401.93   Standard deviation=279.22   Range=0-1000

   DEFINITION: See Variable 54 for definition and note codes.

Variable 59   BLOC MEMBERSHIP 1950

   OSIRIS: location 285 width 5   Card: deck 4, col. 66-70
   Missing data code: 99999   Decimal place: none
   N=72

   DEFINITION: Rating: 0 = Communist bloc membership; 1 = neutral bloc; 2 = Western bloc. Communist and Western bloc memberships are determined by military treaties or alliances with the Soviet Union or the United States. The neutral bloc, a residual category, consists of those nations with no military treaties or alliances with either of the aforementioned bloc leaders. Statesman's Yearbook; T. N. Dupuy, The Almanac of World Military Power.

Variable 60   BLOC MEMBERSHIP 1955

   OSIRIS: location 290 width 5   Card: deck 4, col. 71-75
   Missing data code: 99999   Decimal place: none
   N=82

   DEFINITION: See Variable 59 for definition.

Variable 61   BLOC MEMBERSHIP 1960

   OSIRIS: location 295 width 5   Card: deck 4, col. 76-80
   Missing data code: 99999   Decimal place: none
   N=87

   DEFINITION: See Variable 59 for definition.

Variable 62   BLOC MEMBERSHIP 1963

   OSIRIS: location 300 width 5   Card: deck 5, col. 6-10
   Missing data code: 99999   Decimal place: none
   N=107

   DEFINITION: See Variable 59 for definition.

Variable 63   BLOC MEMBERSHIP 1965

   OSIRIS: location 305 width 5   Card: deck 5, col. 11-15
   Missing data code: 99999   Decimal place: none
   N=113

   DEFINITION: See Variable 59 for definition.

Variable 64   US AID RECEIVED/USSR AND US AID RECEIVED 1950

    OSIRIS: location 310 width 5   Card: deck 5, col. 16-20
    Missing data code: 99999   Decimal place: none

    N=71   Mean 7399.49   Standard deviation=2304.8   Range=33-9989

    DEFINITION: US aid received is divided by the sum of USSR and US aid received. In order to avoid undefined cases when the denominator is zero, 1 is added to both the US and USSR data. Thus, (10^6 $ + $1/10^6$ $ + 2). The New York Times (March 22, 1959); The Foreign Assistance Program, Annual Report to U. S. Congress; World Economic Survey, UN; Hearings Before the Committee on Foreign Affairs, U. S. House of Representatives; Hearing Before the Committee on Foreign Relations, U. S. Senate.

    The units are ten thousand (10^4) times the index.

    NOTES: Variables 64-68
    A. Estimates
    K. The Net Cost of Soviet Foreign Aid, James Richard Carter, p. 109
    L. Soviet Foreign Aid, Marshall I. Goldman, p. 28
    M. Aid for Development, H.J.P. Arnold, p. 164 (figures are for 1964)
    N. Due to lack of data for Russian aid, ratios for these nations cannot legitimately be calculated.

Variable 65   US AID RECEIVED/USSR AND US AID RECEIVED 1955

    OSIRIS: location 315 width 5   Card: deck 5, col. 21-25
    Missing data code: 99999   Decimal place: none

    N=77   Mean=6865.3   Standard deviation=2860.8   Range=70-9968

    DEFINITION: See Variable 64 for definition and note codes.

Variable 66   US AID RECEIVED/USSR AND US AID RECEIVED 1960

    OSIRIS: location 320 width 5   Card: deck 5, col. 26-30
    Missing data code: 99999   Decimal place: none

    N=73   Mean=6895.9   Standard deviation=3043   Range=26-9965

    DEFINITION: See Variable 64 for definition and note codes.

Variable 67   US AID RECEIVED/USSR AND US AID RECEIVED 1963

    OSIRIS: location 325 width 5   Card: deck 5, col. 31-35
    Missing data code: 99999   Decimal place: none

    N=62   Mean=4972.6   Standard deviation=3133.9   Range=100-9900

    DEFINITION: See Variable 64 for definition and note codes.

Variable 68   US AID RECEIVED/USSR AND US AID RECEIVED 1965

    OSIRIS: location 330 width 5   Card: deck 5, col. 36-40
    Missing data code: 99999   Decimal place: none

    N=112   Mean=6889.6   Standard deviation=2982.6   Range=76-9963

    DEFINITION: See Variable 64 for definition and note codes.

Variable 69   FREEDOM OF OPPOSITION 1950

    OSIRIS: location 335 width 5   Card: deck 5, col. 41-45
    Missing data code: 99999   Decimal place: none
    N=72

    DEFINITION: 0 = political opposition not permitted (groups not allowed
    to organize for political action, e.g., interest groups, political parties);
    1 = restricted political opposition allowed (groups to organize in
    politics, but oppositional role limited and they may not campaign
    for control of government); 2 = political opposition mostly unrestricted
    (groups can organize for political action and may campaign for control
    of government). Statesman's Yearbook; The Worldmark Encyclopedia of
    the Nations; Political Handbook and Atlas of the World.

    NOTES: Variables 69-73
    A. Estimates
    B. Statesman's Yearbook
    P. Politics of the Developing Nations, Fred R. Von der Mihden
    Z. Political Handbook and Atlas of the World (1964)

Variable 70   FREEDOM OF OPPOSITION 1955

    OSIRIS: location 340 width 5   Card: deck 5, col. 46-50
    Missing data code: 99999   Decimal place: none
    N=80

    DEFINITION: See Variable 69 for definition and note codes.

Variable 71   FREEDOM OF OPPOSITION 1960

    OSIRIS: location 345 width 5   Card: deck 5, col. 51-55
    Missing data code: 99999   Decimal place: none
    N=87

    DEFINITION: See Variable 69 for definition and note codes.

Variable 72   FREEDOM OF OPPOSITION 1963

    OSIRIS: location 350 width 5   Card: deck 5, col. 56-60
    Missing data code: 99999   Decimal place: none
    N=107

    DEFINITION: See Variable 69 for definition and note codes.

Variable 73   FREEDOM OF OPPOSITION 1965

    OSIRIS: location 355   width 5   Card: deck 5, col. 61-65
    Missing data code: 99999   Decimal place: none
    N=113

    DEFINITION: See Variable 69 for definition and note codes.

Variable 74   IFC AND IBRD SUBSCRIPTION/$(GNP)^2$ PER CAPITA 1950

    OSIRIS: location 360   width 5   Card: deck 5, col. 66-70
    Missing data code: 99999   Decimal place: none
    N=66   Mean=654.08   Standard deviation=1405.60   Range=0-7862

    DEFINITION: The numerator represents subscriptions of member nations to the International Finance Corporation and the International Bank of Reconstruction and Development. The denominator, GNP^2 per capita is chosen to measure the economic resources of a nation--its need for economic aid or its ability to give aid to other nations. Gross domestic product data are used in place of GNP and differ by the exclusion of incomes received from abroad. These economic resources are believed to be best indexed by an exponential, rather than linear function of GNP. International Finance Corporation Annual Report; International Bank of Reconstruction and Development, Annual Report; Demographic Yearbook, U.N.; Statistical Yearbook, U.N.

    The units are 10^7.

    NOTES: Variables 74-78
    A. Estimates
    B. Yearbook of National Accounts Statistics (1965)
    C. GNP data is not available

Variable 75   IFC AND IBRD SUBSCRIPTION/$(GNP)^2$ PER CAPITA 1955

    OSIRIS: location 365   width 5   Card: deck 5, col. 71-75
    Missing data code: 99999   Decimal place: none
    N=79   Mean=627.59   Standard deviation=1235.8   Range=0-7083

    DEFINITION: See Variable 74 for definition and note codes.

Variable 76   IFC AND IBRD SUBSCRIPTION/$(GNP)^2$ PER CAPITA 1960

    OSIRIS: location 370   width 5   Card: deck 5, col. 76-80
    Missing data code: 99999   Decimal place: none
    N=53   Mean=1114.9   Standard deviation=3585.5   Range=0-26087

    DEFINITION: See Variable 74 for definition and note codes.

Variable 77   IFC AND IBRD SUBSCRIPTION/(GNP)^2 PER CAPITA 1963

    OSIRIS: location 375 width 5   Card: deck 6, col. 6-10
    Missing data code: 99999   Decimal place: none
    N=64   Mean=563.42   Standard deviation=997.15   Range=7-7565

    DEFINITION: See Variable 74 for definition and note codes.

Variable 78   IFC AND IBRD SUBSCRIPTION/(GNP)^2 PER CAPITA 1965

    OSIRIS: location 380 width 5   Card: deck 6, col. 11-15
    Missing data code: 99999   Decimal place: none
    N=69   Mean=1451.8   Standard deviation=2834.2   Range=26-18850

    DEFINITION: See Variable 74 for definition and note codes.

Variable 79   THREATS 1950

    OSIRIS: location 385 width 5   Card: deck 6, col. 16-20
    Missing data code: 99999   Decimal place: none
    N=67   Mean=.29851-1   Standard deviation=0.24   Range=0-2

    DEFINITION: A threat is any official diplomatic communication or governmental statement asserting that if a particular country does or does not do a particular thing it will incur negative sanctions. The New York Timex Index; New International Yearbook; Keesinq's Contemporary Archives; Facts on File; Britannica Book of the Year.

Variable 80   THREATS 1955

    OSIRIS: location 390 width 5   Card: deck 6, col. 21-25
    Missing data code: 99999   Decimal place: none
    N=82   Mean=.17   Standard deviation=.644   Range=0-5

    DEFINITION: See Variable 79 for definition and sources.

Variable 81   THREATS 1960

    OSIRIS: location 395 width 5   Card: deck 6, col. 26-30
    Missing data code: 99999   Decimal place: none
    N=87   Mean=.103   Standard deviation=.483   Range=0-4

    DEFINITION: See Variable 79 for definition and sources.

Variable 82   THREATS 1963

    OSIRIS: location 400 width 5   Card: deck 6, col. 31-35
    Missing data code: 99999   Decimal place: none
    N=107   Mean=.168   Standard deviation=.651   Range=0-5

    DEFINITION: See Variable 79 for definition and sources.

Variable 83   THREATS 1965

   OSIRIS: location 405 width 5   Card: deck 6, col. 36-40
   Missing data code: 99999   Decimal place: none
   N=113   Mean=.212   Standard deviation=.725   Range=0-5

   DEFINITION: See Variable 79 for definition and sources.

Variable 84   ACCUSATIONS 1950

   OSIRIS: location 410 width 5   Card: deck 6, col. 41-45
   Missing data code: 99999   Decimal place: none
   N=68   Mean=5.87   Standard deviation=16.38   Range=0-102

   DEFINITION: An accusation is any official diplomatic or governmental statement involving charges and allegations of a derogatory nature against another country. The New York Times Index; New International Yearbook; Keesing's Contemporary Archives; Facts on File; Britannica Book of the Year.

Variable 85   ACCUSATIONS 1955

   OSIRIS: location 415 width 5   Card: deck 6, col. 46-50
   Missing data code: 99999   Decimal place: none
   N=82   Mean=7.9268   Standard deviation=20.459   Range=0-144

   DEFINITION: See Variable 84 for definition.

Variable 86   ACCUSATIONS 1960

   OSIRIS: location 420 width 5   Card: deck 6, col. 51-55
   Missing data code: 99999   Decimal place: none
   N=87   Mean=4.5632   Standard deviation=13.080   Range=0-89

   DEFINITION: See Variable 84 for definition.

Variable 87   ACCUSATIONS 1963

   OSIRIS: location 425 width 5   Card: deck 6, col. 56-60
   Missing data code: 99999   Decimal place: none
   N=107   Mean=2.0467   Standard deviation=5.4779   Range=0-42

   DEFINITION: See Variable 84 for definition.

Variable 88   ACCUSATIONS 1965

   OSIRIS: location 430 width 5   Card: deck 6, col. 61-64
   Missing data code: 99999   Decimal place: none
   N=113   Mean=3.9292   Standard deviation=10.105   Range=0-71

   DEFINITION: See Variable 84 for definition.

Variable 89   KILLED IN FOREIGN VIOLENCE 1950

   OSIRIS: location 435 width 6   Card: deck 6, col. 65-70
   Missing data code: 999999   Decimal place: none

   N=70   Mean=5772.5   Standard deviation=27900   Range=0-200000

   DEFINITION: Number killed is the total number of deaths resulting directly from any violent interchange between countries. The New York Times Index; New International Yearbook; Keesing's Contemporary Archives; Facts on File; Britannica Book of the Year.

   The units are 10^{-1}.

   NOTES: Variables 89-93
   A. Estimates
   D. Keesing's Contemporary Archives
   G. Kahin & Lewis The United States in Vietnam (1969), pp. 185-188
   H. Annual Register of World Events (1965)
   J. Data and estimates referring to the Korean War were based upon three sources:
      1. David Rees, The Limited War (1964)
      2. Mathew Ridgeway, The Korean War (1967)
      3. Korean Army History (Vol. 1-Vol. 12)

Variable 90   KILLED IN FOREIGN VIOLENCE 1955

   OSIRIS: location 441 width 5   Card: deck 6, col. 71-75
   Missing data code: 99999   Decimal place: none

   N=81   Mean=14.975   Standard deviation=64.746   Range=0-437

   DEFINITION: See Variable 89 for definition and note codes.

Variable 91   KILLED IN FOREIGN VIOLENCE 1960

   OSIRIS: location 446 width 5   Card: deck 6, col. 76-80
   Missing data code: 99999   Decimal place: none

   N=87   Mean=95.805   Standard deviation=596.22   Range=0-4816

   DEFINITION: See Variable 89 for definition and note codes.

Variable 92   KILLED IN FOREIGN VIOLENCE 1963

   OSIRIS: location 451 width 5   Card: deck 7, col. 6-10
   Missing data code: 99999   Decimal place: none

   N=104   Mean=69.115   Standard deviation=561.85   Range=0-5665

   DEFINITION: See Variable 89 for definition and note codes.

Variable 93   KILLED IN FOREIGN VIOLENCE 1965

   OSIRIS: location 456 width 5   Card: deck 7, col. 11-15
   Missing data code: 99999   Decimal place: none

   N=113   Mean=389.16   Standard deviation=1725.7   Range=0-11243

   DEFINITION: See Variable 89 for definition and note codes.

Variable 94   MILITARY ACTION OR NOT 1950

    OSIRIS: LOCATION 461 width 5   Card: deck 7, col. 16-20
    Missing data code: 99999   Decimal place: none
    N=70

    DEFINITION: Rating: 0 = no military action; 1 = military action. Military action is defined as any military clash involving gunfire between countries but short of war. War is defined as any military clash in which more than .02 percent of its population are militarily involved. The New York Times Index; New International Yearbook; Keesing's Contemporary Archives; Facts on File; Britannica Book of the Year.

    NOTES: Variables 94-98
    D. Keesings Contemporary Archives

Variable 95   MILITARY ACTION OR NOT 1955

    OSIRIS: location 466 width 5   Card: deck 7, col. 21-25
    Missing data code: 99999   Decimal place: none
    N=81

    DEFINITION: See Variable 94 for definition and note codes.

Variable 96   MILITARY ACTION OR NOT 1960

    OSIRIS: location 471 width 5   Card: deck 7, col. 26-30
    Missing data code: 99999   Decimal place: none
    N=87

    DEFINITION: See Variable 94 for definition and note codes.

Variable 97   MILITARY ACTION OR NOT 1963

    OSIRIS: location 476 width 5   Card: deck 7, col. 31-35
    Missing data code: 99999   Decimal place: none
    N=104

    DEFINITION: See Variable 94 for definition and note codes.

Variable 98   MILITARY ACTION OR NOT 1965

    OSIRIS: location 481 width 5   Card: deck 7, col. 36-40
    Missing data code: 99999   Decimal place: none
    N=113

    DEFINITION: See Variable 94 for definition and note codes.

Variable 99   PROTESTS 1950

    OSIRIS: location 486 width 5   Card: deck 7, col. 41-45
    Missing data code: 99999   Decimal place: none

    N=66   Mean=1.303   Standard deviation=2.665   Range=0-17

    DEFINITION: Any official diplomatic communication or governmental statement which complains about or objects to the policies of another country. The New York Times Index; New International Yearbook; Britannica Book of the Year.

Variable 100   PROTESTS 1955

    OSIRIS: location 491 width 5   Card: deck 7, col. 46-50
    Missing data code: 99999   Decimal place: none

    N=77   Mean=.818   Standard deviation=2.1320   Range=0-15

    DEFINITION: See Variable 99 for definition and sources.

Variable 101   PROTESTS 1960

    OSIRIS: location 496 width 5   Card: deck 7, col. 51-55
    Missing data code: 99999   Decimal place: none

    N=87   Mean=.770   Standard deviation=1.9272   Range=0-13

    DEFINITION: See Variable 99 for definition and sources.

Variable 102   PROTESTS 1963

    OSIRIS: location 501 width 5   Card: deck 7, col. 56-60
    Missing data code: 99999   Decimal place: none

    N=107   Mean=.93458   Standard deviation=3.3089   Range=0-24

    DEFINITION: See Variable 99 for definition and sources.

Variable 103   PROTESTS 1965

    OSIRIS: location 506 width 5   Card: deck 7, col. 61-65
    Missing data code: 99999   Decimal place: none

    N=113   Mean=1.2566   Standard deviation=4.1807   Range=0-31

    DEFINITION: See Variable 99 for definition and sources.

Variable 104   KILLED IN DOMESTIC VIOLENCE 1950

    OSIRIS: location 511 width 5   Card: deck 7, col. 66-70
    Missing data code: 99999   Decimal place: none

    N=70   Mean=18.2   Standard deviation=62.215   Range=0-293

    DEFINITION: Number killed is the number of deaths that are direct consequences of any domestic inter-group violence in the nature of strikes, riots, coups, banditry, etc. This excludes murders, executions, and suicides. Where only casualty figures are given, killed is assumed to be 20 percent of this number. Where more than one figure for a particular incident, or series of incidents were given, the median value was taken. The New York Times Index; New International Yearbook; Keesing's Contemporary Archives; Facts on File; Britannica Book of the Year.

    NOTES: Variables 104-108
    A. Estimates

Variable 105   KILLED IN DOMESTIC VIOLENCE 1955

    OSIRIS: location 516 width 5   Card: deck 7, col. 71-75
    Missing data code: 99999   Decimal place: none

    N=78   Mean=115.97   Standard deviation=673.00   Range=0-4279

    DEFINITION: See Variable 104 for definition and note codes.

Variable 106   KILLED IN DOMESTIC VIOLENCE 1960

    OSIRIS: location 521 width 5   Card: deck 7, col. 76-80
    Missing data code: 99999   Decimal place: none

    N=84   Mean=11.167   Standard deviation=31.035   Range=0-200

    DEFINITION: See Variable 104 for definition and note codes.

Variable 107   KILLED IN DOMESTIC VIOLENCE 1963

    OSIRIS: location 526 width 5   Card: deck 8, col. 6-10
    Missing data code: 99999   Decimal place: none

    N=107   Mean=480.13   Standard deviation=3517.2   Range=0-36010

    DEFINITION: See Variable 104 for definition and note codes.

Variable 108   KILLED IN DOMESTIC VIOLENCE 1965

    OSIRIS: location 531 width 6   Card: deck 8, col. 11-16
    Missing data code: 999999   Decimal place: none

    N=113   Mean=2331.0   Standard deviation=23524   Range=0-250000

    DEFINITION: See Variable 104 for definition and note codes.

-37-

Variable 109   GENERAL STRIKES 1950

    OSIRIS: location 537 width 5   Card: deck 8, col. 17-20
    Missing data code: 99999   Decimal place: none

    N=72   Mean=.27778   Standard deviation=.87568   Range=0-5

    DEFINITION: A general strike is one in which 1000 or more industrial or service workers and more than one employer are involved. It is aimed at national government policies or authority. (General strikes do not include those whose nature is to force government or private industry to grant wage or working concessions.) The New York Times Index; New International Yearbook; Keesing's Contemporary Archives; Facts on File; Britannica Book of the Year.

Variable 110   GENERAL STRIKES 1955

    OSIRIS: location 542 width 5   Card: deck 8, col. 21-25
    Missing data code: 99999   Decimal place: none

    N=79   Mean=.088   Standard deviation=.68294   Range=0-6

    DEFINITION: See Variable 109 for definition and sources.

Variable 111   GENERAL STRIKES 1960

    OSIRIS: location 547 width 5   Card: deck 8, col.26-30
    Missing data code: 99999   Decimal place: none

    N=87   Mean=.19540   Standard deviation=.60692   Range=0-3

    DEFINITION: See Variable 109 for definition and sources.

Variable 112   GENERAL STRIKES 1963

    OSIRIS: location 552 width 5   Card: deck 8, col. 31-35
    Missing data code: 99999   Decimal place: none

    N=107   Mean=.074766   Standard deviation=.35557   Range=0-2

    DEFINITION: See Variable 109 for definition and sources.

Variable 113   GENERAL STRIKES 1965

    OSIRIS: location 557 width 5   Card: deck 8, col. 36-40
    Missing data code: 99999   Decimal place: none

    N=113   Mean=.088496   Standard deviation=.31503   Range=0-2

    DEFINITION: See Variable 109 for definition and sources.

Variable 114   RIOTS 1950

   OSIRIS: location 562 width 5   Card: deck 8, col. 41-45
   Missing data code: 99999   Decimal place: none
   N=72   Mean=.33333   Standard deviation=.97865   Range=0-5

   DEFINITION: A riot is any violent demonstration or clash or more than 100 citizens involving the use of physical force. <u>The New York Times Index</u>; <u>New International Yearbook</u>; <u>Keesing's Contemporary Archives</u>; <u>Facts on File</u>; <u>Britannica Book of the Year</u>.

Variable 115   RIOTS 1955

   OSIRIS: location 567 width 5   Card: deck 8, col. 46-50
   Missing data code: 99999   Decimal place: none
   N=79   Mean=.39241   Standard deviation=1.9963   Range=0-17

   DEFINITION: See Variable 114 for definition and sources.

Variable 116   RIOTS 1960

   OSIRIS: location 572 width 5   Card: deck 8, col. 51-55
   Missing data code: 99999   Decimal place: none
   N=87   Mean=.66667   Standard deviation=1.8531   Range=0-10

   DEFINITION: See Variable 114 for definition and sources.

Variable 117   RIOTS 1963

   OSIRIS: location 577 width 5   Card: deck 8, col. 56-60
   Missing data code: 99999   Decimal place: none
   N=107   Mean=.83178   Standard deviation=2.7351   Range=0-24

   DEFINITION: See Variable 114 for definition and sources.

Variable 118   RIOTS 1965

   OSIRIS: LOCATION 582 width 5   Card: deck 8, col. 61-65
   Missing data code: 99999   Decimal place: none
   N=113   Mean=.66372   Standard deviation=1.9667   Range-0-16

   DEFINITION: See Variable 114 for definition and sources.

Variable 119   PURGES 1950

    OSIRIS: location 587 width 5　　Card: deck 8, col. 66-70
    Missing data code: 99999　　　　Decimal place: none

    N=72　　Mean=0.125　　Standard deviation=0.37294　　Range=0-2

    DEFINITION: A purge is any systematic elimination by jailing or execution within the ranks of the regime or the opposition. (If elimination of opposition continues over a period of time without a relaxation of more than three months, then it is one purge. The New York Times Index; New International Yearbook; Keesing's Contemporary Archives; Facts on File; Britannica Book of the Year.

Variable 120   PURGES 1955

    OSIRIS: location 592 width 5　　Card: deck 8, col. 71-75
    Missing data code: 99999　　　　Decimal place: none

    N=79　　Mean=.22785　　Standard deviation=.52986　　Range=0-3

    DEFINITION: See Variable 119 for definition and sources.

Variable 121   PURGES 1960

    OSIRIS: location 597 width 5　　Card: deck 8, col. 76-80
    Missing data code: 99999　　　　Decimal place: none

    N=87　　Mean=.11494　　Standard deviation=.41555　　Range=0-2

    DEFINITION: See Variable 119 for definition and sources.

Variable 122   PURGES 1963

    OSIRIS: location 602 width 5　　Card: deck 9, col. 6-10
    Missing data code: 99999　　　　Decimal place: none

    N=107　　Mean=.15888　　Standard deviation=.45866　　Range=0-3

    DEFINITION: See Variable 119 for definition and sources.

Variable 123   PURGES 1965

    OSIRIS: location 607 width 5　　Card: deck 9, col. 11-15
    Missing data code: 99999　　　　Decimal place: none

    N=113　　Mean=.27434　　Standard deviation=.55497　　Range=0-3

    DEFINITION: See Variable 119 for definition and sources.

Variable 124   DEMONSTRATIONS 1950

   OSIRIS: location 612 width 5   Card: deck 9, col. 16-20
   Missing data code: 99999   Decimal place: none
   N=72   Mean=0.0833   Standard deviation=0.32501   Range=0-2

   DEFINITION: A demonstration is any peaceful public gathering of at
   least 100 people for the primary purpose of displaying or voicing their
   opposition to government policies or authority, including those
   demonstrations of a strictly anti-foreign nature. These are discrete
   events limited to one day and to a particular group of people.
   The New York Times Index; New International Yearbook; Keesing's
   Contemporary Archives; Facts on File; Britannica Book of the Year.

Variable 125   DEMONSTRATIONS 1955

   OSIRIS: location 617 width 5   Card: deck 9, col. 21-25
   Missing data code: 99999   Decimal place: none
   N=79   Mean=.50633   Standard deviation=1.3385   Range=0-7

   DEFINITION: See Variable 124 for definition and sources.

Variable 126   DEMONSTRATIONS 1960

   OSIRIS: location 622 width 5   Card: deck 9, col. 26-30
   Missing data code: 99999   Decimal place: none
   N=87   Mean=.41379   Standard deviation=1.6813   Range=0-13

   DEFINITION: See Variable 124 for definition and sources.

Variable 127   DEMONSTRATIONS 1963

   OSIRIS: location 627 width 5   Card: deck 9, col. 31-35
   Missing data code: 99999   Decimal place: none
   N=107   Mean=1.1028   Standard deviation=6.576   Range=0-67

   DEFINITION: See Variable 124 for definition and sources.

Variable 128   DEMONSTRATIONS 1965

   OSIRIS: location 632 width 5   Card: deck 9, col. 36-40
   Missing data code: 99999   Decimal place: none
   N=113   Mean=.69912   Standard deviation=2.310   Range=0-15

   DEFINITION: See Variable 124 for definition and sources.

Variable 129   ROMAN CATHOLICS/POPULATION 1950

    OSIRIS: location 637 width 5   Card: deck 9, col. 41-45
    Missing data code: 99999   Decimal place: none

    N=71   Mean=414.87   Standard deviation=427.94   Range=0-1000

    DEFINITION: For population see Variable 39. Religion may refer to religious application or belief. Christianity is divided into Protestant and Catholic. Catholic Encyclopedia, Supplement II; Demographic Yearbook, UN; Worldmark Encyclopedia of the Nations; National Catholic Almanac.

    The units are % x 10.

    NOTES: Variable 129-133
    A. Estimates
    B. In Afghanistan all inhabitants are subject to the law of Islam
    E. Worldmark Encyclopedia of the Nations

Variable 130   ROMAN CATHOLICS/POPULATION 1955

    OSIRIS: location 642 width 5   Card: deck 9, col. 46-50
    Missing data code: 99999   Decimal place: none

    N=81   Mean=393.44   Standard deviation=426.58   Range=0-995

    DEFINITION: See Variable 129 for definition and note codes.

Variable 131   ROMAN CATHOLICS/POPULATION 1960

    OSIRIS: location 647 width 5   Card: deck 9, col. 51-55
    Missing data code: 99999   Decimal place: none

    N=86   Mean=367.41   Standard deviation=407.60   Range=0-995

    DEFINITION: See Variable 129 for definition and note codes.

Variable 132   ROMAN CATHOLICS/POPULATION 1963

    OSIRIS: location 652 width 5   Card: deck 9, col. 56-60
    Missing data code: 99999   Decimal place: none

    N=107   Mean=319.79   Standard deviation=387.70   Range=0-997

    DEFINITION: See Variable 129 for definition and note codes.

Variable 133   ROMAN CATHOLICS/POPULATION 1965

    OSIRIS: location 657 width 5   Card: deck 9, col. 61-65
    Missing data code: 99999   Decimal place: none

    N=112   Mean=314.90   Standard deviation=369.53   Range=0-994

    DEFINITION: See Variable 129 for definition and note codes.

Variable 134   AIR DISTANCE FROM U.S. 1950

    OSIRIS: location 662 width 5   Card: deck 9, col. 66-70
    Missing data code: 99999   Decimal place: none

    N=72   Mean=10969   Standard deviation=6303.2   Range=0-24500

    DEFINITION: Air distance is the shortest distance between national borders as directly measured from a 24" globe.

    The units are inch x 10^3.

    NOTES: Variable 134-138
    C*. Measured from Alaska
    D*. Measured from Hawaii
        *Became states in 1959, thus changing the measured distance for some nations.

Variable 135   AIR DISTANCE FROM U.S. 1955

    OSIRIS: location 667 width 5   Card: deck 9, col. 71-75
    Missing data code: 99999   Decimal place: none

    N=82   Mean=11523   Standard deviation=6316.4   Range=0-24500

    DEFINITION: See Variable 134 for definition and note codes.

Variable 136   AIR DISTANCE FROM U.S. 1960

    OSIRIS: location 672 width 5   Card: deck 9, col. 76-80
    Missing data code: 99999   Decimal place: none

    N=87   Mean=9594.8   Standard deviation=4774.5   Range=0-19875

    DEFINITION: See Variable 134 for definition and note codes.

Variable 137   AIR DISTANCE FROM U.S. 1963

    OSIRIS: location 677 width 5   Card: deck 10, col. 6-10
    Missing data code: 99999   Decimal place: none

    N=107   Mean=10555   Standard deviation=5002   Range=0-24125

    DEFINITION: See Variable 134 for definition and note codes.

Variable 138   AIR DISTANCE FROM U.S. 1965

    OSIRIS: location 682 width 5   Card: deck 10, col. 11-15
    Missing data code: 99999   Decimal place: none

    N=113   Mean=10673   Standard deviation=5191.7   Range-0-24125

    DEFINITION: See Variable 124 for definition and note codes.

Variable 139   MEDICINE NGO/NGO 1950

   OSIRIS: location 687 width 5   Card: deck 10, col. 16-20
   Missing data code: 99999   Decimal place: none
   N=72   Mean=1004.60   Standard deviation=395.96   Range=0-1901

   DEFINITION: Medicine NGO is the number of medical non-governmental organizations of which a country is a member. NGO refers to a country's total NGO memberships. <u>Yearbook of International Occurrances</u>; <u>Total NGO's in Computer Output for Dyadic Co-occurrances, 1950</u>; <u>Raw Data Sheets for NGO's</u>.

   The Units are % x 10^2.

Variable 140   MEDICINE NGO/NGO 1955

   OSIRIS: location 692 width 5   Card: deck 10, col. 21-25
   Missing data code: 99999   Decimal place: none
   N=82   Mean=1092.9   Standard deviation=539.60   Range=0-3000

   DEFINITION: See Variable 139 for definition and sources.

Variable 141   MEDICINE NGO/NGO 1960

   OSIRIS: location 697 width 5   Card: deck 10, col. 26-30
   Missing data code: 99999   Decimal place: none
   N=87   Mean=847.13   Standard deviation=421.82   Range=0-1532

   DEFINITION: See Variable 139 for definition and sources.

Variable 142   MEDICINE NGO/NGO 1963

   OSIRIS: location 702 width 5   Card: deck 10, col. 31-35
   Missing data code: 99999   Decimal place: none
   N=107   Mean=855.79   Standard deviation=529.29   Range=0-2500

   DEFINITION: See Variable 139 for definition and sources.

Variable 143   MEDICINE NGO/NGO 1965

   OSIRIS: location 707 width 5   Card: deck 10, col. 36-40
   Missing data code: 99999   Decimal place: none
   N=113   Mean=929.08   Standard deviation=512.18   Range=0-2033

   DEFINITION: See Variable 139 for definition and sources.

Variable 144   DIPLOMAT EXPELLED OR RECALLED 1950

OSIRIS: location 712 width 5   Card: deck 10, col. 41-45
Missing data code: 99999   Decimal place: none

N=67   Mean=0.701   Standard deviation=1.74   Range=0-10

DEFINITION: Diplomat refers to ambassadors or lesser officials serving as official representatives of a nation at foreign embassies or other diplomatic legations. The New York Times.

Data are the number of such officials expelled or recalled.

Variable 145   DIPLOMAT EXPELLED OR RECALLED 1955

OSIRIS: location 717 width 5   Card: deck 10, col. 46-50
Missing data code: 99999   Decimal place: none

N=76   Mean=.065789   Standard deviation=.24956   Range=0-1

DEFINITION: See Variable 144 for definition and sources.

Variable 146   DIPLOMAT EXPELLED OR RECALLED 1960

OSIRIS: location 722 width 5   Card: deck 10, col. 51-55
Missing data code: 99999   Decimal place: none

N=87   Mean=.42529   Standard deviation=1.0744   Range=0-7

DEFINITION: See Variable 144 for definition and sources.

Variable 147   DIPLOMAT EXPELLED OR RECALLED 1963

OSIRIS: location 727 width 5   Card: deck 10, col. 56-60
Missing data code: 99999   Decimal place: none

N=107   Mean=.29907   Standard deviation=.67593   Range=0-3

DEFINITION: See Variable 144 for definition and sources.

Variable 148   DIPLOMAT EXPELLED OR RECALLED 1965

OSIRIS: location 732 width 5   Card: deck 10, col. 61-65
Missing data code: 99999   Decimal place: none

N=113   Mean=.31858   Standard deviation=.84795   Range=0-4

DEFINITION: See Variable 144 for definition and sources.

Variable 149   DIVORCES/MARRIAGES 1950

OSIRIS: location 737 width 5   Card: deck 10, col. 66-70
Missing data code: 99999   Decimal place: none
N=51   Mean=756.82   Standard deviation=624.71   Range=0-2310

DEFINITION: A divorce is a final legal dissolution of a marriage
. . . by a judicial decree which confers on the parties the right of
civil and/or religious remarriage . . ." Demographic Yearbook, UN.

The units are divorce per 10^3 (thousand) married pair.

NOTES: Variables 149-153
B. No legal provision for divorces, therefore the numerator is zero.
C. Worldmark Encyclopedia of the Nations
D. Demographic Yearbook, year other than primary source.

Variable 150   DIVORCES/MARRIAGES 1955

OSIRIS: location 742 width 5   Card: deck 10, col. 71-75
Missing data code: 99999   Decimal place: none
N=45   Mean=627.56   Standard deviation=512.31   Range=0-2080

DEFINITION: See Variable 149 for definition and note codes.

Variable 151   DIVORCES/MARRIAGES 1960

OSIRIS: location 747 width 5   Card: deck 10, col. 76-80
Missing data code: 99999   Decimal place: none
N=56   Mean=852.68   Standard deviation=637.81   Range=0-2580

DEFINITION: See Variable 149 for definition and note codes.

Variable 152   DIVORCES/MARRIAGES 1963

OSIRIS: location 752 width 5   Card: deck 11, col. 6-10
Missing data code: 99999   Decimal place: none
N=61   Mean=902.69   Standard deviation=656.29   Range=0-2588

DEFINITION: See Variable 149 for definition and note codes.

Variable 153   DIVORCES/MARRIAGES 1965

OSIRIS: location 757 width 5   Card: deck 11, col. 11-15
Missing data code: 99999   Decimal place: none
N=69   Mean=885.62   Standard deviation=679.58   Range=0-2689

DEFINITION: See Variable 149 for definition and note codes.

Variable 154   POPULATION/NATIONAL LAND AREA 1950

   OSIRIS: location 762 width 5   Card: deck 11, col. 16-20
   Missing data code: 99999   Decimal place: none

   N=72   Mean=52.88   Standard deviation=63.26   Range=1-316

   DEFINITION: National land area relates "to the total area of the specified geographical units, including inland water as well as such uninhabited or uninhabitable stretches of land as may lie within their mainland boundaries." Demographic Yearbook, UN.

   The units are persons per Km^2.

   NOTES: Variables 154-158
   A. Estimates
   E. U.N. Statistical Yearbook

Variable 155   POPULATION/NATIONAL LAND AREA 1955

   OSIRIS: location 767 width 5   Card: deck 11, col. 21-25
   Missing data code: 99999   Decimal place: none

   N=78   Mean=63.551   Standard deviation=73.094   Range=1-331

   DEFINITION: See Variable 154 for definition and note codes.

Variable 156   POPULATION/NATIONAL LAND AREA 1960

   OSIRIS: location 772 width 5   Card: deck 11, col. 26-30
   Missing data code: 99999   Decimal place: none

   N=87   Mean=66.230   Standard deviation=74.582   Range=1-342

   DEFINITION: See Variable 154 for definition and note codes.

Variable 157   POPULATION/NATIONAL LAND AREA 1963

   OSIRIS: location 777 width 5   Card: deck 11, col. 31-35
   Missing data code: 99999   Decimal place: none

   N=107   Mean=59.776   Standard deviation=75.397   Range=1-356

   DEFINITION: See Variable 154 for definition and note codes.

Variable 158   POPULATION/NATIONAL LAND AREA 1965

   OSIRIS: location 782 width 5   Card: deck 11, col. 36-40
   Missing data code: 99999   Decimal place: none

   N=113   Mean=64.248   Standard deviation=78.176   Range=1-366

   DEFINITION: See Variable 154 for definition and note codes.

Variable 159   ARABLE LAND/TOTAL LAND AREA 1950

    OSIRIS: location 787 width 5   Card: deck 11, col. 41-45
    Missing data code: 99999   Decimal place: none

    N=70   Mean=178.51   Standard deviation=154.87   Range=0-628

    DEFINITION: Arable land refers to "land planted to crops . . . land temporarily fallow, temporary meadows for mowing or pasture, garden land, and area under fruit trees, vines, fruit-bearing shrubs, and rubber plantation." For total land area, see Variable 164.
    Yearbook of Food and Agricultural Statistics: Production, FAO;
    Demographic Yearbook, UN.

    The units are % x 10.

    NOTES: Variables 159-163
    A. Estimates
    E. U.N. Statistical Yearbook
    L. Production Yearbook

Variable 160   ARABLE LAND/TOTAL LAND AREA 1955

    OSIRIS: location 792 width 5   Card: deck 11, col. 46-50
    Missing data code: 99999   Decimal place: none

    N=76   Mean=194.21   Standard deviation=153.91   Range=1-634

    DEFINITION: See Variable 159 for definition and note codes.

Variable 161   ARABLE LAND/TOTAL LAND AREA 1960

    OSIRIS: location 797 width 5   Card: deck 11, col. 51-55
    Missing data code: 99999   Decimal place: none

    N=85   Mean=194.71   Standard deviation=151.80   Range=0-650

    DEFINITION: See Variable 159 for definition and note codes.

Variable 162   ARABLE LAND/TOTAL LAND AREA 1963

    OSIRIS: location 802 width 5   Card: deck 11, col. 56-60
    Missing data code: 99999   Decimal place: none

    N=88   Mean=206.95   Standard deviation=159.21   Range=1-651

    DEFINITION: See Variable 159 for definition and note codes.

Variable 163   ARABLE LAND/TOTAL LAND AREA 1965

    OSIRIS: location 807 width 5   Card: deck 11, col. 61-65
    Missing data code: 99999   Decimal place: none

    N=93   Mean=204.26   Standard deviation=154.57   Range=2-630

    DEFINITION: See Variable 159 for definition and note codes.

Variable 164   NATIONAL AREA 1950

   OSIRIS: location 812 width 5   Card: deck 11, col. 66-70
   Missing data code: 99999   Decimal place: none
   N=72   Mean=1420.70   Standard deviation=3386   Range=10-22402

   DEFINITION: National land area related "to the total area of the specified geographical units, including inland water as well as such uninhabited or uninhabitable stretches of land as may lie within their mainland boundaries." Demographic Yearbook, UN; Yearbook of Food and Agricultural Statistics: Production, FAO.

   The units are 10^3 Km^2 (one thousand square Kilometers).

   NOTES: Variables 164-168
   A. Estimates
   E. U.N. Statistical Yearbook
   D. Demographic Yearbook

Variable 165   NATIONAL AREA 1955

   OSIRIS: location 817 width 5   Card: deck 11, col. 71-75
   Missing data code: 99999   Decimal place: none
   N=82   Mean=1288.3   Standard deviation=3194.7   Range=10-22402

   DEFINITION: See Variable 164 for definition and note codes.

Variable 166   NATIONAL AREA 1960

   OSIRIS: location 822 width 5   Card: deck 11, col. 76-80
   Missing data code: 99999   Decimal place: none
   N=87   Mean=1256.7   Standard deviation=3110.5   Range=10-22402

   DEFINITION: See Variable 164 for definition and note codes.

Variable 167   NATIONAL AREA 1963

   OSIRIS: location 827 width 5   Card: deck 12, col. 6-10
   Missing data code: 99999   Decimal place: none
   N=107   Mean=1145.2   Standard deviation=2821.7   Range=10-22402

   DEFINITION: See Variable 164 for definition and note codes.

Variable 168   NATIONAL AREA 1965

   OSIRIS: location 832 width 5   Card: deck 12, col. 11-15
   Missing data code: 99999   Decimal place: none
   N=113   Mean=1108.2   Standard deviation=2756.9   Range=5-22402

   DEFINITION: See Variable 164 for definition and note codes.

Variable 169   ROAD LENGTH/NATIONAL AREA 1950

    OSIRIS: location 837 width 5   Card: deck 12, col. 16-20
    Missing data code: 99999   Decimal place: none
    N=57   Mean=224.96   Standard deviation 329.32   Range=1-1319

    DEFINITION: Road length refers to "'total' road kilometrage."
    Ginsburg, Norton (ed.), Atlas of Economic Development; Steinberg,
    S. H. (ed.), The Statesman's Yearbook; Moody's Governments and
    Municipalities.

    The units are Km per 10^3 Km^2.

Variable 170   ROAD LENGTH/NATIONAL AREA 1955

    OSIRIS: location 842 width 5   Card: deck 12, col. 21-25
    Missing data code: 99999   Decimal place: none
    N=66   Mean=204.70   Standard deviation=291.97   Range=1-1347

    DEFINITION: See Variable 169 for definition and note codes.

Variable 171   ROAD LENGTH/NATIONAL AREA 1960

    OSIRIS: location 847 width 5   Card: deck 12, col. 26-30
    Missing data code: 99999   Decimal place: none
    N=74   Mean=198.36   Standard deviation=277.67   Range=1-1369

    DEFINITION: See Variable 169 for definition and note codes.

Variable 172   ROAD LENGTH/NATIONAL AREA 1963

    OSIRIS: location 852 width 5   Card: deck 12, col. 31-35
    Missing data code: 99999   Decimal place: none
    N=91   Mean=195.45   Standard deviation=292.87   Range=1-1433

    DEFINITION: See Variable 169 for definition and note codes.

Variable 173   ROAD LENGTH/NATIONAL AREA 1965

    OSIRIS: location 857 width 5   Card: deck 12, col. 36-40
    Missing data code: 99999   Decimal place: none
    N=93   Mean=229.18   Standard deviation=341.49   Range=0-1433

    DEFINITION: See Variable 169 for definition and note codes.

Variable 174   RAILROAD LENGTH/NATIONAL AREA 1950

    OSIRIS: location 862 width 5   Card: deck 12, col. 41-45
    Missing data code: 99999   Decimal place: none

    N=67   Mean=30.85   Standard deviation=38.50   Range=0-161

    DEFINITION: Railroad includes all double track without discriminating the width of gauge. <u>Atlas of Economic Development</u>; <u>Moody's Governments and Municipalities</u>; <u>The Statesman's Yearbook</u>; <u>Worldmark Encyclopedia of the Nations</u>.

    The units are Km per $10^4 Km^2$.

Variable 175   RAILROAD LENGTH/NATIONAL AREA 1955

    OSIRIS: location 867 width 5   Card: deck 12, col. 46-50
    Missing data code: 99999   Decimal place: none

    N=79   Mean=31.177   Standard deviation=39.136   Range=0-158

    DEFINITION: See Variable 174 for definition and sources.

Variable 176   RAILROAD LENGTH/NATIONAL AREA 1960

    OSIRIS: location 872 width 5   Card: deck 12, col. 51-55
    Missing data code: 99999   Decimal place: none

    N=84   Mean=31.679   Standard deviation=41.646   Range=0-157

    DEFINITION: See Variable 174 for definition and sources.

Variable 177   RAILROAD LENGTH/NATIONAL AREA 1963

    OSIRIS: location 877 width 5   Card: deck 12, col. 56-60
    Missing data code: 99999   Decimal place: none

    N=96   Mean=27.083   Standard deviation=38.956   Range=0-157

    DEFINITION: See Variable 174 for definition and sources.

Variable 178   RAILROAD LENGTH/NATIONAL AREA 1965

    OSIRIS: location 882 width 5   Card: deck 12, col. 61-65
    Missing data code: 99999   Decimal place: none

    N=99   Mean=27.202   Standard deviation=38.973   Range=0-157

    DEFINITION: See Variable 174 for definition and sources.

Variable 179   RELIGIONS 1950

    OSIRIS: location 887 width 5   Card: deck 12, col. 66-70
    Missing data code: 99999   Decimal place: none

    N=72   Mean=2.22   Standard deviation=1.037   Range=1-5

    DEFINITION: Number of religions with membership exceeding one percent of the population. Christianity is divided into Protestant and Catholic, but otherwise divisions are between major religions (Islam, Hindu, Buddhist, etc.) reported for a country. Demographic Yearbook, UN; The Worldmark Encyclopedia of the Nations.

    NOTES: Variables 179-183
    A. Estimates
    B. Worldmark Encyclopedia of the Nations
    G. Demographic Yearbook

Variable 180   RELIGIONS 1955

    OSIRIS: location 892 width 5   Card: deck 12, col. 71-75
    Missing data code: 99999   Decimal place: none

    N=82   Mean=2.2683   Standard deviation=1.0547   Range=1-5

    DEFINITION: See Variable 179 for definition and note codes.

Variable 181   RELIGIONS 1960

    OSIRIS: location 897 width 5   Card: deck 12, col. 76-80
    Missing data code: 99999   Decimal place: none

    N=87   Mean=2.2759   Standard deviation=1.0195   Range=1-5

    DEFINITION: See Variable 179 for definition and note codes.

Variable 182   RELIGIONS 1963

    OSIRIS: location 902 width 5   Card: deck 13, col. 6-10
    Missing data code: 99999   Decimal place: none

    N=107   Mean=2.3832   Standard deviation=1.0697   Range=1-5

    DEFINITION: See Variable 179 for definition and note codes.

Variable 183   RELIGIONS 1965

    OSIRIS: location 907 width 5   Card: deck 13, col. 11-15
    Missing data code: 99999   Decimal place: none

    N=107   Mean=2.3832   Standard deviation=1.0697   Range=1-5

    DEFINITION: See Variable 179 for definition and note codes.

Variable 184   IMMIGRANTS/MIGRANTS 1950

    OSIRIS: location 912   width 5   Card: deck 13, col. 16-20
    Missing data code: 99999   Decimal place: none
    N=22   Mean=577.45   Standard deviation=334.89   Range=0-1000

    DEFINITION: Immigrants are newly arrived aliens to a country intending to remain for a period exceeding one year. Migrants include immigrants and emigrants. Emigrants are defined as nationals leaving their country with the intention of staying abroad for a period exceeding one year. Demographic Yearbook, UN; Encyclopedia Britannica World Atlas; The Worldmark Encyclopedia of the Nations; Yale Political Data Program.

    The units are % x 10.

    NOTES: Variable 184-188
    A. Estimates
    B. Worldmark Encyclopedia of the Nations

Variable 185   IMMIGRANTS/MIGRANTS 1955

    OSIRIS: location 917   width 5   Card: deck 13, col. 21-25
    Missing data code: 99999   Decimal place: none
    N=33   Mean=529.91   Standard deviation=229.74   Range=0-991

    DEFINITION: See Variable 184 for definition and note codes.

Variable 186   IMMIGRANTS/MIGRANTS 1960

    OSIRIS: location 922   width 5   Card: deck 13, col. 26-30
    Missing data code: 99999   Decimal place: none
    N=33   Mean=461.09   Standard deviation=259.86   Range=13-982

    DEFINITION: See Variable 184 for definition and note codes.

Variable 187   IMMIGRANTS/MIGRANTS 1963

    OSIRIS: location 927   width 5   Card: deck 13, col. 31-35
    Missing data code: 99999   Decimal place: none
    N=53   Mean=347.19   Standard deviation=343.02   Range=0-1000

    DEFINITION: See Variable 184 for definition and note codes.

Variable 188   IMMIGRANTS/MIGRANTS 1965

    OSIRIS: location 932   width 5   Card: deck 13, col. 36-40
    Missing data code: 99999   Decimal place: none
    N=34   Mean=453.59   Standard deviation=263.87   Range=3-998

    DEFINITION: See Variable 184 for definition and note codes.

Variable 189   AVERAGE RAINFALL 1950

   OSIRIS: location 937 width 5   Card: deck 13, col. 41-45
   Missing data code: 99999   Decimal place: none
   N=72   Mean=1067.80   Standard deviation=695.43   Range=79-3429

   DEFINITION: Average rainfall is defined as the mean of the yearly mean of monthly rainfall for the year 1931-1942, which in turn is averaged across all reporting stations. World Weather Records; World Atlas, Rand McNally.

   The units are millimeters.

   NOTES: Variable 189-193
   A. Estimates
   C. Rand McNally's Cosmopolitan World Atlas

Variable 190   AVERAGE RAINFALL 1955

   OSIRIS: location 942 width 5   Card: deck 13, col. 46-50
   Missing data code: 99999   Decimal place: none
   N=82   Mean=1100.2   Standard deviation=686.71   Range=79-3429

   DEFINITION: See Variable 189 for definition and note codes.

Variable 191   AVERAGE RAINFALL 1960

   OSIRIS: location 947 width 5   Card: deck 13, col. 51-55
   Missing data code: 99999   Decimal place: none
   N=87   Mean=1097.7   Standard deviation=698.33   Range=79-3429

   DEFINITION: See Variable 189 for definition and note codes.

Variable 192   AVERAGE RAINFALL 1963

   OSIRIS: location 952 width 5   Card: deck 13, col. 56-60
   Missing data code: 99999   Decimal place: none
   N=107   Mean=1115.9   Standard deviation=690.74   Range=79-3429

   DEFINITION: See Variable 189 for definition and note codes.

Variable 193   AVERAGE RAINFALL 1965

   OSIRIS: location 957 width 5   Card: deck 13, col. 61-65
   Missing data code: 99999   Decimal place: none
   N=107   Mean=1115.9   Standard deviation=690.74   Range=79-3429

   DEFINITION: See Variable 189 for definition and note codes.

Variable 194   MEMBERSHIP OF LARGEST RELIGION/POPULATION 1950

   OSIRIS: location 962 width 5   Card: deck 13, col. 66-70
   Missing data code: 99999   Decimal place: none
   N=69   Mean=82.36   Standard deviation=20.50   Range=17-100

   DEFINITION: The membership exceeds one percent of the population.
   Christianity is divided into Protest and Catholic, but otherwise divisions
   are between major religions (Islam, Hindu, Buddhist, etc.). Population
   is taken from the same census as that for religions. Demographic Yearbook,
   UN; The Worldmark Encyclopedia of the Nations.

   The units are %.

   NOTES: Variables 194-198
   A. Estimates
   B. Worldmark Encyclopedia of the Nations
   H. Information Please Almanac (1962)

Variable 195   MEMBERSHIP OF LARGEST RELIGION/POPULATION 1955

   OSIRIS: location 967 width 5   Card: deck 13, col. 71-75
   Missing data code: 99999   Decimal place: none
   N=75   Mean=82.307   Standard deviation=20.080   Range=17-100

   DEFINITION: See Variable 194 for definition and note codes.

Variable 196   MEMBERSHIP OF LARGEST RELIGION/POPULATION 1960

   OSIRIS: location 972 width 5   Card: deck 13, col. 76-80
   Missing data code: 99999   Decimal place: none
   N=79   Mean=82.177   Standard deviation=19.354   Range=17-100

   DEFINITION: See Variable 194 for definition and note codes.

Variable 197   MEMBERSHIP OF LARGEST RELIGION/POPULATION 1963

   OSIRIS: location 977 width 5   Card: deck 14, col. 6-10
   Missing data code: 99999   Decimal place: none
   N=87   Mean=80.069   Standard deviation=20.602   Range=17-100

   DEFINITION: See Variable 194 for definition and note codes.

Variable 198   MEMBERSHIP OF LARGEST RELIGION/POPULATION 1965

   OSIRIS: location 982 width 5   Card: deck 14, col. 11-15
   Missing data code: 99999   Decimal place: none
   N=106   Mean=75.802   Standard deviation=21.804   Range=17-100

   DEFINITION: See Variable 194 for definition and note codes.

Variable 199   DWELLINGS WITH RUNNING WATER/DWELLINGS 1950

   OSIRIS: location 987 width 5   Card: deck 14, col. 16-20
   Missing data code: 99999   Decimal place: none

   N=24   Mean=418.96   Standard deviation=289.33   Range=1-945

   DEFINITION: "A dwelling is a room or suite of rooms...in a permanent
   building...which...is intended for private habitation and is not...used
   wholly for other purposes. It should have a separate access to a street
   or to a common space within the building..." Running water refers
   to water piped in from the outside. Statistical Yearbook, UN.

   The units are % x 10.

   NOTES: Variables 199-203
   A. Estimates

Variable 200   DWELLINGS WITH RUNNING WATER/DWELLINGS 1955

   OSIRIS: location 992 width 5   Card: deck 14, col. 21-25
   Missing data code: 99999   Decimal place: none

   N=33   Mean=459.06   Standard deviation=285.43   Range=52-988

   DEFINITION: See Variable 199 for definition and note codes.

Variable 201   DWELLINGS WITH RUNNING WATER/DWELLINGS 1960

   OSIRIS: location 997 width 5   Card: deck 14, col. 26-30
   Missing data code: 99999   Decimal place: none

   N=56   Mean=362.91   Standard deviation=319.96   Range=50-987

   DEFINITION: See Variable 199 for definition and note codes.

Variable 202   DWELLINGS WITH RUNNING WATER/DWELLINGS 1963

   OSIRIS: location 1002 width 5   Card: deck 14, col. 31-35
   Missing data code: 99999   Decimal place: none

   N=58   Mean=367.24   Standard deviation=323.44   Range=50-987

   DEFINITION: See Variable 199 for definition and note codes.

Variable 203   DWELLINGS WITH RUNNING WATER/DWELLINGS 1965

   OSIRIS: location 1007 width 5   Card: deck 14, col. 36-40
   Missing data code: 99999   Decimal place: none

   N=48   Mean=522.98   Standard deviation=316.73   Range=81-987

   DEFINITION: See Variable 199 for definition and note codes.

Variable 204   FOREIGN COLLEGE STUDENTS/COLLEGE STUDENTS 1950

    OSIRIS: location 1012 width 5   Card: deck 14, col. 41-45
    Missing data code: 99999   Decimal place: none

    N=24   Mean=38.292   Standard deviation=56.994   Range=0-253

    DEFINITION: Total number of foreign college students divided by college students for the same year. Basic Facts and Figures, UNESCO.

    The units are % x 10.

    NOTES: Variable 204-208
    A. Estimates

Variable 205   FOREIGN COLLEGE STUDENTS/COLLEGE STUDENTS 1955

    OSIRIS: location 1017 width 5   Card: deck 14, col. 46-50
    Missing data code: 99999   Decimal place: none

    N=55   Mean=52.127   Standard deviation=79.975   Range=0-348

    DEFINITION: See Variable 204 for definition and note codes.

Variable 206   FOREIGN COLLEGE STUDENTS/COLLEGE STUDENTS 1960

    OSIRIS: location 1022 width 5   Card: deck 14, col. 51-55
    Missing data code: 99999   Decimal place: none

    N=57   Mean=60.474   Standard deviation=88.417   Range=1-408

    DEFINITION: See Variable 204 for definition and note codes.

Variable 207   FOREIGN COLLEGE STUDENTS/COLLEGE STUDENTS 1963

    OSIRIS: location 1027 width 5   Card: deck 14, col. 56-60
    Missing data code: 99999   Decimal place: none

    N=81   Mean=69.099   Standard deviation=117.45   Range=0-581

    DEFINITION: See Variable 204 for definition and note codes.

Variable 208   FOREIGN COLLEGE STUDENTS/COLLEGE STUDENTS 1965

    OSIRIS: location 1032 width 5   Card: deck 14, col. 61-65
    Missing data code: 99999   Decimal place: none

    N=86   Mean=88.826   Standard deviation=138.07   Range=1-628

    DEFINITION: See Variable 204 for definition and note codes.

Variable 209   MEMBERSHIP IN NEUTRAL BLOC 1950

    OSIRIS: location 1037 width 5   Card: deck 14, col. 66-70
    Missing data code: 99999   Decimal place: none
    N=72

    DEFINITION: Rating: 0 = neutral bloc membership; 1 = non-neutral bloc membership. The neutral bloc nations are those which have no military treaties or alliances with either the United States or the Soviet Union. T. N. Dupuy, The Almanac of World Military Power; Statesman's Yearbook; Treaties and Alliances of the World.

Variable 210   MEMBERSHIP IN NEUTRAL BLOC 1955

    OSIRIS: location 1042 width 5   Card: deck 14, col. 71-75
    Missing data code: 99999   Decimal place: none
    N=76

    DEFINITION: See Variable 209 for definition and sources.

Variable 211   MEMBERSHIP IN NEUTRAL BLOC 1960

    OSIRIS: location 1047 width 5   Card: deck 14, col. 76-80
    Missing data code: 99999   Decimal place: none
    N=87

    DEFINITION: See Variable 209 for definition and sources.

Variable 212   MEMBERSHIP IN NEUTRAL BLOC 1963

    OSIRIS: location 1052 width 5   Card: deck 15, col. 6-10
    Missing data code: 99999   Decimal place: none
    N=107

    DEFINITION: See Variable 209 for definition and sources.

Variable 213   MEMBERSHIP IN NEUTRAL BLOC 1965

    OSIRIS: location 1057 width 5   Card: deck 15, col. 11-15
    Missing data code: 99999   Decimal place: none
    N=113

    DEFINITION: See Variable 209 for definition and sources.

Variable 214   AGE OF COUNTRY 1950

   OSIRIS: location 1062 width 5   Card: deck 15, col. 16-20
   Missing data code: 99999   Decimal place: none

   N=70   Mean=2.0429   Standard deviation=1.3981   Range=0-5

   DEFINITION: Date at which country became a politically recognizable unit, according to the following scale: 0=B.C.; 1=1-1499 A.D.; 2=1500-1799 A.D.; 3=1800-1899 A.D.; 4=1900-1945 A.D.; 5=1946-1955 A.D. A political unit is defined as having an internationally recognized border and some form of central administration. Thus, independence is a sufficient, but not a necessary condition of a political unit. For example, Pakistan became a politically recognizable unit as of her independence in 1948, but India, although gaining independence at the same time, has been a politically recognizable unit for centuries. An Encyclopedia of World History; Statesman's Yearbook; The Worldmark Encyclopedia of the Nations.

Variable 215   AGE OF COUNTRY 1955

   OSIRIS: location 1067 width 5   Card: deck 15, col. 21-25
   Missing data code: 99999   Decimal place: none

   N=81   Mean=1.9506   Standard deviation=1.4483   Range=0-5

   DEFINITION: See Variable 214 for definition and sources.

Variable 216   AGE OF COUNTRY 1960

   OSIRIS: location 1072 width 5   Card: deck 15, col. 26-30
   Missing data code: 99999   Decimal place: none

   N=87   Mean=2.0920   Standard deviation=1.5449   Range=0-5

   DEFINITION: See Variable 214 for definition and sources.

Variable 217   AGE OF COUNTRY 1963

   OSIRIS: location 1077 width 5   Card: deck 15, col. 31-35
   Missing data code: 99999   Decimal place: none

   N=107   Mean=2.6355   Standard deviation=1.7983   Range=0-5

   DEFINITION: See Variable 214 for definition and sources.

Variable 218   AGE OF COUNTRY 1965

   OSIRIS: location 1082 width 5   Card: deck 15, col. 36-40
   Missing data code: 99999   Decimal place: none

   N=113   Mean=2.7611   Standard deviation=1.8287   Range=0-5

   DEFINITION: See Variable 214 for definition and sources.

Variable 219   RELIGIOUS TITLES PUBLISHED/BOOK TITLES 1950

    OSIRIS: location 1087 width 5   Card: deck 15, col. 41-45
    Missing data code: 99999   Decimal place: none

    N=31   Mean=653.00   Standard deviation=427.59   Range=23-2270

    DEFINITION: Book titles "cover all non-periodical publications, including pamphlets, first editions of originals and new translations, re-editions and the more important government reports." Statistical Yearbook, UN.

    The units are % x 10^2.

Variable 220   RELIGIOUS TITLES PUBLISHED/BOOK TITLES 1955

    OSIRIS: location 1092 width 5   Card: deck 15, col. 46-50
    Missing data code: 99999   Decimal place: none

    N=61   Mean=594.59   Standard deviation=547.69   Range=0-2900

    DEFINITION: See Variable 219 for definition and sources.

Variable 221   RELIGIOUS TITLES PUBLISHED/BOOK TITLES 1960

    OSIRIS: location 1097 width 5   Card: deck 15, col. 51-55
    Missing data code: 99999   Decimal place: none

    N=59   Mean=666.78   Standard deviation=518.10   Range=10-2170

    DEFINITION: See Variable 219 for definition and sources.

Variable 222   RELIGIOUS TITLES PUBLISHED/BOOK TITLES 1963

    OSIRIS: location 1102 width 5   Card: deck 15, col. 56-60
    Missing data code: 99999   Decimal place: none

    N=73   Mean=667.81   Standard deviation=637.26   Range=0-3102

    DEFINITION: See Variable 219 for definition and sources.

Variable 223   RELIGIOUS TITLES PUBLISHED/BOOK TITLES 1965

    OSIRIS: location 1107 width 5   Card: deck 15, col. 61-65
    Missing data code: 99999   Decimal place: none

    N=73   Mean=698.92   Standard deviation=805.84   Range=0-3564

    DEFINITION: See Variable 219 for definition and sources.

Variable 224   EMIGRANTS/POPULATION 1950

   OSIRIS: location 1112 width 5   Card: deck 15, col. 66-70
   Missing data code: 99999   Decimal place: none

   N=37   Mean=438.19   Standard deviation=878.43   Range=0-3985

   DEFINITION: Emigrants are defined as nationals leaving their country with the intention of staying abroad for a period exceeding one year. Demographic Yearbook, UN; Encyclopedia Britannica World Atlas; The Worldmark Encyclopedia of the Nations.

   The units are % x 10^3.

   NOTES: Variables 224-228
   A. Estimates
   B. Worldmark Encyclopedia of the Nations

Variable 225   EMIGRANTS/POPULATION 1955

   OSIRIS: location 1117 width 5   Card: deck 15, col. 71-75
   Missing data code: 99999   Decimal place: none

   N=44   Mean=557.39   Standard deviation=1050.3   Range=0-4151

   DEFINITION: See Variable 224 for definition and note codes.

Variable 226   EMIGRANTS/POPULATION 1960

   OSIRIS: location 1122 width 5   Card: deck 15, col. 76-80
   Missing data code: 99999   Decimal place: none

   N=30   Mean=246.67   Standard deviation= 241.74   Range=0-800

   DEFINITION: See Variable 224 for definition and note codes.

Variable 227   EMIGRANTS/POPULATION 1963

   OSIRIS: location 1127 width 5   Card: deck 16, col. 6-10
   Missing data code: 99999   Decimal place: none

   N=57   Mean=141.54   Standard deviation=237.56   Range=0-1180

   DEFINITION: See Variable 224 for definition and note codes.

Variable 228   EMIGRANTS/POPULATION 1965

   OSIRIS: location 1132 width 5   Card: deck 16, col. 11-15
   Missing data code: 99999   Decimal place: none

   N=37   Mean=252.19   Standard deviation=335.36   Range=0-1371

   DEFINITION: See Variable 224 for definition and note codes.

Variable 229   SEABORNE GOODS/GNP 1950

    OSIRIS: location 1137 width 5   Card: deck 16, col. 16-20
    Missing data code: 99999   Decimal place: none
    N=38   Mean=364.05   Standard deviation=410.22   Range=50-2235

    DEFINITION: Seaborne goods are defined as the "weight of goods (including packing) in external trade loaded onto and unloaded from sea-going vessels of all flags at the parts of the country in question." Statistical Yearbook, UN. For GNP, see Variable 24.

    The units are % x 10^3.

    NOTES: Variables 229-233
    A. Estimates
    D. Yearbook of National Accounts Statistics, 1965, UN: N.Y., 1966
    J. "Indicators of Market Size for 88 Countries," Business International, N.Y., 1965
    K. Gross National Product Aid, Office of Programs Coord., Statistics and Reports Division

Variable 230   SEABORNE GOODS/GNP 1955

    OSIRIS: location 1142 width 5   Card: deck 16, col. 21-25
    Missing data code: 99999   Decimal place: none
    N=67   Mean=345.82   Standard deviation=620.81   Range=0-4347

    DEFINITION: See Variable 229 for definition and note codes.

Variable 231   SEABORNE GOODS/GNP 1960

    OSIRIS: location 1147 width 5   Card: deck 16, col. 26-30
    Missing data code: 99999   Decimal place: none
    N=67   Mean=418.37   Standard deviation=636.06   Range=2-3624

    DEFINITION: See Variable 229 for definition and note codes.

Variable 232   SEABORNE GOODS/GNP 1963

    OSIRIS: location 1152 width 5   Card: deck 16, col. 31-35
    Missing data code: 99999   Decimal place: none
    N=79   Mean=529.22   Standard deviation=892.25   Range=22-4626

    DEFINITION: See Variable 229 for definition and note codes.

Variable 233   SEABORNE GOODS/GNP 1965

    OSIRIS: location 1157 width 5   Card: deck 16, col. 36-40
    Missing data code: 99999   Decimal place: none
    N=89   Mean=720.94   Standard deviation=1254.3   Range=29-7246

Variable 234   LAW NGO'S/NGO'S 1950

   OSIRIS: location 1162 width 5   Card: deck 16, col. 41-45
   Missing data code: 99999   Decimal place: none

   N=72   Mean=508.10   Standard deviation=306.03   Range=0-1428

   DEFINITION: Total number of law NGO's of which a nation is a member divided by total number of NGO's of which the nation is a member. <u>Union of International Associations</u>; <u>Yearbook of International Organizations</u>.

   The units are % $\times 10^2$.

Variable 235   LAW NGO'S/NGO'S 1955

   OSIRIS: location 1167 width 5   Card: deck 16, col. 46-50
   Missing data code: 99999   Decimal place: none

   N=82   Mean=399.88   Standard deviation=223.48   Range=0-909

   DEFINITION: See Variable 234 for definition and note codes.

Variable 236   LAW NGO'S/NGO'S 1960

   OSIRIS: location 1172 width 5   Card: deck 16, col. 51-55
   Missing data code: 99999   Decimal place: none

   N=87   Mean=510.29   Standard deviation=416.75   Range=0-3333

   DEFINITION: See Variable 234 for definition and note codes.

Variable 237   LAW NGO'S/NGO'S 1963

   OSIRIS: location 1177 width 5   Card: deck 16, col. 56-60
   Missing data code: 99999   Decimal place: none

   N=107   Mean=401.86   Standard deviation 215.79   Range=0-1020

   DEFINITION: See Variable 234 for definition and note codes.

Variable 238   LAW NGO'S/NGO'S 1965

   OSIRIS: location 1182 width 5   Card: deck 16, col. 61-65
   Missing data code: 99999   Decimal place: none

   N=113   Mean=440.75   Standard deviation=301.82   Range=0-2667

   DEFINITION: See Variable 234 for definition and note codes.

Variable 239   UNEMPLOYED/ECONOMICALLY ACTIVE POPULATION 1950

OSIRIS: location 1187 width 5   Card: deck 16, col. 66-70
Missing data code: 99999   Decimal place: none

N=20   Mean=213.55   Standard deviation=340.07   Range=0-1364

DEFINITION: The number of unemployed divided by economically active population. Statistical Yearbook; The Worldmark Encyclopedia of the Nations; Yearbook of Labour Statistics. See variable 279 for definition of "economically active population."

The units are % x 10^2.

NOTES: Variables 239-243
A. Estimates
B. Worldmark Encyclopedia of the Nations
E. Yearbook of Labour Statistics, International Labour Office: Geneva, 1962
F. Moody's Municipal and Government Manual
G. Encyclopedia Britannica World Atlas
H. The Middle East, 1962
I. Overseas Economic Survey

Variable 240   UNEMPLOYED/ECONOMICALLY ACTIVE POPULATION 1955

OSIRIS: location 1192 width 5   Card: deck 16, col. 71-75
Missing data code: 99999   Decimal place: none

N=44   Mean=368.18   Standard deviation=518.88   Range=0-2330

DEFINITION: See Variable 239 for definition and note codes.

Variable 241   UNEMPLOYED/ECONOMICALLY ACTIVE POPULATION 1960

OSIRIS: location 1197 width 5   Card: deck 16, col. 76-80
Missing data code: 99999   Decimal place: none

N=36   Mean=219.42   Standard deviation=224.77   Range=0-740

DEFINITION: See Variable 239 for definition and note codes.

Variable 242   UNEMPLOYED/ECONOMICALLY ACTIVE POPULATION 1963

OSIRIS: location 1202 width 5   Card: deck 17, col. 6-10
Missing data code: 99999   Decimal place: none

N=50   Mean=186.02   Standard deviation=237.21   Range=0-1051

DEFINITION: See Variable 239 for definition and note codes.

Variable 243   UNEMPLOYED/ECONOMICALLY ACTIVE POPULATION 1965

OSIRIS: location 1207 width 5   Card: deck 17, col. 11-15
Missing data code: 99999   Decimal place: none

N=25   Mean=397.60   Standard deviation=314.22   Range=60-1400

DEFINITION: See Variable 239 for definition and note codes.

Variable 244   LEADING EXPORT/EXPORTS 1950

    OSIRIS: location 1212 width 5   Card: deck 17, col. 16-20
    Missing data code: 99999   Decimal place: none

    N=62   Mean=3978.70   Standard deviation=2510.54   Range=512-9205

    DEFINITION: Largest SITC (Standard International Trade Classification) category or largest commodity export (not identified by SITC label) divided by total exports. Yearbook of International Trade Statistics; Worldmark Encyclopedia of the Nations.

    The units are % x 10^2.

    NOTES: Variables 244-248
    A. Estimates
    B. Worldmark Encyclopedia of the Nations
    C. Moody's Governments and Municipalities
    D. Statesman's Yearbook
    E. U. S. Economic Assistance Programs Administered by AID and Predecessor Agencies, 1948-1968.

Variable 245   LEADING EXPORT/EXPORTS 1955

    OSIRIS: location 1217 width 5   Card: deck 17, col. 21-25
    Missing data code: 99999   Decimal place: none

    N=66   Mean=4458.3   Standard deviation=2284.3   Range=1290-9900

    DEFINITION: See Variable 244 for definition and note codes.

Variable 246   LEADING EXPORT/EXPORTS 1960

    OSIRIS: location 1222 width 5   Card: deck 17, col. 26-30
    Missing data code: 99999   Decimal place: none

    N=77   Mean=3536.7   Standard deviation=2043.5   Range=933-9654

    DEFINITION: See Variable 244 for definition and note codes.

Variable 247   LEADING EXPORT/EXPORTS 1963

    OSIRIS: location 1227 width 5   Card: deck 17, col. 31-35
    Missing data code: 99999   Decimal place: none

    N=98   Mean=3751.4   Standard deviation=2189.4   Range=440-9872

    DEFINITION: See Variable 244 for definition and note codes.

Variable 248   LEADING EXPORT/EXPORTS 1965

    OSIRIS: location 1232 width 5   Card: deck 17, col. 36-40
    Missing data code: 99999   Decimal place: none

    N=93   Mean=3479.4   Standard deviation=2302.3   Range=418-9940

    DEFINITION: See Variable 244 for definition and note codes.

Variable 249   LANGUAGES 1950

    OSIRIS: location 1237 width 5   Card: deck 17, col. 41-45
    Missing data code: 99999   Decimal place: none

    N=61   Mean=2.8525   Standard deviation=2.7070   Range=1-12

    DEFINITION: Number of languages with membership exceeding one percent of the population. Demographic Yearbook, UN; The Worldmark Encyclopedia of the Nations.

    NOTES: Variables 249-253
    A. Estimates
    B. Worldmark Encyclopedia of the Nations

Variable 250   LANGUAGES 1955

    OSIRIS: location 1242 width 5   Card: deck 17, col. 46-50
    Missing data code: 99999   Decimal place: none

    N=68   Mean=2.75   Standard deviation=2.6052   Range=1-12

    DEFINITION: See Variable 249 for definition and note codes.

Variable 251   LANGUAGES 1960

    OSIRIS: location 1247 width 5   Card: deck 17, col. 51-55
    Missing data code: 99999   Decimal place: none

    N=86   Mean=3.0116   Standard deviation=2.6279   Range=1-12

    DEFINITION: See Variable 249 for definition and note codes.

Variable 252   LANGUAGES 1963

    OSIRIS: location 1252 width 5   Card: deck 17, col. 56-60
    Missing data code: 99999   Decimal place: none

    N=106   Mean=3.4057   Standard deviation=2.7317   Range=1-12

    DEFINITION: See Variable 249 for definition and note codes.

Variable 253   LANGUAGES 1965

    OSIRIS: location 1257 width 5   Card: deck 17, col. 61-65
    Missing data code: 99999   Decimal place: none

    N=113   Mean=3.2832   Standard deviation=2.5721   Range=1-12

    DEFINITION: See Variable 249 for definition and note codes.

Variable 254   MEMBERSHIP OF LARGEST LANGUAGE GROUP/POPULATION 1950

    OSIRIS: location 1262 width 5   Card: deck 17, col. 66-70
    Missing data code: 99999   Decimal place: none
    N=61   Mean=785.74   Standard deviation=226.83   Range=200-999

    DEFINITION: The number of largest language group divided by total population. *Demographic Yearbook*, UN; *The Worldmark Encyclopedia of the Nations*.

    The units are % x 10.

    NOTES: Variables 254-258
    A. Estimates

Variable 255   MEMBERSHIP OF LARGEST LANGUAGE GROUP/POPULATION 1955

    OSIRIS: location 1267 width 5   Card: deck 17, col. 71-75
    Missing data code: 99999   Decimal place: none
    N=68   Mean=763.6   Standard deviation=242.84   Range=168-999

    DEFINITION: See Variable 254 for definition and note codes.

Variable 256   MEMBERSHIP OF LARGEST LANGUAGE GROUP/POPULATION 1960

    OSIRIS: location 1272 width 5   Card: deck 17, col. 76-80
    Missing data code: 99999   Decimal place: none
    N=71   Mean=757.68   Standard deviation=242.86   Range=168-999

    DEFINITION: See Variable 254 for definition and note codes.

Variable 257   MEMBERSHIP OF LARGEST LANGUAGE GROUP/POPULATION 1963

    OSIRIS: location 1277 width 5   Card: deck 18, col. 6-10
    Missing data code: 99999   Decimal place: none
    N=72   Mean=752.67   Standard deviation=244.86   Range=168-999

    DEFINITION: See Variable 254 for definition and note codes.

Variable 258   MEMBERSHIP OF LARGEST LANGUAGE GROUP/POPULATION 1965

    OSIRIS: location 1282 width 5   Card: deck 18, col. 11-15
    Missing data code: 99999   Decimal place: none
    N=71   Mean=769.72   Standard deviation=230.12   Range=168-999

    DEFINITION: See Variable 254 for definition and note codes.

Variable 259   ETHNIC GROUPS 1950

    OSIRIS: location 1287 width 5   Card: deck 18, col. 16-20
    Missing data code: 99999   Decimal place: none

    N=63   Mean=2.9683   Standard deviation=2.14   Range=0-11

    DEFINITION: Number of ethnic or racial groups with membership exceeding one percent of the population. Data are taken as reported by nations according to what they consider their major ethnic or racial divisions. Demographic Yearbook, UN; The Worldmark Encyclopedia of the Nations.

    NOTES: Variables 259-263
    A. Estimates
    B. Worldmark Encyclopedia of the Nations

Variable 260   ETHNIC GROUPS 1955

    OSIRIS: location 1292 width 5   Card: deck 18, col. 21-25
    Missing data code: 99999   Decimal place: none

    N=72   Mean=2.9028   Standard deviation=2.0567   Range=1-11

    DEFINITION: See Variable 259 for definition and note codes.

Variable 261   ETHNIC GROUPS 1960

    OSIRIS: location 1297 width 5   Card: deck 18, col. 26-30
    Missing data code: 99999   Decimal place: none

    N=81   Mean=3.5432   Standard deviation=3.5322   Range=1-23

    DEFINITION: See Variable 259 for definition and note codes.

Variable 262   ETHNIC GROUPS 1963

    OSIRIS: location 1302 width 5   Card: deck 18, col. 31-35
    Missing data code: 99999   Decimal place: none

    N=98   Mean=4.5918   Standard deviation=4.5517   Range=1-24

    DEFINITION: See Variable 259 for definition and note codes.

Variable 263   ETHNIC GROUPS 1965

    OSIRIS: location 1307 width 5   Card: deck 18, col. 36-40
    Missing data code: 99999   Decimal place: none

    N=105   Mean=4.4286   Standard deviation=4.2784   Range=1-24

    DEFINITION: See Variable 259 for definition and note codes.

Variable 264   ECONOMIC AID RECEIVED 1950

    OSIRIS: location 1312 width 5 Card: deck 18, col. 41-45
    Missing data code: 99999 Decimal place: none

    N=58   Mean=889.97   Standard deviation=1902.80   Range=0-9573

DEFINITION: Data including amounts expended in grants or long term loans "in cash and in kind, including within the latter category the provision of services as well as of commodities... Long term loans are...those for which there is a schedule of repayments extending beyond a period of five years from the date the loan becomes effective. Grants and loans specifically linked to the defense of the recipient country such as transfer of military equipment, direct military expenditure and financial contributions for the support of military forces are excluded." <u>Statistical Yearbook</u>, UN.

The units are 10^5 (hundred thousand) US dollars.

NOTES: Variables 264-268
A. Estimates
E. <u>U. S. Economic Assistance Programs Administered by AID and Predecessor Agencies, 1948-1968</u>
F. <u>U. S. Foreign Assistance and Assistance from International Organizations: July 1, 1945 - June 3, 1960</u>
G. <u>U. S. Overseas Loans and Grants and Assistance from International Organizations: July 1, 1945 - June 30, 1966</u>
P. <u>International Aid</u>, I. M. D. Little, Ch. IV
Q. <u>Development Assistance Efforts and Policies 1965</u>, OECD
R. <u>Flow of Financial Resources to Less Developed Countries, 1961-1965</u>

Variable 265   ECONOMIC AID RECEIVED 1955

    OSIRIS: location 1317 width 5 Card: deck 18, col. 46-50
    Missing data code: 99999 Decimal place: none

    N=47   Mean=787.51   Standard deviation=1778.2   Range=-325-10467

DEFINITION: See Variable 264 for definition and note codes.

Variable 266   ECONOMIC AID RECEIVED 1960

    OSIRIS: location 1322 width 5 Card: deck 18, col. 51-55
    Missing data code: 99999 Decimal place: none

    N=67   Mean=308.64   Standard deviation=704.30   Range=-118-4478

DEFINITION: See Variable 264 for definition and note codes.

Variable 267   ECONOMIC AID RECEIVED 1963

    OSIRIS: location 1327 width 5 Card: deck 18, col. 56-60
    Missing data code: 99999 Decimal place: none

    N=57   Mean=826.14   Standard deviation=1495.0   Range=0-9780

DEFINITION: See Variable 264 for definition and note codes.

Variable 268   ECONOMIC AID RECEIVED 1965

    OSIRIS: location 1332 width 5   Card: deck 18, col. 61-65
    Missing data code: 99999   Decimal place: none

    N=93   Mean=806.27   Standard deviation=1640.4   Range=-294-13110

    DEFINITION: See Variable 264 for definition and note codes.

Variable 269   TECHNICAL ASSISTANCE RECEIVED 1950

    OSIRIS: location 1337 width 5   Card: deck 18, col. 66-70
    Missing data code: 99999   Decimal place: none

    N=12   Mean=448.33   Standard deviation=618.00   Range=0-2000

    DEFINITION: Technical assistance includes all domestic technical assistance and relief projects. <u>United Nations Assistance Committee Report of the Technical Assistance Board</u>.

    The units are 10^3 (thousands) US dollars.

    NOTES: Variable 269-273
    A. Estimates
    H. Data given only as "less than $50,000"; recorded as $40,000.
    S. Data given only as "less than $100,000"; recorded as $90,000.

Variable 270   TECHNICAL ASSISTANCE RECEIVED 1955

    OSIRIS: location 1342 width 5   Card: deck 18, col. 71-75
    Missing data code: 99999   Decimal place: none

    N=82   Mean=199.51   Standard deviation=258.92   Range=0-992

    DEFINITION: See Variable 269 for definition and note codes.

Variable 271   TECHNICAL ASSISTANCE RECEIVED 1960

    OSIRIS: location 1347 width 5   Card: deck 18, col. 76-80
    Missing data code: 99999   Decimal place: none

    N=76   Mean=304.47   Standard deviation=339.96   Range=0-2150

    DEFINITION: See Variable 269 for definition and note codes.

Variable 272   TECHNICAL ASSISTANCE RECEIVED 1963

    OSIRIS: location 1352 width 5   Card: deck 19, col. 6-10
    Missing data code: 99999   Decimal place: none

    N=84   Mean=356.52   Standard deviation=289.04   Range=0-1545

    DEFINITION: See Variable 269 for definition and note codes.

Variable 273   TECHNICAL ASSISTANCE RECEIVED 1965

    OSIRIS: location 1357 width 5   Card: deck 19, col. 11-15
    Missing data code: 99999   Decimal place: none

    N=97   Mean=3794.5   Standard deviation=9380.7   Range=0-44200

    DEFINITION: See Variable 269 for definition and note codes.

Variable 274   GOVERNMENT EDUCATION EXPENDITURES/GOVERNMENT EXPENDITURES 1950

    OSIRIS: location 1362 width 5   Card: deck 19, col. 16-20
    Missing data code: 99999   Decimal place: none

    N=56   Mean=993.36   Standard deviation=494.95   Range=81-2652

    DEFINITION: Governmental educational expenditures divided by total government expenditures. Statistical Yearbook, UN.

The units are $\% \times 10^2$

NOTES: Variables 274-278
A. Estimates
B. Worldmark Encyclopedia of the Nations
D. Statesman's Yearbook
I. U. N. Statistical Yearbook
K. Professional Manpower and Education in Communist China, p. 14
L. U. N. Economic Survey of Latin America, 1955
M. U. N. Economic Survey of Asia and the Far East, 1960
N. Overseas Economic Surveys, HMSO, 1954

Variable 275   GOVERNMENT EDUCATION EXPENDITURES/GOVERNMENT EXPENDITURES 1955

    OSIRIS: location 1367 width 5   Card: deck 19, col. 21-25
    Missing data code: 99999   Decimal place: none

    N=66   Mean=1220.4   Standard deviation=531.99   Range=290-2800

    DEFINITION: See Variable 274 for definition and note codes.

Variable 276   GOVERNMENT EDUCATION EXPENDITURES/GOVERNMENT EXPENDITURES 1960

    OSIRIS: location 1372 width 5   Card: deck 19, col. 26-30
    Missing data code: 99999   Decimal place: none

    N=51   Mean=1272.5   Standard deviation=521.59   Range=418-2808

    DEFINITION: See Variable 274 for definition and note codes.

Variable 277   GOVERNMENT EDUCATION EXPENDITURES/GOVERNMENT EXPENDITURES 1963

    OSIRIS: location 1377 width 5   Card: deck 19, col. 31-35
    Missing data code: 99999   Decimal place: none

    N=89   Mean=1393.0   Standard deviation=574.12   Range=117-2883

    DEFINITION: See Variable 274 for definition and note codes.

Variable 278   GOVERNMENT EDUCATION EXPENDITURES/GOVERNMENT EXPENDITURES 1965

    OSIRIS: location 1382 width 5   Card: deck 19, col. 36-40
    Missing data code: 99999   Decimal place: none

    N=84   Mean=1537.8   Standard deviation=544.22   Range=329-2710

    DEFINITION: See Variable 274 for definition and note codes.

Variable 279   FEMALE WORKERS/ECONOMICALLY ACTIVE 1950

    OSIRIS: location 1387 width 5   Card: deck 19, col. 41-45
    Missing data code: 99999   Decimal place: none

    N=55   Mean=2755.8   Standard deviation=1150.9   Range=581-4914

    DEFINITION: Economically active "consists of all persons who are or who seek to be engaged in producing goods and services, whether employed or unemployed at the time of the census inquiry." Demographic Yearbook, UN; The Worldmark Encyclopedia of the Nations; Yearbook of Labor Statistics.

    The units are % x 10^2.

    NOTES: Variable 279-283
    A. Estimates
    B. Yearbook of Labor Statistics (1954)

Variable 280   FEMALE WORKERS/ECONOMICALLY ACTIVE 1955

    OSIRIS: location 1392 width 5   Card: deck 19, col. 46-50
    Missing data code: 99999   Decimal place: none

    N=65   Mean=2800.6   Standard deviation=1116.3   Range=580-4900

    DEFINITION: See Variable 279 for definition and note codes.

Variable 281   FEMALE WORKERS/ECONOMICALLY ACTIVE 1960

    OSIRIS: location 1397 width 5   Card: deck 19, col. 51-55
    Missing data code: 99999   Decimal place: none

    N=58   Mean=2699.7   Standard deviation=1064.1   Range=500-5184

    DEFINITION: See Variable 279 for definition and note codes.

Variable 282   FEMALE WORKERS/ECONOMICALLY ACTIVE 1963

    OSIRIS: location 1402 width 5   Card: deck 19, col. 56-60
    Missing data code: 99999   Decimal place: none

    N=73   Mean=2928.8   Standard deviation=1204.0   Range=500-5208

    DEFINITION: See Variable 279 for definition and note codes.

Variable 283   FEMALE WORKERS/ECONOMICALLY ACTIVE 1965

   OSIRIS: location 1407 width 5   Card: deck 19, col. 61-65
   Missing data code: 99999   Decimal place: none

   N=94   Mean=2469.7   Standard deviation=1428.7   Range = 180-5620

   DEFINITION: See Variable 279 for definition and note codes.

Variable 284   EXPORTS/GNP 1950

   OSIRIS: location 1412 width 5   Card: deck 19, col. 66-70
   Missing data code: 99999   Decimal place: none

   N=50   Mean=1526.20   Standard deviation=1236   Range=2-5910

   DEFINITION: Total exports f.o.b. divided by Gross National Product.
   For GNP see Variable 24. Norton Ginsburg, Atlas of Economic Development;
   Statistical Yearbook, UN.

   NOTES: Variable 284-288
   A. Estimates

Variable 285   EXPORTS/GNP 1955

   OSIRIS: location 1417 width 5   Card: deck 19, col. 71-75
   Missing data code: 99999   Decimal place: none

   N=69   Mean=1716.5   Standard deviation=1107.3   Range=70-5190

   DEFINITION: See Variable 284 for definition and note codes.

Variable 286   EXPORTS/GNP 1960

   OSIRIS: location 1422 width 5   Card: deck 19, col. 76-80
   Missing data code: 99999   Decimal place: none

   N=49   Mean=1695.6   Standrad deviation=981.12   Range=399-4953

   DEFINITION: See Variable 284 for definition and note codes.

Variable 287   EXPORTS/GNP 1963

   OSIRIS: location 1427 width 5   Card: deck 20, col. 6-10
   Missing data code: 99999   Decimal place: none

   N=68   Mean=1899.4   Standard deviation=1406.9   Range=309-9560

   DEFINITION: See Variable 284 for definition and note codes.

Variable 288   EXPORTS/GNP 1965

   OSIRIS: location 1432 width 5   Card: deck 20, col. 11-15
   Missing data code: 99999   Decimal place: none

   N=104   Mean=1893.2   Standard deviation=1417.6   Range=57-7668

   DEFINITION: See Variable 284 for definition and note codes.

Variable 289   FOREIGN MAIL SENT/FOREIGN MAIL 1950

OSIRIS: location 1437 width 5   Card: deck 20, col. 16-20
Missing data code: 99999   Decimal place: none

N=35   Mean=43.286   Standard deviation=9.6758   Range=17-64

DEFINITION: Mail covers letters (air mail, ordinary mail, and registered) post cards, printed matter, business papers, small merchandise samples, small packets, and phonopost packets. They include mail carried without charge, but exclude ordinary packages with a declared value. The denominator, foreign mail, includes mail sent and received. Statistical Yearbook, UN.

The units are %.

NOTES: Variables 289-293
A. Estimates

Variable 290   FOREIGN MAIL SENT/FOREIGN MAIL 1955

OSIRIS: location 1442 width 5   Card: deck 20, col. 21-25
Missing data code: 99999   Decimal place: none

N=46   Mean=44.087   Standard deviation=12.318   Range=4-72

DEFINITION: See Variable 289 for definition and note codes.

Variable 291   FOREIGN MAIL SENT/FOREIGN MAIL 1960

OSIRIS: location 1447 width 5   Card: deck 20, col. 26-30
Missing data code: 99999   Decimal place: none

N=41   Mean=42.049   Standard deviation=12.110   Range=3-69

DEFINITION: See Variable 289 for definition and note codes.

Variable 292   FOREIGN MAIL SENT/FOREIGN MAIL 1963

OSIRIS: location 1452 width 5   Card: deck 20, col. 31-35
Missing data code: 99999   Decimal place: none

N=48   Mean=43.292   Standard deviation=9.5203   Range=23-68

DEFINITION: See Variable 289 for definition and note codes.

Variable 293   FOREIGN MAIL SENT/FOREIGN MAIL 1965

OSIRIS: location 1457 width 5   Card: deck 20, col. 36-40
Missing data code: 99999   Decimal place: none

N=52   Mean=45.000   Standard deviation=12.613   Range=17-83

DEFINITION: See Variable 289 for definition and note codes.

Variable 294   IMPORTS/TRADE 1950

    OSIRIS: location 1462 width 5   Card: deck 20, col. 41-45
    Missing data code: 99999   Decimal place: none

    N=62   Mean=5172.6   Standard deviation=1361.9   Range=2142-9085

DEFINITION: Trade includes imports c.i.f. and exports f.o.b. Data for most countries exclude goods imported into the customs area and re-exported without being cleared for domestic consumption. Goods passing through a country only for the purposes of transport are excluded from all figures.

The units are $\% \times 10^2$.

NOTES: Variables 294-298
A. Estimates
I. Imports include foreign aid

Variable 295   IMPORTS/TRADE 1955

    OSIRIS: location 1467 width 5   Card: deck 20, col. 46-50
    Missing data code: 99999   Decimal place: none

    N=75   Mean=5453.9   Standard deviation=1311.9   Range=2430-9500

DEFINITION: See Variable 294 for definition and note codes.

Variable 296   IMPORTS/TRADE 1960

    OSIRIS: location 1472 width 5   Card: deck 20, col. 51-55
    Missing data code: 99999   Decimal place: none

    N=79   Mean=5657.9   Standard deviation=1241.8   Range=3036-9839

DEFINITION: See Variable 294 for definition and note codes.

Variable 297   IMPORTS/TRADE 1963

    OSIRIS: location 1477 width 5   Card: deck 20, col. 56-60
    Missing data code: 99999   Decimal place: none

    N=97   Mean=5600   Standard deviation=1250.8   Range=2462-9667

DEFINITION: See Variable 294 for definition and note codes.

Variable 298   IMPORTS/TRADE 1965

    OSIRIS: location 1482 width 5   Card: deck 20, col. 61-65
    Missing data code: 99999   Decimal place: none

    N=104   Mean=5454   Standard deviation=1174.3   Range=2867-9706

DEFINITION: See Variable 294 for definition and note codes.

Variable 299   CALORIES CONSUMED MINUS CALORIES REQUIRED/CALORIES REQUIRED 1950

OSIRIS: location 1487 width 5   Card: deck 20, col. 66-70
Missing data code: 99999   Decimal place: none

N=31   Mean=803.52   Standard deviation=1328   Range=-2613-3359

DEFINITION: Calorie requirement is calculated by the UN on the basis of climate, work load and average body build. Report on the World Social Situation, UN.

The units are % x 10^2.

Variable 300   CALORIES CONSUMED MINUS CALORIES REQUIRED/CALORIES REQUIRED 1955

OSIRIS: location 1492 width 5   Card: deck 20, col. 71-75
Missing data code: 99999   Decimal place: none

N=40   Mean=672.88   Standard deviation=1396.9   Range=-1853-3206

DEFINITION: See Variable 299 for definition and sources.

Variable 301   CALORIES CONSUMED MINUS CALORIES REQUIRED/CALORIES REQUIRED 1960

OSIRIS: location 1497 width 5   Card: deck 20, col. 76-80
Missing data code: 99999   Decimal place: none

N=58   Mean= 701.16   Standard deviation=1461.6   Range=-2375-3321

DEFINITION: See Variable 299 for definition and sources.

Variable 302   CALORIES CONSUMED MINUS CALORIES REQUIRED/CALORIES REQUIRED 1963

OSIRIS: location 1502 width 5   Card: deck 21, col. 6-10
Missing data code: 99999   Decimal place: none

N=61   Mean=800.67   Standard deviation=1395.4   Range=-2250-3244

DEFINITION: See Variable 299 for definition and sources.

Variable 303   CALORIES CONSUMED MINUS CALORIES REQUIRED/CALORIES REQUIRED 1965

OSIRIS: location 1507 width 5   Card: deck 21, col. 11-15
Missing data code: 99999   Decimal place: none

N=61   Mean=842.49   Standrad deviation=1365.4   Range=-2250-3144

DEFINITION: See Variable 299 for definition and sources.

Variable 304   PROTEINS/CALORIES 1950

   OSIRIS: location 1512 width 5   Card: deck 21, col. 16-20
   Missing data code: 99999   Decimal place: none

   N=31   Mean=315.71   Standard deviation=51.648   Range=203-394

   DEFINITION: The calorie data are for foodstuffs, excluding alcoholic beverages. The data are given as proteins per capita and calories per capita. Statistical Yearbook, UN; Norton Ginsburg, Atlas of Economic Development; Encyclopedia Britannica World Atlas. Units are % x 10^2.

   NOTES: Variables 304-308
   A. Estimates

Variable 305   PROTEINS/CALORIES 1955

   OSIRIS: location 1517 width 5   Card: deck 21, col. 21-25
   Missing data code: 99999   Decimal place: none

   N=49   Mean=284.47   Standard deviation=30.584   Range=212-346

   DEFINITION: See Variable 304 for definition and note codes.

Variable 306   PROTEINS/CALORIES 1960

   OSIRIS: location 1522 width 5   Card: deck 21, col. 26-30
   Missing data code: 99999   Decimal place: none

   N=47   Mean=277   Standard deviation=28.444   Range=212-333

   DEFINITION: See Variable 304 for definition and note codes.

Variable 307   PROTEINS/CALORIES 1963

   OSIRIS: location 1527 width 5   Card: deck 21, col. 31-35
   Missing data code: 99999   Decimal place: none

   N=44   Mean=279.05   Standard deviation=28.566   Range=219-338

   DEFINITION: See Variable 304 for definition and note codes.

Variable 308   PROTEINS/CALORIES 1965

   OSIRIS: location 1532 width 5   Card: deck 21, col. 36-40
   Missing data code: 99999   Decimal place: none

   N=79   Mean=272.85   Standard deviation=34.294   Range=192-368

   DEFINITION: See Variable 304 for definition and note codes.

Variable 309   RUSSIAN TITLES TRANSLATED/FOREIGN TITLES TRANSLATED 1950

OSIRIS: location 1537 width 5   Card: deck 21, col. 41-45
Missing data code: 99999   Decimal place: none

N=29   Mean=1353.6   Standard deviation=2566.7   Range=0-8505

DEFINITION: Book titles "cover all non-periodical publications, including pamphlets, first editions of originals and new translations, re-editions and the more important government reports." Statistical Yearbook, UN. The units are % x 10^2.

NOTES: Variables 309-313
A. Estimates
B. Russian is Native Language
R. Index Translationum, UNESCO, Vol. 18 (1965)

Variable 310   RUSSIAN TITLES TRANSLATED/FOREIGN TITLES TRANSLATED 1955

OSIRIS: location 1542 width 5   Card: deck 21, col. 46-50
Missing data code: 99999   Decimal place: none

N=35   Mean=1267.1   Standard deviation=2080.6   Range=0-6970

DEFINITION: See Variable 309 for definition and note codes.

Variable 311   RUSSIAN TITLES TRANSLATED/FOREIGN TITLES TRANSLATED 1960

OSIRIS: location 1547 width 5   Card: deck 21, col. 51-55
Missing data code: 99999   Decimal place: none

N=36   Mean=889   Standard deviation=1180.3   Range=81-4639

DEFINITION: See Variable 309 for definition and note codes.

Variable 312   RUSSIAN TITLES TRANSLATED/FOREIGN TITLES TRANSLATED 1963

OSIRIS: location 1552 width 5   Card: deck 21, col. 56-60
Missing data code: 99999   Decimal place: none

N=47   Mean=699.81   Standard deviation=1097.6   Range=0-5292

DEFINITION: See Variable 309 for definition and note codes.

Variable 313   RUSSIAN TITLES TRANSLATED/FOREIGN TITLES TRANSLATED 1965

OSIRIS: location 1557 width 5   Card: deck 21, col. 61-65
Missing data code: 99999   Decimal place: none

N=64   Mean=542.78   Standard deviation=933.60   Range=0-4375

DEFINITION: See Variable 309 for definition and note codes.

Variable 314   MILITARY PERSONNEL/POPULATION 1950

    OSIRIS: location 1562 width 5   Card: deck 21, col. 66-70
    Missing data code: 99999   Decimal place: none

    N=57   Mean=90.16   Standrad deviation=102.08   Range=0-587

DEFINITION: Military personnel data exclude civilians employed by the armed forces Statesman's Yearbook; The Worldmark Encyclopedia of the Nations.

The units are % x 10.

NOTES: Variables 314-318
A. Estimates
C. Statesman's Yearbook (1951)
D. Brassey's Armed Forces Annual (1952)
E. Encyclopedia Britannica Book of the Year
F. Yearbook of the Commonwealth of Australia No. 38 (1951)
G. Whitaker's Almanac (1950)
J. Naval data missing
K. Air Force data missing
M. The Military Balance, The Institute for Strategic Studies, London
N. Army data only
P. Air Force data only

Variable 315   MILITARY PERSONNEL/POPULATION 1955

    OSIRIS: location 1567 width 5   Card: deck 21, col. 71-75
    Missing data code: 99999   Decimal place: none

    N=79   Mean=90.924   Standrad deviation=99.414   Range=0-569

DEFINITION: See Variable 314 for definition and note codes.

Variable 316   MILITARY PERSONNEL/POPULATION 1960

    OSIRIS: location 1572 width 5   Card: deck 21, col. 76-80
    Missing data code: 99999   Decimal place: none

    N=76   Mean=87.947   Standard deviation=87.229   Range=7-472

DEFINITION: See Variable 314 for definition and note codes.

Variable 317   MILITARY PERSONNEL/POPULATION 1963

    OSIRIS: location 1577 width 5   Card: deck 22, col. 6-10
    Missing data code: 99999   Decimal place: none

    N=79   Mean=102.44   Standard deviation=142.17   Range=0-1050

DEFINITION: See Variable 314 for definition and note codes.

Variabls 318   MILITARY PERSONNEL/POPULATION 1965

    OSIRIS: location 1582 width 5   Card: deck 22, col. 11-15
    Missing data code: 99999   Decimal place: none

    N=101   Mean=80.099   Standard deviation=123.19   Range=0-1050

DEFINITION: See Variable 314 for definition and note codes.

Variable 319   BALANCE OF INVESTMENTS/GOLD STOCK 1950

    OSIRIS: location 1587 width 5   Card: deck 22, col. 16-20
    Missing data code: 99999   Decimal place: none

    N=43   Mean=-173.83   Standard deviation=643.08   Range=-4100-153

    DEFINITION: Balance of investments is the annual average of income from investments in other nations minus payments on foreign domestic investments. Data on gold stocks were averaged for liquid holdings over three year periods around the data year. Nations which had zero gold stock during this period were given one million in the denominator to avoid an indeterminate ratio. International Financial Statistics.

    The units are %.

    NOTES: Variables 319-323
    H. $1 million U. S. has been assumed for those countries with no gold stock to avoid an indeterminate ratio.
    Q. Statistical Yearbook (1968)

Variable 320   BALANCE OF INVESTMENTS/GOLD STOCK 1955

    OSIRIS: location 1592 width 5   Card: deck 22, col. 21-25
    Missing data code: 99999   Decimal place: none

    N=56   Mean=-530.36   Standard deviation=1503.1   Range=-8100-500

    DEFINITION: See Variable 319 for definition and note codes.

Variable 321   BALANCE OF INVESTMENTS/GOLD STOCK 1960

    OSIRIS: location 1597 width 5   Card: deck 22, col. 26-30
    Missing data code: 99999   Decimal place: none

    N=66   Mean=-167.32   Standard deviation=1144.9   Range=-6700-5700

    DEFINITION: See Variable 319 for definition and note codes.

Variable 322   BALANCE OF INVESTMENTS/GOLD STOCK 1963

    OSIRIS: location 1602 width 5   Card: deck 22, col. 31-35
    Missing data code: 99999   Decimal place: none

    N=55   Mean=-220   Standard deviation=921.84   Range=-6800-210

    DEFINITION: See Variable 319 for definition and note codes.

Variable 323   BALANCE OF INVESTMENTS/GOLD STOCK 1965

    OSIRIS: location 1607 width 5   Card: deck 22, col. 36-40
    Missing data code: 99999   Decimal place: none

    N=73   Mean=-721.95   Standard deviation=1612.9   Range=-9999-238.00

    DEFINITION: See Variable 319 for definition and note codes.

Variable 324   POLITICAL PARTIES 1950

    OSIRIS: location 1612 width 5   Card: deck 22, col. 41-45
    Missing data code: 99999   Decimal place: none

    N=68   Mean=3.00   Standard deviation=2.46   Range=0-14

    DEFINITION: Number of political parties with a membership of more than one percent of the population. Political Handbook and Atlas of the World; Statesman's Yearbook; The Worldmark Encyclopedia of the Nations.

    NOTES: Variables 324-328
    A. Estimates
    H. Mehden, Politics of the Developing Nations
    I. Burnett & Johnson, Political Forces in Latin America
    K. Furnivall, Governance of Modern Burma (1958)
    L. Wignon, Party Politics in India (1957)
    M. Bindn, Politics in Lebanon
    N. Fgin, Israel (1967)
    P. Ngorawardana, Ceylon General Election 1956 (1960)
    Q. Marlowe, Iran (1963)
    R. Majid Khaddrri, Independent Iraq (1955)
    S. Seale, The Struggle for Syria (1965)
    T. Little, Modern Egypt
    U. Robinson, The First Turkish Republic (1965)
    V. Ingrams, The Yemen (1963)
    W. R. F. Smith, Background to Revolution (1966)
    X. Tinker, India and Pakistan (1962)
    Y. Muron, A History of Venezuela (1964)
    Z. Kogan, The Government of Italy (1962)

Variable 325   POLITICAL PARTIES, 1955

    OSIRIS: location 1617 width 5   Card: deck 22, col. 46-50
    Missing data code: 99999   Decimal place: none

    N=79   Mean=3.8354   Standard deviation=2.4674   Range=0-12

    DEFINITION: See Variable 324 for definition and note codes.

Variable 326   POLITICAL PARTIES 1960

    OSIRIS: location 1622 width 5   Card: deck 22, col. 51-55
    Missing data code: 99999   Decimal place: none

    N=87   Mean=3.0920   Standard deviation=2.7603   Range=0-13

    DEFINITION: See Variable 324 for definition and note codes.

Variable 327   POLITICAL PARTIES 1963

    OSIRIS: location 1627 width 5   Card: deck 22, col. 56-60
    Missing data code: 99999   Decimal place: none

    N=105   Mean=2.6857   Standard deviation=2.4586   Range=0-10

    DEFINITION: See Variable 324 for definition and note codes.

Variable 328   POLITICAL PARTIES, 1965

    OSIRIS: location 1632 width 5　　　Card: deck 22, col. 61-65
    Missing data code: 99999　　　　　　Decimal place: none
    N=113　　Mean=2.8938　　Standard deviation=2.4508　　Range=0-10

    DEFINITION: See Variable 324 for definition and note codes.

Variable 329   ARTS AND CULTURE NGO/NGO 1950

    OSIRIS: location 1637 width 5　　　Card: deck 22, col. 66-70
    Missing data code: 99999　　　　　　Decimal place: none
    N=72　　Mean=271.49　　Standard deviation=193.21　　Range=0-567

    DEFINITION: Total of all arts and culture international non-governmental organizations for each nation divided by total of all NGO's for the nation. Yearbook of International Organization.

    The units are % x 10^2.

Variable 330   ARTS AND CULTURE NGO/NGO 1955

    OSIRIS: location 1642 width 5　　　Card: deck 22, col. 71-75
    Missing data code: 99999　　　　　　Decimal place: none
    N=82　　Mean=315.72　　Standard deviation=226.37　　Range=0-1250

    DEFINITION: See Variable 329 for definition and sources.

Variable 331   ARTS AND CULTURE NGO/NGO 1960

    OSIRIS: location 1647 width 5　　　Card: deck 22, col. 76-80
    Missing data code: 99999　　　　　　Decimal place: none
    N=87　　Mean=492.08　　Standard deviation=277.68　　Range=0-1429

    DEFINITION: See Variable 329 for definition and sources.

Variable 332   ARTS AND CULTURE NGO/NGO 1963

    OSIRIS: location 1652 width 5　　　Card: deck 23, col. 6-10
    Missing data code: 99999　　　　　　Decimal place: none
    N=107　　Mean=422.02　　Standard deviation=299.16　　Range=0-1429

    DEFINITION: See Variable 329 for definition and sources.

Variable 333   ARTS AND CULTURE NGO/NGO 1965

    OSIRIS: location 1657 width 5　　　Card: deck 23, col. 11-15
    Missing data code: 99999　　　　　　Decimal place: none
    N=113　　Mean=443.63　　Standard deviation=230.32　　Range=0-1364

    DEFINITION: See Variable 329 for definition and sources.

Variable 334   COMMUNIST PARTY MEMBERSHIP/POPULATION 1950

   OSIRIS: location 1662 width 5   Card: deck 23, col. 16-20
   Missing data code: 99999   Decimal place: none
   N=70   Mean=1144.6   Standard deviation=2577.00   Range=0-13590

   DEFINITION: Communist party membership divided by total population.
   U. S. State Department World Strength of the Communist Party
   Organizations; Demographic Yearbook, UN.

   The units are % x 10^3.

   NOTES: Variables 334-338
   A. Estimates
   J. Since the Communist Party of the United States was outlawed in
      1954, no reliable data sources have been located. FBI information
      is classified.

Variable 335   COMMUNIST PARTY MEMBERSHIP/POPULATION 1955

   OSIRIS: location 1667 width 5   Card: deck 23, col. 21-25
   Missing data code: 99999   Decimal place: none
   N=81   Mean=1071.5   Standard deviation=2428.6   Range=0-12362

   DEFINITION: See Variable 334 for definition and note codes.

Variable 336   COMMUNIST PARTY MEMBERSHIP/POPULATION 1960

   OSIRIS: location 1672 width 5   Card: deck 23, col. 26-30
   Missing data code: 99999   Decimal place: none
   N=86   Mean=982.67   Standard deviation=2259.4   Range=0-11321

   DEFINITION: See Variable 334 for definition and note codes.

Variable 337   COMMUNIST PARTY MEMBERSHIP/POPULATION 1963

   OSIRIS: location 1677 width 5   Card: deck 23, col. 31-35
   Missing data code: 99999   Decimal place: none
   N=103   Mean=883.74   Standard deviation=2278.9   Range=0-11641

   DEFINITION: See Variable 334 for definition and note codes.

Variable 338   COMMUNIST PARTY MEMBERSHIP/POPULATION 1965

   OSIRIS: location 1682 width 5   Card: deck 23, col. 36-40
   Missing data code: 99999   Decimal place: none
   N=112   Mean=837.02   Standard deviation=2347.9   Range=0-13223

   DEFINITION: See Variable 334 for definition and note codes.

Variable 339   GOVERNMENT EXPENDITURE/GNP 1950

   OSIRIS: location 1687 width 5   Card: deck 23, col. 41-45
   Missing data code: 99999   Decimal place: none
   N=48   Mean=1515.0   Standard deviation=714.62   Range=534-3333

   DEFINITION: Government expenditures refers to the budgeted current and
   capital outlays of the national government. Redemption of debt is
   excluded as are also certain capital transfers. Grants to foreign
   governments are included. For GNP see Variable 24. Norton Ginsburg,
   Atlas of Economic Development; Statistical Yearbook, UN.

   NOTES: Variables 339-343
   A. Estimates
   B. Statesman's Yearbook
   D. Monthly Bulletin of Statistics, Jan-June 1965
   E. Yearbook of National Account Statistics, 1966
   F. Europa Yearbook, 1967

Variable 340   GOVERNMENT EXPENDITURE/GNP 1955

   OSIRIS: location 1692 width 5   Card: deck 23, col. 46-50
   Missing data code: 99999   Decimal place: none
   N=64   Mean=1711.8   Standard deviation=768.74   Range=496-4977

   DEFINITION: See Variable 339 for definition and note codes.

Variable 341   GOVERNMENT EXPENDITURE/GNP 1960

   OSIRIS: location 1697 width 5   Card: deck 23, col. 51-55
   Missing data code: 99999   Decimal place: none
   N=49   Mean=1772.1   Standard deviation=679.73   Range=701-3243

   DEFINITION: See Variable 339 for definition and note codes.

Variable 342   GOVERNMENT EXPENDITURE/GNP 1963

   OSIRIS: location 1702 width 5   Card: deck 23, col. 56-60
   Missing data code: 99999   Decimal place: none
   N=72   Mean=2116.9   Standard deviation=1296.0   Range=7-7270

   DEFINITION: See Variable 339 for definition and note codes.

Variable 343   GOVERNMENT EXPENDITURE/GNP 1965

   OSIRIS: location 1707 width 5   Card: deck 23, col. 61-65
   Missing data code: 99999   Decimal place: none
   N=84   Mean=2092.8   Standard deviation=1033.9   Range=668-5896

   DEFINITION: See Variable 339 for definition and note codes.

Variable 344   MONARCHY OR NOT 1950

    OSIRIS: location 1712 width 5   Card: deck 23, col. 66-70
    Missing data code: 99999   Decimal place: none
    N=72

    DEFINITION: Rating: 0 = non-monarchy; 1 = monarchy. A country is considered a monarchy if heredity is the primary means of succession to the chief of state and/or chief executive position. No distinction is made between constitutional and absolute monarchies. Statesman's Yearbook; The Worldmark Encyclopedia of the Nations.

    NOTES: Variables 344-348
    G. Political Handbook and Atlas of the World, 1964

Variable 345   MONARCHY OR NOT 1955

    OSIRIS: location 1717 width 5   Card: deck 23, col. 71-75
    Missing data code: 99999   Decimal place: none
    N=82

    DEFINITION: See Variable 344 for definition and note codes.

Variable 346   MONARCHY OR NOT 1960

    OSIRIS: location 1722 width 5   Card: deck 23, col. 76-80
    Missing data code: 99999   Decimal place: none
    N=87

    DEFINITION: See Variable 344 for definition and note codes.

Variable 347   MONARCHY OR NOT 1963

    OSIRIS: location 1727 width 5   Card: deck 24, col. 6-10
    Missing data code: 99999   Decimal place: none
    N=107

    DEFINITION: See Variable 344 for definition and note codes.

Variable 348   MONARCHY OR NOT 1965

    OSIRIS: location 1732 width 5   Card: deck 24, col. 11-15
    Missing data code: 99999   Decimal place: none
    N=113

    DEFINITION: See Variable 344 for definition and note codes.

Variable 349   PUPILS IN PRIMARY SCHOOL/PRIMARY SCHOOL TEACHERS 1950

OSIRIS: location 1737 width 5   Card: deck 24, col. 16-20
Missing data code: 99999   Decimal place: none
N=63   Mean=3420.9   Standard deviation=1106.1   Range=1017-7033

DEFINITION: Pupils in primary school divided by primary school teachers. Basic Facts and Figures, UNESCO; Arthur S. Banks, Cross-Polity Time-Series Data; Report on the World Social Situation, UN.

The units are $x10^2$.

NOTES: Variables 349-353
A. Estimates
B. Statesman's Yearbook
C. Worldmark Encyclopedia of the Nations
F. Europa Yearbook, 1967

Variable 350   PUPILS IN PRIMARY SCHOOL/PRIMARY SCHOOL TEACHERS 1955

OSIRIS: location 1742 width 5   Card: deck 24, col. 21-25
Missing data code: 99999   Decimal place: none
N=79   Mean=3434.2   Standard deviation=1038.5   Range=1700-8600

DEFINITION: See Variable 349 for definition and note codes.

Variable 351   PUPILS IN PRIMARY SCHOOL/PRIMARY SCHOOL TEACHERS 1960

OSIRIS: location 1747 width 5   Card: deck 24, col. 26-30
Missing data code: 99999   Decimal place: none
N=84   Mean=3383.3   Standard deviation=860.77   Range=2000-6200

DEFINITION: See Variable 349 for definition and note codes.

Variable 352   PUPILS IN PRIMARY SCHOOL/PRIMARY SCHOOL TEACHERS 1963

OSIRIS: location 1752 width 5   Card: deck 24, col. 31-35
Missing data code: 99999   Decimal place: none
N=104   Mean=3720.9   Standard deviation=1414.7   Range=1392-10471

DEFINITION: See Variable 349 for definition and note codes.

Variable 353   PUPILS IN PRIMARY SCHOOL/PRIMARY SCHOOL TEACHERS 1965

OSIRIS: location 1757 width 5   Card: deck 24, col. 36-40
Missing data code: 99999   Decimal place: none
N=106   Mean=3584.0   Standard deviation=1212.2   Range=1800-8300

DEFINITION: See Variable 349 for definition and note codes.

Variable 354   LEGALITY OF GOVERNMENT CHANGE 1950

   OSIRIS: location 1762 width 5   Card: deck 24, col. 41-45
   Missing data code: 99999   Decimal place: none
   N=72

   DEFINITION: Rating based on previous and present government:
   0=previous and present government came into being through non-legal
   means (e.g., illegal elections, revolutions), or if there has been only
   one government since independence, it came into being illegally.
   1=previous or present government came into being through non-legal
   means, or if there has been only one government since independence,
   present government came into power legally. 2=previous and present
   government came into being through legal means. Government refers to
   the executive head of government; legality refers to the constitutional
   provisions for transferring power, or in the absence of a constitution,
   the traditional practice of a country (e.g., hereditary transferrance of
   power). The Worldmark Encyclopedia of the Nations; Statesman's Yearbook;
   Political Handbook and Atlas of the World; Britannica Book of the Year.

Variable 355   LEGALITY OF GOVERNMENT CHANGE 1955

   OSIRIS: location 1767 width 5   Card: deck 24, col. 46-50
   Missing data code: 99999   Decimal place: none
   N=79

   DEFINITION: See Variable 354 for definition and sources.

Variable 356   LEGALITY OF GOVERNMENT CHANGE 1960

   OSIRIS: location 1772 width 5   Card: deck 24, col. 51-55
   Missing data code: 99999   Decimal place: none
   N=87

   DEFINITION: See Variable 354 for definition and sources.

Variable 357   LEGALITY OF GOVERNMENT CHANGE 1963

   OSIRIS: location 1777 width 5   Card: deck 24, col. 56-60
   Missing data code: 99999   Decimal place: none
   N=107

   DEFINITION: See Variable 354 for definition and sources.

Variable 358   LEGALITY OF GOVERNMENT CHANGE 1965

   OSIRIS: location 1782 width 5   Card: deck 24, col. 61-65
   Missing data code: 99999   Decimal place: none
   N=113

   DEFINITION: See Variable 354 for definition and sources.

Variable 359   LEGITIMACY OF PRESENT GOVERNMENT 1950

    OSIRIS: location 1787 width 5   Card: deck 24, col. 66-70
    Missing data code: 99999   Decimal place: none
    N=72

    DEFINITION: Rating: 0=present government came into being through means other than revolution; 1=present government came into being through revolution. Government refers to the executive head of government; revolution refers to any illegal or forced change in the top governmental elite, any attempt at such a change, or any successful or unsuccessful armed rebellion whose aim is independence from the central government. The Worldmark Encyclopedia of the Nations; Statesman's Yearbook; Political Handbook and Atlas of the World; Britannica Book of the Year.

    NOTES: Variables 359-363
    A. Estimates
    F. An Atlas of Middle Eastern Affairs, R. C. Kingsbury and
       V. J.G. Pounds

Variable 360   LEGITIMACY OF PRESENT GOVERNMENT 1955

    OSIRIS: location 1792 width 5   Card: deck 24, col. 71-75
    Missing data code: 99999   Decimal place: none
    N=77

    DEFINITION: See Variable 359 for definition and note codes.

Variable 361   LEGITIMACY OF PRESENT GOVERNMENT 1960

    OSIRIS: location 1797 width 5   Card: deck 24, col. 76-80
    Missing data code: 99999   Decimal place: none
    N=87

    DEFINITION: See Variable 359 for definition and note codes.

Variable 362   LEGITIMACY OF PRESENT GOVERNMENT 1963

    OSIRIS: location 1802 width 5   Card: deck 25, col. 6-10
    Missing data code: 99999   Decimal place: none
    N=107

    DEFINITION: See Variable 359 for definition and note codes.

Variable 363   LEGITIMACY OF PRESENT GOVERNMENT 1965

    OSIRIS: location 1807 width 5   Card: deck 25, col. 11-15
    Missing data code: 99999   Decimal place: none
    N=113

    DEFINITION: See Variable 359 for definition and note codes.

Variable 364   LARGEST ETHNIC GROUP MEMBERSHIP/POPULATION 1950

OSIRIS: location 1812 width 5   Card: deck 25, col. 16-20
Missing data code: 99999   Decimal place: none

N=72   Mean=715.19   Standard deviation=251.56   Range=100-1000

DEFINITION: Number of ethnic or racial groups with membership exceeding one percent of the population divided by total population. <u>Demographic Yearbook</u>, UN; <u>The Worldmark Encyclopedia of the Nations</u>.

The units are % x 10.

NOTES: Variables 364-368
A. Estimates
C. 37% of Filipinos speak English and 37% speak Tagalog.
E. <u>The Gallatin Annual of International Business</u>

Variable 365   LARGEST ETHNIC GROUP MEMBERSHIP/POPULATION 1955

OSIRIS: location 1817 width 5   Card: deck 25, col. 21-25
Missing data code: 99999   Decimal place: none

N=82   Mean=730.74   Standard deviation=244.91   Range=100-1000

DEFINITION: See Variable 364 for definition and note codes.

Variable 366   LARGEST ETHNIC GROUP MEMBERSHIP/POPULATION 1960

OSIRIS: location 1822 width 5   Card: deck 25, col. 26-30
Missing data code: 99999   Decimal place: none

N=87   Mean=708.63   Standard deviation=257.88   Range=100-1000

DEFINITION: See Variable 364 for definition and note codes.

Variable 367   LARGEST ETHNIC GROUP MEMBERSHIP/POPULATION 1963

OSIRIS: location 1827 width 5   Card: deck 25, col. 31-35
Missing data code: 99999   Decimal place: none

N=107   Mean=645.40   Standard deviation 286.79   Range=100-1000

DEFINITION: See Variable 364 for definition and note codes.

Variable 368   LARGEST ETHNIC GROUP MEMBERSHIP/POPULATION 1965

OSIRIS: location 1832 width 5   Card: deck 25, col. 36-40
Missing data code: 99999   Decimal place: none

N=113   Mean=649.54   Standard deviation=285.87   Range=100-1000

DEFINITION: See Variable 364 for definition and note codes.

Variable 369   ASSASSINATIONS 1950

    OSIRIS: location 1837 width 5   Card: deck 25, col. 41-45
    Missing data code: 99999   Decimal place: none
    N=72   Mean=0.12500   Standard deviation=.37294   Range=0-2

    DEFINITION: The politically motivated murder or attempted murder of a high government official or politician. Among high government officials are included the governors of states or provinces, the mayors of large cities, members of the cabinet, and members of the national legislature. Among high politicians are included members of the inner core of the ruling party or group and leaders of the opposition. The New York Times Index; New International Yearbook; Britannica Book of the Year; Keesing's Contemporary Archives; Facts on File.

    NOTES: Variables 369-373
    G. The Politics of Assassination, Murray Clark Havens, Carl Leiden, Karl M. Schmitt, Prentice-Hall, N.H. (1970), Appendix A.

Variable 370   ASSASSINATIONS 1955

    OSIRIS: location 1842 width 5   Card: deck 25, col. 46-50
    Missing data code: 99999   Decimal place: none
    N=79   Mean=.13924   Standard deviation=.49959   Range=0-3

    DEFINITION: See Variable 369 for definition and note codes.

Variable 371   ASSASSINATIONS 1960

    OSIRIS: location 1847 width 5   Card: deck 25, col. 51-55
    Missing data code: 99999   Decimal place: none
    N=87   Mean=.24138   Standard deviation=1.2197   Range=0-11

    DEFINITION: See Variable 369 for definition and note codes.

Variable 372   ASSASSINATIONS 1963

    OSIRIS: location 1852 width 5   Card: deck 25, col. 56-60
    Missing data code: 99999   Decimal place: none
    N=107   Mean=.084112-1   Standard deviation-.31086   Range=0-2

    DEFINITION: See Variable 369 for definition and note codes.

Variable 373   ASSASSINATIONS 1965

    OSIRIS: location 1857 width 5   Card: deck 25, col. 61-65
    Missing data code: 99999   Decimal place: none
    N=112   Mean=.28571   Standard deviation=.91463   Range=0-6

    DEFINITION: See Variable 369 for definition and note codes.

Variable 374   MAJOR GOVERNMENT CRISIS 1950

   OSIRIS: location 1862 width 5   Card: deck 25, col. 66-70
   Missing data code: 99999   Decimal place: none

   N=72   Mean=0.13889   Standard deviation=.34826   Range-0-1

   DEFINITION: Any rapidly developing situation (excluding revolution) which threatens to bring the immediate downfall of the present government. A vote of no confidence by a parliamentary majority, or the forced resignation or impeachment of top officials are also considered major government crises. A new major government crisis is not counted unless at least three months of stability have intervened since the previous crisis. The New York Times Index; New International Yearbook; Britannica Book of the Year.

Variable 375   MAJOR GOVERNMENT CRISIS 1955

   OSIRIS: location 1867 width 5   Card: deck 25, col. 71-75
   Missing data code: 99999   Decimal place: none

   N=79   Mean=.13924   Standard deviation=.41559   Range=0-2

   DEFINITION: See Variable 374 for definition and sources.

Variable 376   MAJOR GOVERNMENT CRISIS 1960

   OSIRIS: location 1872 width 5   Card: deck 25, col. 76-80
   Missing data code: 99999   Decimal place: none

   N=87   Mean=.26437   Standard deviation=.55948   Range=0-3

   DEFINITION: See Variable 374 for definition and sources.

Variable 377   MAJOR GOVERNMENT CRISIS 1963

   OSIRIS: location 1877 width 5   Card: deck 26, col. 6-10
   Missing data code: 99999   Decimal place: none

   N=107   Mean=.14953   Standard deviation=.57959   Range=0-5

   DEFINITION: See Variable 374 for definition and sources.

Variable 378   MAJOR GOVERNMENT CRISIS 1965

   OSIRIS: location 1882 width 5   Card: deck 26, col. 11-15
   Missing data code: 99999   Decimal place: none

   N=112   Mean=.33036   Standard deviation=.55974   Range=0-2

   DEFINITION: See Variable 374 for definition and sources.

Variable 379   UN PAYMENT DELINQUENCIES/ASSESSMENTS 1950

OSIRIS: location 1887 width 5   Card: deck 26, col. 16-20
Missing data code: 99999   Decimal place: none
N=72   Mean=2.3194   Standard deviation=15.254   Range=0-122

DEFINITION: Delinquencies include total outstanding against UN assessments prior to 1955. Information Annex II; Statesman's Yearbook.

The units are %.

NOTES: Variables 379-383
D. The UN continues to hold $140,000 in a suspended account for India and Pakistan, relating to a payment made in 1947 towards a Working Capital Fund.

Variable 380   UN PAYMENT DELINQUENCIES/ASSESSMENTS 1955

OSIRIS: location 1892 width 5   Card: deck 26, col. 21-25
Missing data code: 99999   Decimal place: none
N=82   Mean=12.780   Standard deviation=29.311   Range=0-99

DEFINITION: See Variable 379 for definition and note codes.

Variable 381   UN PAYMENT DELINQUENCIES/ASSESSMENTS 1960

OSIRIS: location 1897 width 5   Card: deck 26, col. 26-30
Missing data code: 99999   Decimal place: none
N=87   Mean=35.621   Standard deviation=56.522   Range=0-214

DEFINITION: See Variable 379 for definition and note codes.

Variable 382   UN PAYMENT DELINQUENCIES/ASSESSMENTS 1963

OSIRIS: location 1902 width 5   Card: deck 26, col. 31-35
Missing data code: 99999   Decimal place: none
N=107   Mean=32.981   Standard deviation=56.292   Range=0-459

DEFINITION: See Variable 379 for definition and note codes.

Variable 383   UN PAYMENT DELINQUENCIES/ASSESSMENTS 1965

OSIRIS: location 1907 width 5   Card: deck 26, col. 36-40
Missing data code: 99999   Decimal place: none
N=113   Mean=43.531   Standard deviation=37.000   Range=0-89

DEFINITION: See Variable 379 for definition and note codes.

Variable 384   BALANCE OF PAYMENTS/GOLD STOCK 1950

    OSIRIS: location 1912 width 5   Card: deck 26, col. 41-45
    Missing data code: 99999   Decimal place: none

    N=46   Mean=-7.4130   Standard deviation=46.894   Range=-220-116

DEFINITION: Average short term balance of payments over three-year periods around the data year. Data on gold stocks were averaged for liquid holdings over three-year periods around the data year. Nations which had zero gold stock during this period were given one million in the denominator to avoid an indeterminate ratio. Therefore, the ratios are biased slightly in the direction of being too high for countries with no gold stock. <u>International Financial Statistics</u>.

The units are % x 10^{-1}.

NOTES: Variables 384-388
A. Estimates
B. Nation's total holdings are in U. S. dollars

Variable 385   BALANCE OF PAYMENTS/GOLD STOCK 1955

    OSIRIS: location 1917 width 5   Card: deck 26, col. 46-50
    Missing data code: 99999   Decimal place: none

    N=59   Mean=-3.3559   Standard deviation=75.291   Range=-404-279

DEFINITION: See Variable 384 for definition and note codes.

Variable 386   BALANCE OF PAYMENTS/GOLD STOCK 1960

    OSIRIS: location 1922 width 5   Card: deck 26, col. 51-55
    Missing data code: 99999   Decimal place: none

    N=68   Mean=-6.2206   Standard deviation=257.98   Range=-1480-1329

DEFINITION: See Variable 384 for definition and note codes.

Variable 387   BALANCE OF PAYMENTS/GOLD STOCK 1963

    OSIRIS: location 1927 width 5   Card: deck 26, col. 56-60
    Missing data code: 99999   Decimal place: none

    N=67   Mean=8.8657   Standard deviation=60.495   Range=-212-307

DEFINITION: See Variable 384 for definition and note codes.

Variable 388   BALANCE OF PAYMENTS/GOLD STOCK 1965

    OSIRIS: location 1932 width 5   Card: Deck 26, col. 61-65
    Missing data code: 99999   Decimal place: none

    N=76   Mean=-19.895   Standard deviation=186.08   Range=-1590-258

DEFINITION: See Variable 384 for definition and note codes.

Variable 389   BALANCE OF INVESTMENTS 1950

OSIRIS: location 1937 width 5   Card: deck 26, col. 66-70
Missing data code: 99999   Decimal place: none

N=51   Mean=8.0196   Standard deviation=256.71   Range=-363-1693

DEFINITION: Annual average of income from investments in other nations minus payments on foreign domestic investments. Balance of Payments Yearbook, IMG.

NOTES: Variables 389-393
A. Estimates
D. Data available for 1967 only.

Variable 390   BALANCE OF INVESTMENTS 1955

OSIRIS: location 1942 width 5   Card: deck 26, col. 71-75
Missing data code: 99999   Decimal place: none

N=62   Mean=35.839   Standard deviation=1069.4   Range=-1825-7966

DEFINITION: See Variable 389 for definition and note codes.

Variable 391   BALANCE OF INVESTMENTS 1960

OSIRIS: location 1947 width 5   Card: deck 26, col. 76-80
Missing data code: 99999   Decimal place: none

N=65   Mean=13.785   Standard deviation=458.75   Range=-538-3443

DEFINITION: See Variable 389 for definition and note codes.

Variable 392   BALANCE OF INVESTMENTS 1963

OSIRIS: location 1952 width 5   Card: deck 27, col. 6-10
Missing data code: 99999   Decimal place: none

N=74   Mean=14.649   Standard deviation=581.23   Range=-667-4654

DEFINITION: See Variable 389 for definition and note codes.

Variable 393   BALANCE OF INVESTMENTS 1965

OSIRIS: location 1957 width 5   Card: deck 27, col. 11-15
Missing data code: 99999   Decimal place: none

N=75   Mean=18.827   Standard deviation=667.40   Range=-789-5348

DEFINITION: See Variable 389 for definition and note codes.

Variable 394   SYSTEM STYLE 1950

    OSIRIS: location 1962 width 5   Card: deck 27, col. 16-20
    Missing data code: 99999   Decimal place: none
    N=72

    DEFINITION: Rating: 0=non-mobilizational; 1=limited mobilizational; 2=mobilizational. Banks and Textor, A Cross-Polity Survey; DON estimates.

    NOTES: Variables 394-398
    A. Estimates
    B. Political Forces in Latin America, Barnett and Johnson (1968)

Variable 395   SYSTEM STYLE 1955

    OSIRIS: location 1967 width 5   Card: deck 27, col. 21-25
    Missing data code: 99999   Decimal place: none
    N=82

    DEFINITION: See Variable 394 for definition and note codes.

Variable 396   SYSTEM STYLE 1960

    OSIRIS: location 1972 width 5   Card: deck 27, col. 26-30
    Missing data code: 99999   Decimal place: none
    N=86

    DEFINITION: See Variable 394 for definition and note codes.

Variable 397   SYSTEM STYLE 1963

    OSIRIS: location 1977 width 5   Card: deck 27, col. 31-35
    Missing data code: 99999   Decimal place: none
    N=107

    DEFINITION: See Variable 394 for definition and note codes.

Variable 398   SYSTEM STYLE 1965

    OSIRIS: location 1982 width 5   Card: deck 27, col. 36-40
    Missing data code: 99999   Decimal place: none
    N=113

    DEFINITION: See Variable 394 for definition and note codes.

Variable 399   CONSTITUTIONAL STATUS 1950

   OSIRIS: location 1987 width 5   Card: deck 27, col. 41-45
   Missing data code: 99999   Decimal place: none
   N=72

   DEFINITION: Rating: 0=totaliarian; 1=authoritarian; 2=constitutional.
   Banks and Textor, A Cross-Polity Survey; DON estimates.

   NOTES: Variables 399-403
   A. Estimates
   C. World Almanac (1971)

Variable 400   CONSTITUTIONAL STATUS 1955

   OSIRIS: location 1992 width 5   Card: deck 27, col. 46-50
   Missing data code: 99999   Decimal place: none
   N=82

   DEFINITION: See Variable 399 for definition and note codes.

Variable 401   CONSTITUTIONAL STATUS 1960

   OSIRIS: location 1997 width 5   Card: deck 27, col. 51-55
   Missing data code: 99999   Decimal place: none
   N=85

   DEFINITION: See Variable 399 for definition and note codes.

Variable 402   CONSTITUTIONAL STATUS 1963

   OSIRIS: location 2002 width 5   Card: deck 27, col. 56-60
   Missing data code: 99999   Decimal place: none
   N=107

   DEFINITION: See Variable 399 for definition and note codes.

Variable 403   CONSTITUTIONAL STATUS 1965

   OSIRIS: location 2007 width 5   Card: deck 27, col. 61-65
   Missing data code: 99999   Decimal place: none
   N=113

   DEFINITION: See Variable 399 for definition and note codes.

Variable 404   ELECTORAL SYSTEM 1950

    OSIRIS: location 2012 width 5   Card: deck 27, col. 66-70
    Missing data code: 99999   Decimal place: none
    N=72

    DEFINITION: Rating: 0=non-competitive; 1=partially competitive; 2=competitive. Banks and Textor, <u>A Cross-Polity Survey</u>; DON estimates.

    NOTES: Variables 404-408
    A. Estimates
    B. <u>Political Forces in Latin America,</u> Barnett and Johnson (1968)
    C. <u>World Almanac</u> (1971)

Variable 405   ELECTORAL SYSTEM 1955

    OSIRIS: location 2017 width 5   Card: deck 27, col. 71-75
    Missing data code: 99999   Decimal place: none
    N=82

    DEFINITION: See Variable 404 for definition and note codes.

Variable 406   ELECTORAL SYSTEM 1960

    OSIRIS: location 2022 width 5   Card: deck 27, col. 76-80
    Missing data code: 99999   Decimal place: none
    N=78

    DEFINITION: See Variable 404 for definition and note codes.

Variable 407   ELECTORAL SYSTEM 1963

    OSIRIS: location 2027 width 5   Card: deck 28, col. 6-10
    Missing data code: 99999   Decimal place: none
    N=107

    DEFINITION: See Variable 404 for definition and note codes.

Variable 408   ELECTORAL SYSTEM 1965

    OSIRIS: location 2032 width 5   Card: deck 28, col. 11-15
    Missing data code: 99999   Decimal place: none
    N=113

    DEFINITION: See Variable 404 for definition and note codes.

Variable 409   NON-COMMUNIST REGIME 1950

    OSIRIS: location 2037 width 5   Card: deck 28, col. 16-20
    Missing data code: 99999   Decimal place: none

    N=72

    DEFINITION: Rating: 0=no; 1=yes. Banks and Textor, A Cross-Polity Survey; DON estimates.

    NOTES: Variables 409-413
    A. Estimates

Variable 410   NON-COMMUNIST REGIME 1955

    OSIRIS: location 2042 width 5   Card: deck 28, col. 21-25
    Missing data code: 99999   Decimal place: none

    N=82

    DEFINITION: See Variable 409 for definition and note codes.

Variable 411   NON-COMMUNIST REGIME 1960

    OSIRIS: location 2047 width 5   Card: deck 28, col. 26-30
    Missing data code: 99999   Decimal place: none

    N=86

    DEFINITION: See Variable 409 for definition and note codes.

Variable 412   NON-COMMUNIST REGIME 1963

    OSIRIS: location 2052 width 5   Card: deck 28, col. 31-35
    Missing data code: 99999   Decimal place: none

    N=107

    DEFINITION: See Variable 409 for definition and note codes.

Variabls 413   NON-COMMUNIST REGIME 1965

    OSIRIS: location 2057 width 5   Card: deck 28, col. 36-40
    Missing data code: 99999   Decimal place: none

    N=113

    DEFINITION: See Variable 409 for definition and note codes.

Variable 414   POLITICAL LEADERSHIP 1950

    OSIRIS: location 2062 width 5   Card: deck 28, col. 41-45
    Missing data code: 99999   Decimal place: none
    N=69

    DEFINITION: Rating: 0=elitist; 1=moderately elitist; 2=non-elite. Banks and Textor, A Cross-Polity Survey; DON estimates.

    NOTES: Variables 414-418
    A. Estimates
    B. Political Forces in Latin America, Barnett and Johnson (1968)

Variable 415   POLITICAL LEADERSHIP 1955

    OSIRIS: location 2067 width 5   Card: deck 28, col. 46-50
    Missing data code: 99999   Decimal place: none
    N=82

    DEFINITION: See Variable 414 for definition and note codes.

Variable 416   POLITICAL LEADERSHIP 1960

    OSIRIS: location 2072 width 5   Card: deck 28, col. 51-55
    Missing data code: **99999**   Decimal place: none
    N=84

    DEFINITION: See Variable 414 for definition and note codes.

Variable 417   POLITICAL LEADERSHIP 1963

    OSIRIS: location 2077 width 5   Card: deck 28, col. 56-60
    Missing data code: 99999   Decimal place: none
    N=106

    DEFINITION: See Variable 414 for definition and note codes.

Variable 418   POLITICAL LEADERSHIP 1965

    OSIRIS: location 2082 width 5   Card: deck 28, col. 61-65
    Missing data code: 99999   Decimal place: none
    N=113

    DEFINITION: See Variable 414 for definition and note codes.

Variable 419   HORIZONTAL POWER DISTRIBUTION 1950

    OSIRIS: location 2087 width 5   Card: deck 28, col. 66-70
    Missing data code: 99999   Decimal place: none
    N=71

    DEFINITION: Rating: 0=negligible; 1=limited; 2=significant.
    Banks and Textor, A Cross-Polity Survey; DON estimates.

    NOTES: Variables 419-423
    A. Estimates
    B. Political Forces in Latin America, Barnett and Johnson (1968)

Variable 420   HORIZONTAL POWER DISTRIBUTION 1955

    OSIRIS: location 2092 width 5   Card: deck 28, col. 71-75
    Missing data code: 99999   Decimal place: none
    N=82

    DEFINITION: See Variable 419 for definition and note codes.

Variable 421   HORIZONTAL POWER DISTRIBUTION 1960

    OSIRIS: location 2097 width 5   Card: deck 28, col. 76-80
    Missing data code: 99999   Decimal place: none
    N=85

    DEFINITION: See Variable 419 for definition and note codes.

Variable 422   HORIZONTAL POWER DISTRIBUTION 1963

    OSIRIS: location 2102 width 5   Card: deck 29, col. 6-10
    Missing data code: 99999   Decimal place: none
    N=106

    DEFINITION: See Variable 419 for definition and note codes.

Variable 423   HORIZONTAL POWER DISTRIBUTION 1965

    OSIRIS: location 2107 width 5   Card: deck 29, col. 11-15
    Missing data code: 99999   Decimal place: none
    N=113

    DEFINITION: See Variable 419 for definition and note codes.

Variable 424   MILITARY PARTICIPATION 1950

    OSIRIS: location 2112 width 5   Card: deck 29, col. 16-20
    Missing data code: 99999   Decimal place: none
    N=72

    DEFINITION: Rating: 0=neutral; 1=supportive; 2=interventive. The Almanac of World Military Power; Banks and Textor, A Cross-Polity Survey; Cross-Polity Time-Series Data.

    NOTES: Variables 424-428
    A. Estimates
    B. Encyclopedia Britannica
    C. "Toward Expanding Military Intervention in Latin American Politics," Robert Putnam, World Politics, XX, No. 1 (Oct. 1967)

Variable 425   MILITARY PARTICIPATION 1955

    OSIRIS: location 2117 width 5   Card: deck 29, col. 21-25
    Missing data code: 99999   Decimal place: none
    N=82

    DEFINITION: See Variable 424 for definition and note codes.

Variable 426   MILITARY PARTICIPATION 1960

    OSIRIS: location 2122 width 5   Card: deck 29, col. 26-30
    Missing data code: 99999   Decimal place: none
    N=82

    DEFINITION: See Variable 424 for definition and note codes

Variable 427   MILITARY PARTICIPATION 1963

    OSIRIS: location 2127 width 5   Card: deck 29, col. 31-35
    Missing data code: 99999   Decimal place: none
    N=100

    DEFINITION: See Variable 424 for definition and note codes.

Variable 428   MILITARY PARTICIPATION 1965

    OSIRIS: location 2132 width 5   Card: deck 29, col. 36-40
    Missing data code: 99999   Decimal place: none
    N=113

    DEFINITION: See Variable 424 for definition and note codes.

Variable 429   BUREAUCRACY 1950

    OSIRIS: location 2137 width 5   Card: deck 29, col. 41-45
    Missing data code: 99999   Decimal place: none
    N=72

    DEFINITION: Rating: 0=traditional or postcolonial; 1=semi-modern; 2=modern. Banks and Textor, A Cross-Polity Survey; Cross-Polity Time-Series Data.

    NOTES: Variables 429-433
    A. Estimates

Variable 430   BUREAUCRACY 1955

    OSIRIS: location 2142 width 5   Card: deck 29, col. 46-50
    Missing data code: 99999   Decimal place: none
    N=82

    DEFINITION: See Variable 429 for definition and note codes.

Variable 431   BUREAUCRACY 1960

    OSIRIS: location 2147 width 5   Card: deck 29, col. 51-55
    Missing data code: 99999   Decimal place: none
    N=82

    DEFINITION: See Variable 429 for definition and note codes.

Variable 432   BUREAUCRACY 1963

    OSIRIS: location 2152 width 5   Card: deck 29, col. 56-60
    Missing data code: 99999   Decimal place: none
    N=101

    DEFINITION: See Variable 429 for definition and note codes.

Variable 433   BUREAUCRACY 1965

    OSIRIS: location 2157 width 5   Card: deck 29, col. 61-65
    Missing data code: 99999   Decimal place: none
    N=113

    DEFINITION: See Variable 429 for definition and note codes.

Variable 434   CENSORSHIP SCORE 1950

    OSIRIS: location 2162 width 5   Card: deck 29, col. 66-70
    Missing data code: 99999   Decimal place: none
    N=69

    DEFINITION: Rating: 0=complete or fairly complete censorship of news; 1=some censorship of the news; 2=no censorship, other than usual laws about libel and the controlling of news of a national security nature. Journalism Quarterly, Vol. 37 (1960); The New York Times Index; The Worldmark Encyclopedia of the Nations.

    NOTES: Variables 434-438
    A. Estimates

Variable 435   CENSORSHIP SCORE 1955

    OSIRIS: location 2167 width 5   Card: deck 29, col. 71-75
    Missing data code: 99999   Decimal place: none
    N=82

    DEFINITION: See Variable 434 for definition and note codes.

Variable 436   CENSORSHIP SCORE 1960

    OSIRIS: location 2172 width 5   Card: deck 29, col. 76-80
    Missing data code: 99999   Decimal place: none
    N=87

    DEFINITION: See Variable 434 for definition and note codes.

Variable 437   CENSORSHIP SCORE 1963

    OSIRIS: location 2177 width 5   Card: deck 30, col. 6-10
    Missing data code: 99999   Decimal place: none
    N=102

    DEFINITION: See Variable 434 for definition and note codes.

Variable 438   CENSORSHIP SCORE 1965

    OSIRIS: location 2182 width 5   Card: deck 30, col. 11-15
    Missing data code: 99999   Decimal place: none
    N=113

    DEFINITION: See Variable 434 for definition and note codes.

Variable 439   GEOGRAPHY-X 1950

    OSIRIS: location 2187 width 5   Card: deck 30, col. 16-20
    Missing data code: 99999   Decimal place: none
    N=72   Mean=1385.5   Standard deviation=1546.8   Range=-2975-3881

DEFINITION: The geographical location of the city or place containing the administrative seat of the central government of the nation is represented on the surface of a sphere by utilizing three dimensional space. North latitude and east longitude are given the positive sense.

$$GEOG\text{-}X = R \cos\phi \cos\theta$$
$$GEOG\text{-}Y = R \cos\phi \sin\theta$$
$$GEOG\text{-}Z = R \sin\phi$$

where ϕ is latitude, θ is longitude, and R = 3,963 miles (equatorial radius of the Earth).

NOTES: Variables 439-453
A. *The International Atlas*, Rand McNally, pp. I.8 - I.11, I.28-I.223
B. Name of Administrative Seat of Government taken from *Worldmark Encyclopedia* (1963)

Variable 440   GEOGRAPHY-X 1955

    OSIRIS: location 2192 width 5   Card: deck 30, col. 21-25
    Missing data code: 99999   Decimal place: none
    N=82   Mean=1247.2   Standard deviation=1658.5   Range=-2975-3881

DEFINITION: See Variable 439 for definition and note codes.

Variable 441   GEOGRAPHY-X 1960

    OSIRIS: location 2197 width 5   Card: deck 30, col. 26-30
    Missing data code: 99999   Decimal place: none
    N=87   Mean=1323.7   Standard deviation=1689.1   Range=-2975-3948

DEFINITION: See Variable 439 for definition and note codes.

Variable 442   GEOGRAPHY-X 1963

    OSIRIS: location 2202 width 5   Card: deck 30, col. 31-35
    Missing data code: 99999   Decimal place: none
    N=107   Mean=1764.3   Standard deviation=1787.5   Range=-2975-3948

DEFINITION: See Variable 439 for definition and note codes.

Variable 443   GEOGRAPHY-X 1965

    OSIRIS: location 2207 width 5   Card: deck 30, col. 36-40
    Missing data code: 99999   Decimal place: none
    N=113   Mean=1813.7   Standard deviation=1766.1   Range=-2975-3948

DEFINITION: See Variable 439 for definition and note codes.

Variable 444   GEOGRAPHY-Y 1950

    OSIRIS: location 2212 width 5   Card: deck 30, col. 41-45
    Missing data code: 99999   Decimal place: none

    N=72   Mean=67.319   Standard deviation=2590.8   Range=-3881-3874

    DEFINITION: See Variable 439 for definition and note codes.

Variable 445   GEOGRAPHY-Y 1955

    OSIRIS: location 2217 width 5   Card: deck 30, col. 46-50
    Missing data code: 99999   Decimal place: none

    N=82   Mean=331.10   Standard deviation=2576.9   Range=-3881-3874

    DEFINITION: See Variable 439 for definition and note codes.

Variable 446   GEOGRAPHY-Y 1960

    OSIRIS: location 2222 width 5   Card: deck 30, col. 51-55
    Missing data code: 99999   Decimal place: none

    N=87   Mean=379.94   Standard deviation=2539.8   Range=-3881-3885

    DEFINITION: See Variable 439 for definition and note codes.

Variable 447   GEOGRAPHY-Y 1963

    OSIRIS: location 2227 width 5   Card: deck 30, col. 56-60
    Missing data code: 99999   Decimal place: none

    N=107   Mean=396.77   Standard deviation=2342.9   Range=-3881-3885

    DEFINITION: See Variable 439 for definition and note codes.

Variable 448   GEOGRAPHY-Y 1965

    OSIRIS: location 2232 width 5   Card: deck 30, col. 61-65
    Missing data code: 99999   Decimal place: none

    N=113   Mean=368   Standard deviation=2354.1   Range=-3881-3885

    DEFINITION: See Variable 439 for definition and note codes.

Variable 449   GEOGRAPHY-Z 1950

    OSIRIS: location 2237 width 5   Card: deck 30, col. 66-70
    Missing data code: 99999   Decimal place: none

    N=72   Mean=1468.6   Standard deviation=1638.2   Range=-2600-3432

    DEFINITION: See Variable 439 for definition and note codes.

Variable 450   GEOGRAPHY-Z 1955

    OSIRIS: location 2242 width 5   Card: deck 30, col. 71-75
    Missing data code: 99999   Decimal place: none

    N=82   Mean=1524.8   Standard deviation=1571.4   Range=-2600-3432

    DEFINITION: See Variable 439 for definition and note codes.

Variable 451   GEOGRAPHY-Z 1960

    OSIRIS: location 2247 width 5   Card: deck 30, col. 76-80
    Missing data code: 99999   Decimal place: none
    N=87   Mean=1513.4   Standard deviation=1532.6   Range=-2600-3432

    DEFINITION: See Variable 439 for definition and note codes.

Variable 452   GEOGRAPHY-Z 1963

    OSIRIS: location 2252 width 5   Card: deck 31, col. 6-10
    Missing data code: 99999   Decimal place: none
    N=107   Mean=1292.9   Standard deviation=1476.9   Range=-2600-3432

    DEFINITION: See Variable 439 for definition and note codes.

Variable 453   GEOGRAPHY-Z 1965

    OSIRIS: location 2257 width 5   Card: deck 31, col. 11-15
    Missing data code: 99999   Decimal place: none
    N=113   Mean=1259.1   Standard deviation=1459.2   Range=-2600-3432

    DEFINITION: See Variable 439 for definition and note codes.

SECTION I

APPENDICES: A & B

SECTION I

APPENDIX A: DATA FORMAT AND SUMMARY STATISTICS

Variable Number	Variable Name	OSIRIS Location	Width	Deck	Card-Image Col.	Missing Data Code	N	Mean	Standard Deviation	Range
1	CCODE	1	3	1	6-8	---				
2	RUMMEL	4	3	1	9-11	---				
3	RSSCODE	7	3	all	3-5	---				
4	TEL-PC50	10	5	1	12-16	99999	72	345.79	631.32	0-2846
5	TEL-PC55	15	5	1	17-21	99999	81	428.25	746.86	0-3390
6	TEL-PC60	20	5	1	22-26	99999	86	519.12	876.20	0-4115
7	TEL-PC63	25	5	1	27-31	99999	107	490.28	913.95	2-4458
8	TEL-PC65	30	5	1	32-36	99999	113	523.49	978.02	3-4813
9	%A-POP50	35	5	1	37-41	99999	61	49.73	24.13	6-95
10	%A-POP55	40	5	1	42-46	99999	69	49.18	24.34	6-95
11	%A-POP60	45	5	1	47-51	99999	84	47.73	23.70	4-94
12	%A-POP63	50	5	1	52-56	99999	105	56.05	26.05	6-97
13	%A-POP65	55	5	1	57-61	99999	113	54.14	26.34	4-95
14	ENC-PC50	60	5	1	62-66	99999	68	975.87	1533	0-7543
15	ENC-PC55	65	5	1	67-71	99999	79	1068.3	1491.7	0-7745
16	ENC-PC60	70	5	1	72-76	99999	84	1179.9	1565.4	4-8047
17	ENC-POP63	75	5	1	6-10	99999	107	1086.6	1638.1	5-8508
18	ENC-POP65	80	5	2	11-15	99999	111	1191.6	1767.6	0-9203
19	ILLITE50	85	5	2	16-20	99999	72	41.11	31.76	2-97
20	ILLITE55	90	5	2	21-25	99999	82	41.32	32.20	2-97
21	ILLITE60	95	5	2	26-30	99999	87	36.87	31.60	0-96
22	ILLITE63	100	5	2	31-35	99999	106	43.98	35.52	1-98
23	ILLITE65	105	5	2	36-40	99999	113	46.31	35.53	1-99
24	GNP-PC50	110	5	2	41-45	99999	52	386.71	376.24	43-1908
25	GNP-PC55	115	5	2	46-50	99999	73	413.92	432.32	45-2334
26	GNP-PC60	120	5	2	51-55	99999	87	512.49	550.37	45-2830
27	GNP-PC63	125	5	2	56-60	99999	99	486.34	593.71	40-3048
28	GNP-PC65	130	5	2	61-65	99999	113	568.18	693.85	39-3520
29	EXPP50	135	5	2	66-70	99999	57	3994.8	324.36	3883-6121
30	EXPP55	140	5	2	71-75	99999	81	4004	332.60	3879-6113
31	EXPP60	145	5	2	76-80	99999	82	4012.4	378.96	3873-6065
32	EXPP63	150	5	3	6-10	99999	107	4004.1	358.33	3883-6299
33	EXPP65	155	5	3	11-15	99999	113	4004.3	359.97	3885-6335

-107-

SECTION I
APPENDIX A: DATA FORMAT AND SUMMARY STATISTICS

Variable Number	Variable Name	OSIRIS Location	Width	Deck	Card-Image Col.	Missing Data Code	N	Mean	Standard Deviation	Range
34	NI 50	160	5	3	16-20	99999	51	85.25	336.75	1-2410
35	NI 55	165	5	3	21-25	99999	67	111.03	408.84	1-3302
36	NI 60	170	5	3	26-30	99999	82	136.77	498.75	1-4170
37	NI 63	175	5	3	31-35	99999	88	157.94	551.24	2-4750
38	NI 65	180	5	3	36-40	99999	105	154.66	604.04	1-5684
39	POPULA50	185	5	3	41-45	99999	72	2829.4	7256	80-46350
40	POPULA55	190	5	3	46-50	99999	82	3075.1	8312.6	83-60819
41	POPULA60	195	5	3	51-55	99999	87	3198.7	8695	94-65000
42	POPULA63	200	5	3	56-60	99999	107	2875.3	8336.8	46-68000
43	POPULA65	205	5	3	61-65	99999	113	2853.2	8427.3	46-70000
44	%CT-UN50	210	5	3	66-70	99999	72	130.43	493.29	0-3979
45	%CT-UN55	215	5	3	71-75	99999	64	156.05	480.47	0-3333
46	%CT-UN60	220	5	3	76-80	99999	84	116.06	395.57	0-3251
47	%CT-UN63	225	5	4	6-10	99999	107	91.15	352.21	0-3202
48	%CT-UN65	230	5	4	11-15	99999	110	95.18	351.62	0-3191
49	DEFEX50	235	5	4	16-20	99999	57	774.75	3153.8	1-20717
50	DEFEX55	240	5	4	21-25	99999	58	1384.8	6007.1	2-44428
51	DEFEX60	245	5	4	26-30	99999	48	1440	6876.8	2-47690
52	DEFEX63	250	5	4	31-35	99999	104	1030.4	5474.9	0-53429
53	DEFEX65	255	5	4	36-40	99999	113	1280.4	6523.3	0-51884
54	E/TRSL50	260	5	4	41-45	99999	25	570.40	854.41	10-714
55	E/TRSL55	265	5	4	46-50	99999	27	379.56	203.77	30-692
56	E/TRSL60	270	5	4	51-55	99999	40	456.25	222.54	33-933
57	E/TRSL63	275	5	4	56-60	99999	51	355.39	250.87	0-827
58	E/TRSL65	280	5	4	61-65	99999	61	401.93	279.22	0-1000
59	BLOC50	285	5	4	66-70	99999	72			
60	BLOC55	290	5	4	71-75	99999	82	The mean, standard deviation and range statistics are inapplicable to this categorical variable.		
61	BLOC60	295	5	4	76-80	99999	87			
62	BLOC63	300	5	5	6-10	99999	107			
63	BLOC65	305	5	5	11-15	99999	113			
64	US/AID50	310	5	5	16-20	99999	71	7399.5	2304.8	33-9989
65	US/AID55	315	5	5	21-25	99999	77	6865.3	2860.8	70-9968
66	US/AID60	320	5	5	26-30	99999	73	6895.9	3043	26-9965
67	US/AID63	325	5	5	31-35	99999	62	4972.6	3133.9	100-9900
68	US/AID65	330	5	5	36-40	99999	112	6889.6	2982.6	76-9963

SECTION I

APPENDIX A: DATA FORMAT AND SUMMARY STATISTICS

Variable Number	Variable Name	OSIRIS Location	Width	Deck	Card-Image Col.	Missing Data Code	N	Mean	Standard Deviation	Range
69	TOTAL150	335	5	5	41-45	99999	72	The mean, standard deviation and range statistics are inapplicable to this categorical variable.		0-7862
70	TOTAL155	340	5	5	46-50	99999	80			0-7083
71	TOTAL160	345	5	5	51-55	99999	87			0-26087
72	TOTAL163	350	5	5	56-60	99999	107			7-7565
73	TOTAL165	355	5	5	61-65	99999	113			26-18850
74	TFC/GP50	360	5	5	66-70	99999	66	654.08	1405.6	0-7862
75	TFC/GP55	365	5	5	71-75	99999	79	627.59	1235.8	0-7083
76	TFC/GP60	370	5	5	76-80	99999	53	1114.9	3585.5	0-26087
77	TFC/GP63	375	5	6	6-10	99999	64	563.42	997.15	7-7565
78	TFC/GP65	380	5	6	11-15	99999	69	1451.8	2834.2	26-18850
79	THREAT50	385	5	6	16-20	99999	67	.29 -1	.24	0-2
80	THREAT55	390	5	6	21-25	99999	82	.17	.64	0-5
81	THREAT60	395	5	6	26-30	99999	87	.10	.48	0-4
82	THREAT63	400	5	6	31-35	99999	107	.16	.65	0-5
83	THREAT65	405	5	6	36-40	99999	113	.21	.72	0-5
84	ACCUSA50	410	5	6	41-45	99999	68	5.86	16.31	0-102
85	ACCUSA55	415	5	6	46-50	99999	82	7.92	20.45	0-144
86	ACCUSA60	420	5	6	51-55	99999	87	4.56	13.08	0-89
87	ACCUSA63	425	5	6	56-60	99999	107	2.04	5.47	0-42
88	ACCUSA65	430	6	6	61-64	99999	113	3.92	10.10	0-71
89	F-KILL50	435	6	6	65-70	999999	70	5772.5	27900	0-.20+6
90	F-KILL55	441	5	6	71-75	99999	81	14.97	64.74	0-437
91	F-KILL60	446	5	6	76-80	99999	87	95.80	596.22	0-4816
92	F-KILL63	451	5	7	6-10	99999	104	69.11	561.85	0-5665
93	F-KILL65	456	5	7	11-15	99999	113	389.16	1725.7	0-11243
94	MILACT50	461	5	7	16-20	99999	70	The mean, standard deviation and range statistics are inapplicable to this categorical variable.		
95	MILACT55	466	5	7	21-25	99999	81			
96	MILACT60	471	5	7	26-30	99999	87			
97	MILACT63	476	5	7	31-35	99999	104			
98	MILACT65	481	5	7	36-40	99999	113			
99	PROTST50	486	5	7	41-45	99999	66	1.3030	2.66	0-17
100	PROTST55	491	5	7	46-50	99999	77	.81	2.13	0-15
101	PROTST60	496	5	7	51-55	99999	87	.77	1.92	0-13
102	PROTST63	501	5	7	56-60	99999	107	.93	3.30	0-24
103	PROTST65	506	5	7	61-65	99999	113	1.25	4.18	0-31
104	D-KILL50	511	5	7	66-70	99999	70	18.20	62.215	0-293
105	D-KILL55	516	5	7	71-75	99999	78	115.97	673	0-4279
106	D-KILL60	521	5	7	76-80	99999	84	11.16	31.03	0-200
107	D-KILL63	526	5	8	6-10	99999	107	480.13	3517.2	0-36010
108	D-KILL65	531	6	8	11-16	99999	113	2331.0	23524	0-.25000+6

-109-

SECTION I

APPENDIX A: DATA FORMAT AND SUMMARY STATISTICS

Variable Number	Variable Name	OSIRIS Location	Width	Deck	Card-Image Col.	Missing Data Code	N	Mean	Standard Deviation	Range
109	STRIKE50	537	5	8	17-20	99999	72	.27	.87	0-5
110	STRIKE55	542	5	8	21-25	99999	79	.88 -1	.68	0-6
111	STRIKE60	547	5	8	26-30	99999	87	.19	.60	0-3
112	STRIKE63	552	5	8	31-35	99999	107	.74 -1	.35	0-2
113	STRIKE65	557	5	8	36-40	99999	113	.88 -1	.31	0-2
114	RIOTS50	562	5	8	41-45	99999	72	.33	.97	0-5
115	RIOTS55	567	5	8	46-50	99999	79	.39	1.99	0-17
116	RIOTS60	572	5	8	51-55	99999	87	.66	1.85	0-10
117	RIOTS63	577	5	8	56-60	99999	107	.83	2.73	0-24
118	RIOTS65	582	5	8	61-65	99999	113	.66	1.96	0-16
119	PURGES50	587	5	8	66-70	99999	72	.12	.37	0-2
120	PURGES55	592	5	8	71-75	99999	79	.22	.52	0-3
121	PURGES60	597	5	8	76-80	99999	87	.11	.41	0-2
122	PURGES63	602	5	9	6-10	99999	107	.15	.45	0-3
123	PURGES65	607	5	9	11-15	99999	113	.27	.55	0-3
124	DEMONS50	612	5	9	16-20	99999	72	.83 -1	.32	0-2
125	DEMONS55	617	5	9	21-25	99999	79	.50	1.33	0-7
126	DEMONS60	622	5	9	26-30	99999	87	.41	1.68	0-13
127	DEMONS63	627	5	9	31-35	99999	107	1.10	6.57	0-67
128	DEMONS65	632	5	9	36-40	99999	113	.69	2.31	0-15
129	%CATH50	637	5	9	41-45	99999	71	414.87	427.94	0-1000
130	%CATH55	642	5	9	46-50	99999	81	393.44	426.58	0-995
131	%CATH60	647	5	9	51-55	99999	86	367.41	407.60	0-995
132	%CATH63	652	5	9	56-60	99999	107	319.79	387.70	0-997
133	%CATH65	657	5	9	61-65	99999	112	314.90	369.53	0-994
134	US-DIS50	662	5	9	66-70	99999	72	10969	6303.09	2-24500
135	US-DIS55	667	5	9	71-75	99999	82	11523	6316.4	0-24500
136	US-DIS60	672	5	9	76-80	99999	87	9594.8	4774.5	0-19875
137	US-DIS63	677	5	10	6-10	99999	107	10555	5002	0-24125
138	US-DIS65	682	5	10	11-15	99999	113	10673	5191.7	0-24125
139	MED/NG50	687	5	10	16-20	99999	72	1004.6	395.96	0-1901
140	MED/NG55	692	5	10	21-25	99999	82	1092.9	539.60	0-3000
141	MED/NG60	697	5	10	26-30	99999	87	847.12	421.82	0-1532
142	MED/NG63	702	5	10	31-35	99999	107	855.79	529.29	0-2500
143	MED/NG65	707	5	10	36-40	99999	113	929.08	512.18	0-2033
144	ER-AMB50	712	5	10	41-45	99999	67	.70	1.74	0-10
145	ER-AMB55	717	5	10	46-50	99999	76	.65 -1	.24	0-1
146	ER-AMB60	722	5	10	51-55	99999	87	.42	1.07	0-7
147	ER-AMB63	727	5	10	56-60	99999	107	.29	.67	0-3
148	ER-AMB65	732	5	10	61-65	99999	113	.31	.84	0-4

SECTION I

APPENDIX A. DATA FORMAT AND SUMMARY STATISTICS

Variable Number	Variable Name	OSIRIS Location	Width	Deck	Card-Image Col.	Missing Data Code	N	Mean	Standard Deviation	Range
149	DIV-MR50	737	5	10	66-70	99999	51	756.82	624.71	0-2310
150	DIV-MR55	742	5	10	71-75	99999	45	627.56	512.31	0-2080
151	DIV-MR60	747	5	10	76-80	99999	56	852.68	637.81	0-2580
152	DIV-MR63	752	5	11	6-10	99999	61	902.69	656.29	0-2588
153	DIV-MR65	757	5	11	11-15	99999	69	885.62	679.58	0-2689
154	DNSITY50	762	5	11	16-20	99999	72	52.87	63.25	1-316
155	DNSITY55	767	5	11	21-25	99999	78	63.55	73.09	1-331
156	DNSITY60	772	5	11	26-30	99999	87	66.23	74.58	1-342
157	DNSITY63	777	5	11	31-35	99999	107	59.77	75.39	1-356
158	DNSITY65	782	5	11	36-40	99999	113	64.24	78.17	1-366
159	%ARABL50	787	5	11	41-45	99999	70	178.51	154.87	0-628
160	%ARABL55	792	5	11	46-50	99999	76	194.21	153.91	1-634
161	%ARABL60	797	5	11	51-55	99999	85	194.71	151.80	0-650
162	%ARABL63	802	5	11	56-60	99999	88	206.95	159.21	1-651
163	%ARABL65	807	5	11	61-65	99999	93	204.26	154.57	2-630
164	AREA50	812	5	11	66-70	99999	72	1420.7	3386.0	10-22402
165	AREA55	817	5	11	71-75	99999	82	1288.3	3194.7	10-22402
166	AREA60	822	5	11	76-80	99999	87	1256.7	3110.5	10-22402
167	AREA63	827	5	12	6-10	99999	107	1145.2	2821.7	10-22402
168	AREA65	832	5	12	11-15	99999	113	1108.2	2756.9	5-22402
169	RDS-KM50	837	5	12	16-20	99999	57	224.96	329.32	1-1319
170	RDS-KM55	842	5	12	21-25	99999	66	204.70	291.97	1-1347
171	RDS-KM60	847	5	12	26-30	99999	74	198.36	277.67	1-1369
172	RDS-KM63	852	5	12	31-35	99999	91	195.45	292.87	1-1433
173	RDS-KM65	857	5	12	36-40	99999	93	229.18	341.49	0-1433
174	RR-KM50	862	5	12	41-45	99999	67	30.85	38.50	0-161
175	RR-KM55	867	5	12	46-50	99999	79	31.17	39.13	0-158
176	RR-KM60	872	5	12	51-55	99999	84	31.67	41.64	0-157
177	RR-KM63	877	5	12	56-60	99999	96	27.08	38.95	0-157
178	RR-KM65	882	5	12	61-65	99999	99	27.20	38.97	0-157
179	RELGRP50	887	5	12	66-70	99999	72	2.22	1.03	1-5
180	RELGRP55	892	5	12	71-75	99999	82	2.26	1.05	1-5
181	RELGRP60	897	5	12	76-80	99999	87	2.27	1.01	1-5
182	RELGRP63	902	5	13	6-10	99999	107	2.38	1.06	1-5
183	RELGRP65	907	5	13	11-15	99999	107	2.38	1.06	1-5

-112-

SECTION I

APPENDIX A: DATA FORMAT AND SUMMARY STATISTICS

Variable Number	Variable Name	OSIRIS Location	Width	Deck	Card-Image Col.	Missing Data Code	N	Mean	Standard Deviation	Range
184	IM/I+E50	912	5	13	16-20	99999	22	577.45	334.89	0-1000
185	IM/I+E55	917	5	13	21-25	99999	33	529.91	229.74	0-991
186	IM/I+E60	922	5	13	26-30	99999	33	461.09	259.86	13-982
187	IM/I+E63	927	5	13	31-35	99999	53	347.19	343.02	0-1000
188	IM/I+E65	932	5	13	36-40	99999	34	453.59	263.87	3-998
189	RAIN50	937	5	13	41-45	99999	72	1067.8	695.42	79-3429
190	RAIN55	942	5	13	46-50	99999	82	1100.2	686.71	79-3429
191	RAIN60	947	5	13	51-55	99999	87	1097.7	698.33	79-3429
192	RAIN63	952	5	13	56-60	99999	107	1115.9	690.74	79-3429
193	RAIN65	957	5	13	61-65	99999	107	1115.9	690.74	79-3429
194	RGRP/P50	962	5	13	66-70	99999	69	82.36	20.50	17-100
195	RGRP/P55	967	5	13	71-75	99999	75	82.30	20.08	17-100
196	RGRP/P60	972	5	13	76-80	99999	79	82.17	19.35	17-100
197	RGRP/P63	977	5	14	6-10	99999	87	80.06	20.60	17-100
198	RGRP/P65	982	5	14	11-15	99999	106	75.80	21.80	17-100
199	%D-WTR50	987	5	14	16-20	99999	24	418.96	289.33	1-945
200	%D-WTR55	992	5	14	21-25	99999	33	459.06	285.43	52-988
201	%D-WTR60	997	5	14	26-30	99999	56	362.91	319.96	50-987
202	%D-WTR63	1002	5	14	31-35	99999	58	367.24	323.44	50-987
203	%D-WTR65	1007	5	14	36-40	99999	48	522.98	316.73	81-987
204	FST/ST50	1012	5	14	41-45	99999	24	38.29	56.99	0-253
205	FST/ST55	1017	5	14	46-50	99999	55	52.12	79.97	0-348
206	FST/ST60	1022	5	14	51-55	99999	57	60.47	88.41	1-408
207	FST/ST63	1027	5	14	56-60	99999	81	69.09	117.45	0-581
208	FST/ST65	1032	5	14	61-65	99999	86	88.82	138.07	1-628
209	NEUTRL50	1037	5	14	66-70	99999	72			
210	NEUTRL55	1042	5	14	71-75	99999	76	The mean, standard deviation and range statistics are inapplicable to this categorical variable.		
211	NEUTRL60	1047	5	14	76-80	99999	87			
212	NEUTRL63	1052	5	15	6-10	99999	107			
213	NEUTRL65	1057	5	15	11-15	99999	113			
214	NATAGE50	1062	5	15	16-20	99999	70	2.04	1.39	0-5
215	NATAGE55	1067	5	15	21-25	99999	81	1.95	1.44	0-5
216	NATAGE60	1072	5	15	26-30	99999	87	2.09	1.54	0-5
217	NATAGE63	1077	5	15	31-35	99999	107	2.63	1.79	0-5
218	NATAGE65	1082	5	15	36-40	99999	113	2.76	1.82	0-5

SECTION I

APPENDIX A: DATA FORMAT AND SUMMARY STATISTICS

Variable Number	Variable Name	OSIRIS Location	Width	Deck	Card-Image Col.	Missing Data Code	N	Mean	Standard Deviation	Range
219	REL/TI50	1087	5	15	41-45	99999	31	653	427.59	23-2270
220	REL/TI55	1092	5	15	46-50	99999	61	594.59	547.69	0-2900
221	REL/TI60	1097	5	15	51-55	99999	59	666.78	518.10	10-2170
222	REL/TI63	1102	5	15	56-60	99999	73	667.81	637.26	0-3102
223	REL/TI65	1107	5	15	61-65	99999	73	698.92	805.84	0-3564
224	EMG/PP50	1112	5	15	66-70	99999	37	438.19	878.43	0-3985
225	EMG/PP55	1117	5	15	71-75	99999	44	557.39	1050.3	0-4151
226	EMG/PP60	1122	5	15	76-80	99999	30	246.67	241.74	0-800
227	EMG/PP63	1127	5	16	6-10	99999	57	141.54	237.56	0-1180
228	EMG/PP65	1132	5	16	11-15	99999	37	252.19	335.36	0-1371
229	SG/GNP50	1137	5	16	16-20	99999	38	364.05	410.22	50-2235
230	SG/GNP55	1142	5	16	21-25	99999	67	345.82	620.81	0-4347
231	SG/GNP60	1147	5	16	26-30	99999	67	418.37	636.06	2-3624
232	SG/GNP63	1152	5	16	31-35	99999	79	529.22	892.25	22-4626
233	SG/GNP65	1157	5	16	36-40	99999	89	720.94	1254.3	29-7246
234	LAW/NG50	1162	5	16	41-45	99999	72	508.10	306.02	0-1428
235	LAW/NG55	1167	5	16	46-50	99999	82	399.88	223.48	0-909
236	LAW/NG60	1172	5	16	51-55	99999	87	510.29	416.75	0-3333
237	LAW/NG63	1177	5	16	56-60	99999	107	401.86	215.79	0-1020
238	LAW/NG65	1182	5	16	61-65	99999	113	440.75	301.82	0-2667
239	%UNEMP50	1187	5	16	66-70	99999	20	213.55	340.07	0-1364
240	%UNEMP55	1192	5	16	71-75	99999	44	368.18	518.88	0-2330
241	%UNEMP60	1197	5	16	76-80	99999	36	219.42	224.77	0-740
242	%UNEMP63	1202	5	17	6-10	99999	50	186.02	237.21	0-1051
243	%ENEMP65	1207	5	17	11-15	99999	25	397.60	314.22	60-1400
244	EX/EPT50	1212	5	17	16-20	99999	62	2510.6	2510.6	512-9205
245	EX/EPT55	1217	5	17	21-25	99999	66	4458.3	2284.3	1290-9900
246	EX/EPT60	1222	5	17	26-30	99999	77	3536.7	2043.5	933-9654
247	EX/EPT63	1227	5	17	31-35	99999	98	3751.4	2189.4	440-9872
248	EX/EPT65	1232	5	17	36-40	99999	93	3479.4	2302.3	418-9940
249	LANGRP50	1237	5	17	41-45	99999	61	2.85	2.70	1-12
250	LANGRP55	1242	5	17	46-50	99999	68	2.75	2.60	1-12
251	LANGRP60	1247	5	17	51-55	99999	86	3.01	2.62	1-12
252	LANGRP63	1252	5	17	56-60	99999	106	3.40	2.73	1-12
253	LANGRP65	1257	5	17	61-65	99999	113	3.28	2.57	1-12
254	LGRP/P50	1262	5	17	66-70	99999	61	785.74	226.83	200-999
255	LGRP/P55	1267	5	17	71-75	99999	68	763.60	242.84	168-999
256	LGRP/P60	1272	5	17	76-80	99999	71	757.68	242.86	168-999
257	LGRP/P63	1277	5	18	6-10	99999	72	752.67	244.86	168-999
258	LGRP/P65	1282	5	18	11-15	99999	71	769.72	230.12	168-999

SECTION I

APPENDIX A: DATA FORMAT AND SUMMARY STATISTICS

Variable Number	Variable Name	OSIRIS Location	Width	Deck	Card-Image Col.	Missing Data Code	N	Mean	Standard Deviation	Range
259	ETHGRP50	1287	5	18	16-20	99999	63	2.96	2.14	0-11
260	ETHGRP55	1292	5	18	21-25	99999	72	2.90	2.05	1-11
261	ETHGRP60	1297	5	18	26-30	99999	81	3.54	3.53	1-23
262	ETHGRP63	1302	5	18	31-35	99999	98	4.59	4.55	1-24
263	ETHGRP65	1307	5	18	36-40	99999	105	4.42	4.27	1-24
264	AIDRVD50	1312	5	18	41-45	99999	58	889.97	1902.8	0-9573
265	AIDRVD55	1317	5	18	46-50	99999	47	787.51	1778.2	-325-10467
266	AIDRVD60	1322	5	18	51-55	99999	67	308.64	704.30	-118-4478
267	AIDRVD63	1327	5	18	56-60	99999	57	826.14	1495	0-9780
268	AIDRVD65	1332	5	18	61-65	99999	93	806.27	1640.4	-294-13110
269	D-TY50	1337	5	18	66-70	99999	12	448.33	618	0-2000
270	D-TY55	1342	5	18	71-75	99999	82	199.51	258.92	0-992
271	D-TY60	1347	5	18	76-80	99999	76	304.47	339.96	0-2150
272	D-TY63	1352	5	19	6-10	99999	84	356.52	289.04	0-1545
273	D-TY65	1357	5	19	11-15	99999	97	3794.5	9380.7	0-44200
274	GE-GVT50	1362	5	19	16-20	99999	56	993.36	494.96	81-2652
275	GE-GVT55	1367	5	19	21-25	99999	66	1220.4	531.99	290-2800
276	GE-GVT60	1372	5	19	26-30	99999	51	1272.5	521.59	418-2808
277	GE-GVT63	1377	5	19	31-35	99999	89	1393	574.12	117-2883
278	GE-GVT65	1382	5	19	36-40	99999	84	1537.8	544.22	329-2710
279	FM/WKS50	1387	5	19	41-45	99999	55	2755.8	1150.9	581-4914
280	FM/WKS55	1392	5	19	46-50	99999	65	2800.6	1116.3	580-4900
281	FM/WKS60	1397	5	19	51-55	99999	58	2699.7	1064.1	500-5184
282	FM/WKS63	1402	5	19	56-60	99999	73	2928.8	1204.0	500-5208
283	FM/WKS65	1407	5	19	61-65	99999	94	2469.7	1428.7	180-5620
284	EP/GNP50	1412	5	19	66-70	99999	50	1526.2	1236.0	2-5910
285	EP/GNP55	1417	5	19	71-75	99999	69	1716.5	1107.3	70-5190
286	EP/GNP60	1422	5	19	76-80	99999	49	1695.6	981.12	399-4953
287	EP/GNP63	1427	5	20	6-10	99999	68	1899.4	1406.9	309-9560
288	EP/GNP65	1432	5	20	11-15	99999	104	1893.2	1417.6	57-7668
289	MSNT/M50	1437	5	20	16-20	99999	35	43.28	9.67	17-64
290	MSNT/M55	1442	5	20	21-25	99999	46	44.08	12.31	4-72
291	MSNT/M60	1447	5	20	26-30	99999	41	42.04	12.11	3-69
292	MSNT/M63	1452	5	20	31-35	99999	48	43.29	9.52	23-68
293	MSNT/M65	1457	5	20	36-40	99999	52	45	12.61	17-83
294	IP/TRD50	1462	5	20	41-45	99999	62	5172.6	1361.9	2142-9085
295	IP/TRD55	1467	5	20	46-50	99999	75	5453.9	1311.9	2430-9500
296	IP/TRD60	1472	5	20	51-55	99999	79	5657.9	1241.8	3036-9839
297	IP/TRD63	1477	5	20	56-60	99999	97	5600	1250.8	2462-9667
298	IP/TRD65	1482	5	20	61-65	99999	104	5454	1174.3	2867-9706

SECTION I
APPENDIX A: DATA FORMAT AND SUMMARY STATISTICS

Variable Number	Variable Name	OSIRIS Location	Width	Deck	Card-Image Col.	Missing Data Code	N	Mean	Standard Deviation	Range
299	CAL-PC50	1487	5	20	66-70	99999	31	803.52	1328	-2613-3359
300	CAL-PC55	1492	5	20	71-75	99999	40	672.88	1396.9	-1853-3206
301	CAL-PC60	1497	5	20	76-80	99999	58	701.16	1461.6	-2375-3321
302	CAL-PC63	1502	5	21	6-10	99999	61	800.67	1395.4	-2250-3244
303	CAL-PC65	1507	5	21	11-15	99999	61	842.49	1365.4	-2250-3144
304	PR/CAL50	1512	5	21	16-20	99999	31	315.71	51.64	203-394
305	PR/CAL55	1517	5	21	21-25	99999	49	284.47	30.58	212-346
306	PR/CAL60	1522	5	21	26-30	99999	47	277	28.44	212-333
307	PR/CAL63	1527	5	21	31-35	99999	44	279.05	28.56	219-338
308	PR/CAL65	1532	5	21	36-40	99999	79	272.85	34.29	192-368
309	R/TRSL50	1537	5	21	41-45	99999	29	1353.6	2566.7	0-8505
310	R/TRSL55	1542	5	21	46-50	99999	35	1267.1	2080.6	0-6970
311	R/TRSL60	1547	5	21	51-55	99999	36	889	1180.3	81-4639
312	R/TRSL63	1552	5	21	56-60	99999	47	699.81	1097.6	0-5292
313	R/TRS165	1557	5	21	61-65	99999	64	542.78	933.60	0-4365
314	MIL/PP50	1562	5	21	66-70	99999	57	90.15	102.08	0-587
315	MIL/PP55	1567	5	21	71-75	99999	79	90.92	99.41	0-569
316	MIL/PP60	1572	5	21	76-80	99999	76	87.94	87.22	7-472
317	MIL/PP63	1577	5	22	6-10	99999	79	102.44	142.17	0-1050
318	MIL/PP65	1582	5	22	11-15	99999	101	80.09	123.19	0-1050
319	BOT/G050	1587	5	22	16-20	99999	43	-173.83	643.08	-4100-153
320	BOT/G055	1592	5	22	21-25	99999	56	-530.36	1503.1	-8100-500
321	BOT/G060	1597	5	22	26-30	99999	66	-167.32	1144.9	-6700-5700
322	BOT/G063	1602	5	22	31-35	99999	55	-220.73	921.84	-6800-210
323	BOT/G065	1607	5	22	36-40	99999	73	-721.95	1612.9	-9999-238
324	PARTYS50	1612	5	22	41-45	99999	68	3.00	2.45	0-14
325	PARTYS55	1617	5	22	46-50	99999	79	3.83	2.46	0-12
326	PARTYS60	1622	5	22	51-55	99999	87	3.09	2.76	0-13
327	PARTYS63	1627	5	22	56-60	99999	105	2.68	2.45	0-10
328	PARTYS65	1632	5	22	61-65	99999	113	2.89	2.45	0-10
329	ART/NG50	1637	5	22	66-70	99999	72	271.49	193.21	0-567
330	ART/NG55	1642	5	22	71-75	99999	82	315.72	226.37	0-1250
331	ART/NG60	1647	5	22	76-80	99999	87	492.08	277.68	0-1429
332	ART/NG63	1652	5	23	6-10	99999	107	422.02	229.16	0-1429
333	ART/NG65	1657	5	23	11-15	99999	113	443.63	230.32	0-1364

SECTION I
APPENDIX A. DATA FORMAT AND SUMMARY STATISTICS

Variable Number	Variable Name	OSIRIS Location	Width	Deck	Card-Image Col.	Missing Data Code	N	Mean	Standard Deviation	Range
334	COM/PP50	1662	5	23	16-20	99999	70	1144.6	2577	0-13590
335	COM/PP55	1667	5	23	21-25	99999	81	1071.5	2428.6	0-12362
336	COM/PP60	1672	5	23	26-30	99999	86	982.67	2259.4	0-11321
337	COM/PP63	1677	5	23	31-35	99999	103	883.74	2278.9	0-11641
338	COM/PP65	1682	5	23	36-40	99999	112	837.02	2347.9	0-13223
339	GUT-PC50	1687	5	23	41-45	99999	48	1515.0	714.62	534-3333
340	GUT-PC55	1692	5	23	46-50	99999	64	1711.8	768.74	496-4977
341	GUT-PC60	1697	5	23	51-55	99999	49	1772.1	679.73	701-3243
342	GUT-PC63	1702	5	23	56-60	99999	72	2116.9	1296.0	7-7270
343	GUT-PC65	1707	5	23	61-65	99999	84	2092.8	1033.9	668-5896
344	MONARC50	1712	5	23	66-70	99999	72	The mean, standard deviation and range statistics are inapplicable to this categorical variable.		
345	MONARC55	1717	5	23	71-75	99999	82			
346	MONARC60	1722	5	23	76-80	99999	87			
347	MONARC63	1727	5	24	6-10	99999	107			
348	MONARC65	1732	5	24	11-15	99999	113			
349	PUP-PT50	1737	5	24	16-20	99999	63	3420.9	1106.1	1017-7033
350	PUP-PT55	1742	5	24	21-25	99999	79	3434.2	1038.5	1700-8600
351	PUP-PT60	1747	5	24	26-30	99999	84	3383.3	860.77	2000-6200
352	PUP-PT63	1752	5	24	31-35	99999	104	3720.9	1414.7	1392-10471
353	PUP-PT65	1757	5	24	36-40	99999	106	3584	1212.2	1800-8300
354	LAWTRA50	1762	5	24	41-45	99999	72	The man, standard deviation and range statistics are inapplicable to this categorical variable.		
355	LAWTRA55	1767	5	24	46-50	99999	79			
356	LAWTRA60	1772	5	24	51-55	99999	87			
357	LAWTRA63	1777	5	24	56-60	99999	107			
358	LAWTRA65	1782	5	24	61-65	99999	113			
359	LEGIT50	1787	5	24	66-70	99999	72	The mean, standard deviation and range statistics are inapplicable to this categorical variable.		
360	LEGIT55	1792	5	24	71-75	99999	77			
361	LEGIT60	1797	5	24	76-80	99999	87			
362	LEGIT63	1802	5	25	6-10	99999	107			
363	LEGIT65	1807	5	25	11-15	99999	113			
364	EGRP/P50	1812	5	25	16-20	99999	72	715.19	251.56	100-1000
365	EGRP/P55	1817	5	25	21-25	99999	82	730.74	244.91	100-1000
366	EGRP/P60	1822	5	25	26-30	99999	87	708.63	257.88	100-1000
367	EGRP/P63	1827	5	25	31-35	99999	107	645.40	286.79	100-1000
368	EGRP/P65	1832	5	25	36-40	99999	113	649.54	285.87	100-1000

SECTION I
APPENDIX A: DATA FORMAT AND SUMMARY STATISTICS

Variable Number	Variable Name	OSIRIS Location	Width	Deck	Card-Image Col.	Missing Data Code	N	Mean	Standard Deviation	Range
369	ASSASS50	1837	5	25	41-45	99999	72	.12	.37	0-2
370	ASSASS55	1842	5	25	46-50	99999	79	.13	.49	0-3
371	ASSASS60	1847	5	25	51-55	99999	87	.24	1.21	0-11
372	ASSASS63	1852	5	25	56-60	99999	107	.84	-1 .31	0-2
373	ASSASS65	1857	5	25	61-65	99999	112	.28	.91	0-6
374	GVTCRS50	1862	5	25	66-70	99999	72	.13	.34	0-1
375	GVTCRS55	1867	5	25	71-75	99999	79	.13	.41	0-2
376	GVTCRS60	1872	5	25	76-80	99999	87	.26	.55	0-3
377	GVTCRS63	1877	5	26	6-10	99999	107	.14	.57	0-5
378	GVTCRS65	1882	5	26	11-15	99999	112	.33	.55	0-2
379	UNDE/C50	1887	5	26	16-20	99999	72	2.31	15.25	0-122
380	UNDE/C55	1892	5	26	21-25	99999	82	12.78	29.31	0-99
381	UNDE/C60	1897	5	26	26-30	99999	87	35.62	56.52	0-214
382	UNDE/C63	1902	5	26	31-35	99999	107	32.98	56.29	0-459
383	UNDE/C65	1907	5	26	36-40	99999	113	43.53	37	0-89
384	BOP/GO50	1912	5	26	41-45	99999	46	-7.41	46.89	-220-116
385	BOP/GO55	1917	5	26	46-50	99999	59	-3.35	75.29	-404-279
386	BOP/GO60	1922	5	26	51-55	99999	68	-6.22	257.98	-1480-1329
387	BOP/GO63	1927	5	26	56-60	99999	67	8.86	60.49	-212-307
388	BOP/GO65	1932	5	26	61-65	99999	76	-19.89	186.08	-1590-258
389	INVBAL50	1937	5	26	66-70	99999	51	8.01	256.71	-363-1693
390	INVBAL55	1942	5	26	71-75	99999	62	35.83	1069.4	-1825-7966
391	INVBAL60	1947	5	26	76-80	99999	65	13.78	458.75	-538-3443
392	INVBAL63	1952	5	27	6-10	99999	74	14.64	581.23	-667-4654
393	INVBAL65	1957	5	27	11-15	99999	75	18.82	667.40	-789-5348
394	STYLE50	1962	5	27	16-20	99999	72			
395	STYLE55	1967	5	27	21-25	99999	82	The mean, standard deviation and range statistics are inapplicable to this categorical variable.		
396	STYLE60	1972	5	27	26-30	99999	86			
397	STYLE63	1977	5	27	31-35	99999	107			
398	STYLE65	1982	5	27	36-40	99999	113			
399	CONSTI50	1987	5	27	41-45	99999	72			
400	CONSTI55	1992	5	27	46-50	99999	82	The mean, standard deviation and range statistics are inapplicable to this categorical variable.		
401	CONSTI60	1997	5	27	51-55	99999	85			
402	CONSTI63	2002	5	27	56-60	99999	107			
403	CONSTI65	2007	5	27	61-65	99999	113			

-118-

SECTION I

APPENDIX A: DATA FORMAT AND SUMMARY STATISTICS

Variable Number	Variable Name	OSIRIS Location	Width	Deck	Card-Image Col.	Missing Data Code	N	Mean	Standard Deviation	Range
404	ELECTO50	2012	5	27	66-70	99999	72			
405	ELECTO55	2017	5	27	71-75	99999	82	The mean, standard deviation and range statistics are inapplicable to this categorical variable.		
406	ELECTO60	2022	5	27	76-80	99999	78			
407	ELECTO63	2027	5	28	6-10	99999	107			
408	ELECTO65	2032	5	28	11-15	99999	113			
409	COMMUN50	2037	5	28	16-20	99999	72			
410	COMMUN55	2042	5	28	21-25	99999	82	The mean, standard deviation and range statistics are inapplicable to this categorical variable.		
411	COMMUN60	2047	5	28	26-30	99999	86			
412	COMMUN63	2052	5	28	31-35	99999	107			
413	COMMUN65	2057	5	28	36-40	99999	113			
414	LEADER50	2062	5	28	41-45	99999	69			
415	LEADER55	2067	5	28	46-50	99999	82			
416	LEADER60	2072	5	28	51-55	99999	84	The mean, standard deviation and range statistics are inapplicable to this categorical variable.		
417	LEADER63	2077	5	28	56-60	99999	106			
418	LEADER65	2082	5	28	61-65	99999	113			
419	POWDIS50	2087	5	28	66-70	99999	71			
420	POWDIS55	2092	5	28	71-75	99999	82			
421	POWDIS60	2097	5	28	76-80	99999	85	The mean, standard deviation and range statistics are inapplicable to this categorical variable.		
422	POWDIS63	2102	5	29	6-10	99999	106			
423	POWDIS65	2107	5	29	11-15	99999	113			
424	MILPAR50	2112	5	29	16-20	99999	72			
425	MILPAR55	2117	5	29	21-25	99999	82			
426	MILPAR60	2122	5	29	26-30	99999	82	The mean, standard deviation and range statistics are inapplicable to this categorical variable.		
427	MILPAR63	2127	5	29	31-35	99999	100			
428	MILPAR65	2132	5	29	36-40	99999	113			
429	BUREAU50	2137	5	29	41-45	99999	72			
430	BUREAU55	2142	5	29	46-50	99999	82			
431	BUREAU60	2147	5	29	51-55	99999	82	The mean, standard deviation and range statistics are inapplicable to this categorical variable.		
432	BUREAU63	2152	5	29	56-60	99999	101			
433	BUREAU65	2157	5	29	61-65	99999	113			
434	CENSOR50	2162	5	29	66-70	99999	69			
435	CENSOR55	2167	5	29	71-75	99999	82			
436	CENSOR60	2172	5	29	76-80	99999	87	The mean, standard deviation and range statistics are inapplicable to this categorical variable.		
437	CENSOR63	2177	5	30	6-10	99999	102			
438	CENSOR65	2182	5	30	11-15	99999	113			

SECTION I

APPENDIX A: DATA FORMAT AND SUMMARY STATISTICS

Variable Number	Variable Name	OSIRIS Location	Width	Deck	Card-Image Col.	Missing Data Code	N	Mean	Standard Deviation	Range
439	GEOG-X50	2187	5	30	16-20	99999	72	1385.5	1546.8	-2975-3881
440	GEOG-X55	2192	5	30	21-25	99999	82	1247.2	1658.5	-2975-3881
441	GEOG-X60	2197	5	30	26-30	99999	87	1323.7	1689.1	-2975-3948
442	GEOG-X63	2202	5	30	31-35	99999	107	1764.3	1787.5	-2975-3948
443	GEOG-X65	2207	5	30	36-40	99999	113	1813.7	1766.1	-2975-3948
444	GEOG-Y50	2212	5	30	41-45	99999	72	67.31	2590.8	-3881-3874
445	GEOG-Y55	2217	5	30	46-50	99999	82	331.10	2576.9	-3881-3874
446	GEOG-Y60	2222	5	30	51-55	99999	87	379.94	2539.8	-3881-3885
447	GEOG-Y63	2227	5	30	56-60	99999	107	396.77	2342.9	-3881-3885
448	GEOG-Y65	2232	5	30	61-65	99999	113	368	2354.1	-3881-3885
449	GEOG-250	2237	5	30	66-70	99999	72	1468.6	1638.2	-2600-3432
450	GEOG-255	2242	5	30	71-75	99999	82	1524.8	1571.4	-2600-3432
451	GEOG-260	2247	5	30	76-80	99999	87	1513.4	1532.6	-2600-3432
452	GEOG-263	2252	5	31	6-10	99999	107	1292.9	1476.9	-2600-3432
453	GEOG-265	2257	5	31	11-15	99999	113	1259.1	1459.2	-2600-3432

SECTION I

APPENDIX B: NOTES

SECTION I

APPENDIX A: NOTES

-122-

SECTION I
APPENDIX A: NOTES

ATTRIBUTES OF NATIONS, 1950-1965: NOTES, VARIABLES 29-58

	1	29	31	32	33	34	35	36	37	38	39	40	41	43	44	45	46	49	50	51	52	53	54	55	56	57	58	3
USA																		C										002
CAN																		C										020
CUB								A		B	A	A	A					D	H	S								040
HAI					A				C		A	A	A					D		A								041
DOM											A	A	A					D									I	042
JAM																												051
TRI																		AC										052
MEX								A			A	A	A					C										070
GUA												A	A					AC									I	090
HON	A										A	A	A					C										091
ELS													A															092
NIC													A							S								093
COS	A										A	A	A					C		S								094
PAN	A										A	A	A															095
COL											A		A															100
VEN									C				A					C									I	101
ECU								A			A	Q	A					B		A								130
PER	A								D		A	A	A					AC		A								135
BRA	A								C		A	A	A					AC		A						I	140
BOL	A										A	A	A					B		A	S							145
PAR					A								A					B		A	S							150
CHL					B								A					AC			S							155
ARG	A												A					AC										160
URA	A								C				A					B	A									165
UNK					A													C									I	200
IRE												A						C	H			J	J	J	J	J	J	205
NTH												A						C	H									210
BEL																		AC	H									211
FRN																		C										220
SWZ																		C				J	J	J	J	J	I	225
SPN					A						A		A					D										230
POR								A			A							C										235
GMW							A	A	AC	E								C										255
GME							A	AC	AB								AC										265
POL																				B								290
AUS																		B		A								305
HUN	A							A	AC	B	A	A	A					AC	P	A								310
CZE								A	C		A	A	A					C										315
ITA										B										R								325
ALB	A							A					A															339
YUG							A	A	B				A					D		S								345
GRC	A						A	A	C		A	A	A					C										350
BUL	A						A	A		B	A	A	A					B	H	AC								355
RUM	A							A	B			A	A					B		R								360
USR																		C										365
FIN										E								D										375
SWD																		C	H									380
NOR																		C										385
DEN																		D	H									390
SEN								A												S								433
DAH													A							S								434
MAU													A							S								435
NIR													A							S								436
IVC													A							S								437
GUI														B	B													438
UPP													A							S								439

-123-

SECTION I

APPENDIX A: NOTES

ATTRIBUTES OF NATIONS, 1950-1965: NOTES, VARIABLES 29-58

	29	31	32	33	34	35	36	37	38	39	40	41	43	44	45	46	49	50	51	52	53	54	55	56	57	58	
LBR																											450
SIE								C		A		A	A							S							451
GHA							A	A				A	A							S						I	452
TOG													A							A							461
CAC													A							S							471
NIG								A					A							S						I	475
GAM													A							S							481
CEN													A							S							482
MLI													A							S							483
CHA													A							S							484
CON													A														490
ZAI							D	A					A							S						I	500
UGA													A							S						I	510
TAZ													A														516
BUI													A														517
RWA													A								A						520
SOM						A	A				A		A							S						I	530
ETH													A				C			S							560
SAP													Q														580
MAG												A	A														600
MOR											A	A	A							S						I	615
ALG							C				A	A	A							S							616
TUN						A	A				A	A	A							S							620
LBY												A	A														625
SUD												A	A						A	A							630
IRN											A	A	A				AC		A	A							640
TUR							C				A	A	A				C										645
IRQ							D				A	A	A				C			A							651
UAR													A				D		C	AS						I	652
SYR					A	A	A					A	A				AC			A							660
LEB							D					A	A							A							663
JOR							A						A							S							666
ISR						C	A				A	AC					C			A							670
SAU						A						A	A							S							678
YEM						C	A					A	A							AS							700
APG				B	A	A					A	A	A							AS							710
CHN			B	B								A	A							S							712
MON													A							S							713
CHT													A							AS							711
KON										A			A														732
KOS													A														740
JAP							A				A	A	A				C			S							750
IND												A	A				C			S							770
PAK												A	A				C										775
BUR													A				C									I	780
CEY							A	A			A	A	A														790
NEP											A	A	A				C			S							800
TAI							A	C				A	A							S							811
CAM							C	A				A	A							S							812
LAO													A														816
VTN											A	A	A														817
VTS											A	A	A				C										820
MAL								C			A	A	A				D										840
PHI							A	A			A	A	A				C			S							850
INS																	C										
AUL																						J	J	J	J	J	900
NEW																						J	J	J	J	J	920

SECTION I

APPENDIX A: NOTES

SECTION I

APPENDIX A: NOTES

SECTION I

APPENDIX A: NOTES

-127-

SECTION I

APPENDIX A: NOTES

ATTRIBUTES OF NATIONS, 1950-1965: NOTES, VARIABLES 149-187

1	149	150	151	152	153	154	155	159	160	161	162	163	164	166	167	179	180	182	183	184	185	187	3
LBR						A											B	B	B				450
SIE											L							B					451
GHA												L							B				452
TOG												L							B				461
CAO																			B				471
NIG												L						B	B				475
GAM												L							B				481
CEN												L							B				482
MLI																			B				483
CHA											L								B				484
CON																			B				490
ZAI																			B				500
UGA																							510
TAZ												L							B				516
BUI																							517
BWA												L											520
SOM																		D					530
ETH																			B				560
SAF			A																				580
MAG																			D				600
MOR							D					L											615
ALG					D							L							D				616
TUN					D						L												620
LBY																		P					625
SUD																		D					630
IRN					A													B					640
TUR												L											645
IRQ					D																		651
UAR												L					A		B				652
SYR																	A	A	A				660
LEB					A		D					L					A	B	B				663
JOR					A			A									B	B					666
ISR					E			E										B					670
SAU																		B					678
YEM					A		D	A			L	A				A	B	A					700
AFG					AD			A					A					B	B					710
CHN																		B					712
MON																		B					713
CHT										L							A	B					731
KON																		B	B				732
KOS											L												740
JAP											L												750
IND											L												770
PAK											L												775
BUR																							780
CEY				A	D						L						B						790
NEP				A	D			D									B						800
TAI												↓						A					811
CAM											AL							B	B				812
LAO																	A	A	B				816
VTN											L												817
VTS																							820
MAL																							840
PHI	BD			B	B																		850
INS												L						B					900
AUL												L											904
NEW																							920

SECTION I

APPENDIX A: NOTES

SECTION I

APPENDIX A: NOTES

SECTION I

APPENDIX A: NOTES

SECTION I

APPENDIX A: NOTES

SECTION I

APPENDIX A: NOTES

ATTRIBUTES OF NATIONS, 1950-1965: NOTES, VARIABLES 274-318

	1	274	275	276	277	278	279	280	281	284	289	290	291	293	294	295	296	305	306	309	310	313	314	315	316	317	318	3
USA					A			B	A														A			A		002
CAN																												020
CUB					E																				N		N	040
HAI					A																					A		041
DOM								B													R							042
JAM																												051
TRI																												052
MEX					A			B	A																	A		070
GUA																												090
HON								B													R				N		P	091
ELS					A			B	A														A		J		J	092
NIC					B				A														C		J		N	093
COS								B	B																		J	094
PAN								B	B																			095
COL											A																	100
VEN		D						B	A		A							A				R	C					101
ECU					A				A		A							A				R	C					130
PER								E	A				A					A										135
BRA					A				A													R						140
BOL					B																				J		J	145
PAH														A									A			A		150
CHL																												155
ARG		L			B			A	A		A													K				160
URA		N						A																				165
UNK		D																			5							200
IRE		E																										205
NTH					A				A														AE					210
BEL		I						A															E		K			211
FRN								B																				220
SWZ								B										A										225
SPN		D									A													P	P	A	P	230
POR											A												D			A		235
GMW					E			B			A												B			H		255
GME								B																		A		265
POL		L																										290
AUS					E			A	A		A												E		J	J	J	305
HUN								A	A		A														J		J	310
CZE					E			A	A		A														K	A		315
ITA								A	A																	H		325
ALB																						A						339
YUG		A						A	A														C			A		345
GRC								A	A														G		K	A		350
BUL								A			A												A		A	A		355
RUM		E						A																				360
USR		I																		B	B	B	C					365
FIN								B															AE		A	A		375
SWD								B															E		A	A		380
NOR								B			A															A		385
DEN					E				A																			390
SEN					B				A																			433
DAH									A																			434
MAU					E				A		A																	435
NIR					B				A		A																	436
IVC																												437
GUI																												438
UPP					E																						N	439

-132-

SECTION I

APPENDIX A: NOTES

SECTION I

APPENDIX A: NOTES

ATTRIBUTES OF NATIONS, 1950-1965: NOTES, VARIABLES 319-363

	1	319	320	321	322	323	324	326	327	334	335	336	337	338	339	340	341	342	343	347	350	351	352	353	359	362	363	3
USA													J									A						002
CAN			H	H									J															020
CUB			H		Q	W							J									A						040
HAI							I																					041
DOM								H					J															042
JAM					E																							051
TRI					H																							052
MEX																												070
GUA																												090
HON					Q									A														091
ELS																												092
NIC					Q		I							A														093
COS			H	H	H										E													094
PAN					H		I																					095
COL							I																					100
VEN						Y																						101
ECU							I																					130
PER							I																		B			135
BRA							I					A																140
BOL			H		A		I											P										145
PAR					Q		I																					150
CHL												A						P		A								155
ARG							I											E										160
URA																				A								165
UNK																		D		A								200
IRE																												205
NTH																												210
BEL																												211
FRN																				P								220
SWZ																												225
SPN											A							P	G									230
POR											A							P										235
GMW																												255
GME																		P										265
POL																												290
AUS										A																		305
HUN																												310
CZE															A													315
ALB					N																							325
ITA																												339
YUG																A												345
GRC															A													350
BUL				H														P										355
RUM																				C								360
USR																												365
FIN																						A						375
SWD																												380
NOR																												385
DEN																												390
SEN																												433
DAH																												434
MAU																												435
NZR																												436
IVC					H																							437
GUI				H																								438
UPP																												439

-134-

SECTION I

APPENDIX A: NOTES

SECTION I

APPENDIX A: NOTES

ATTRIBUTES OF NATIONS, 1950-1965: NOTES, VARIABLES 364-398

	1	364	365	366	367	368	371	372	373	382	384	385	386	387	388	389	390	393	394	395	396	397	398	3
USA								G																002
CAN																								020
CUB																				B				040
HAI															A									041
DOM															A					B				042
JAM														B										051
TRI														B										052
MEX			A		X	A														B				070
GUA			A		X	A									A					B				090
HON																				B				091
ELS																								092
NIC																			A					093
COS					E							B	B	B	B									094
PAN															A									095
COL															A			A						101
VEN			X	X	A		G													B				130
ECU			X	X	E																			135
PER					A																			140
BRA															A					B				145
BOL																				B				150
PAR															A				A					155
CHL																			A	B				160
ARG																			A					165
URA			A																A					200
UNK			A																					205
IRE																								210
NTH																								211
BEL																		D						220
FRN																								221
SWZ																			A			A	A	225
SPN			A	A	A	A																		230
POR			A	A	A	A									A			A						235
GMW																								255
GME																								265
POL			A	A	A	A																	A	290
AUS																								305
HUN			X	X																				310
CZE			X	X																				315
ITA				A																				325
ALB																								339
YUG																								345
GRC																								350
BUL																								355
RUM																								360
USR																								365
FIN																								375
SWD																								380
NOR																								385
DEN			A																					390
SEN															B									433
CAH															B									434
MAU															B									435
NIR				A	A			G							B									436
IVC				A	A										A			A						437
GUI																								438
UPP															B									439

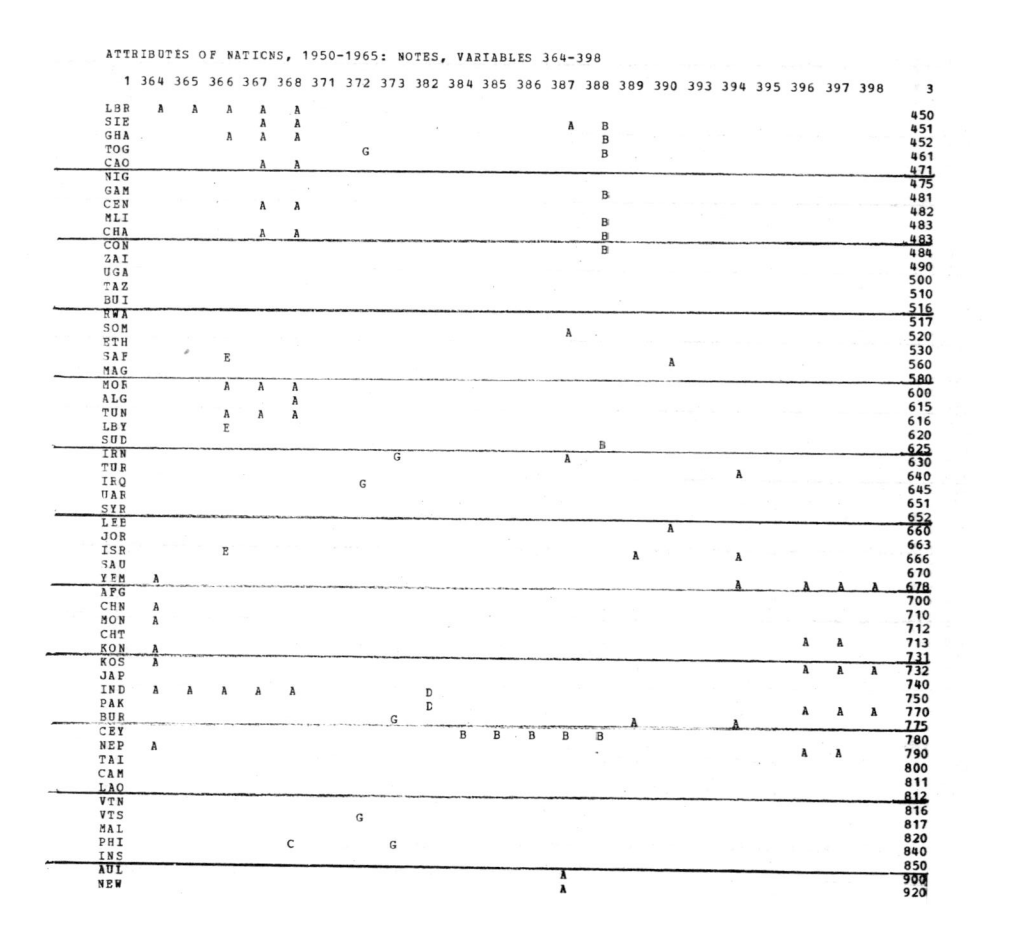

SECTION I

APPENDIX A: NOTES

SECTION I

APPENDIX A: NOTES

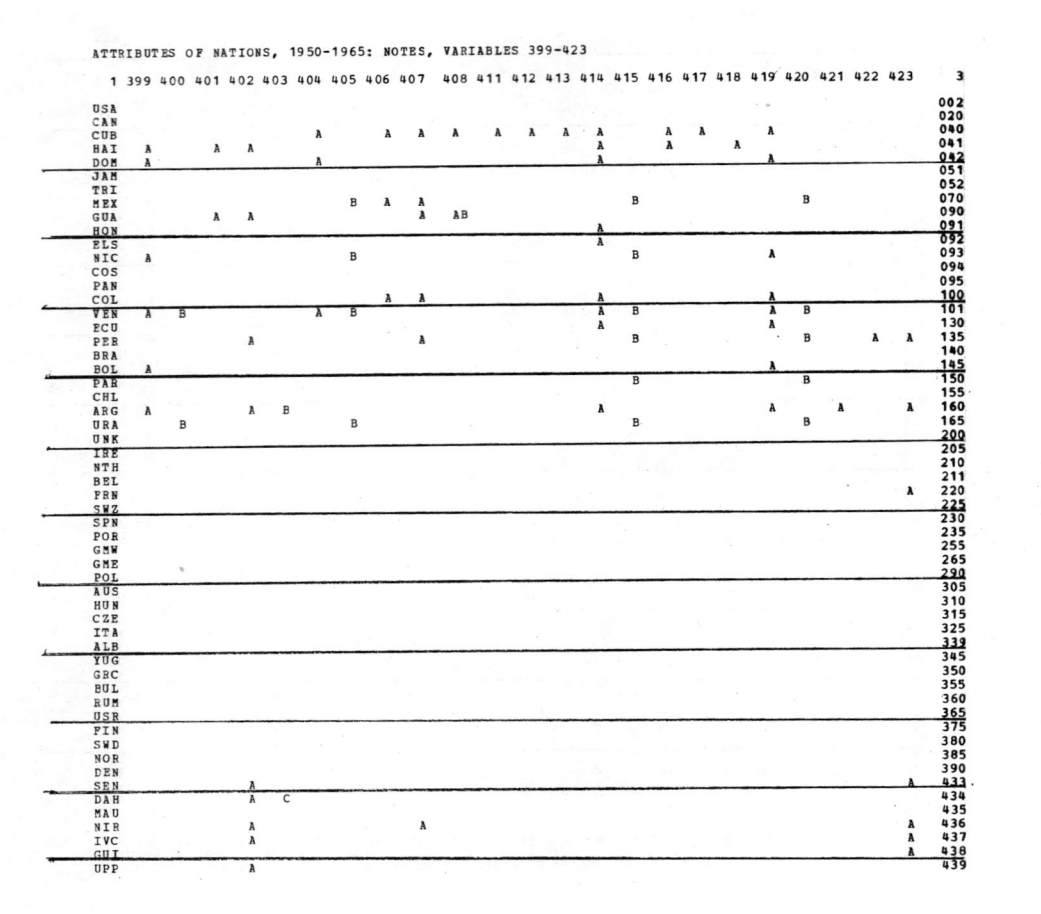

ATTRIBUTES OF NATIONS, 1950-1965: NOTES, VARIABLES 399-423

	399	400	401	402	403	404	405	406	407	408	411	412	413	414	415	416	417	418	419	420	421	422	423	
USA																								002
CAN																								020
CUB			A			A			A		A	A	A	A	A	A	A	A						040
HAI	A		A			A			A		A	A	A	A	A	A	A							041
DOM	A					A			A		A	A	A	A	A									042
JAM																								051
TRI																								052
MEX				A		B	A	A	AB					B				B						070
GUA				A		A	A	A						A										090
HON													A											091
ELS			A			B								A	B			A						092
NIC	A																							093
COS																								094
PAN																								095
COL								A	A					A				A	A B					100
VEN	A	B		A		A	B	A	A					A				A	B					101
ECU				A																				130
PER						A	B		A					A	B			A	B		A	A		135
BRA														A				B						140
BOL	A																							145
PAR															B				B					150
CHL														A	B			A	B	A		A		155
ARG		B		A	B	B																		160
URA																								165
UNK																							A	200
IRE																								205
NTH																								210
BEL																							A	211
FRN																								220
SWZ																								225
SPN																								230
POR																								235
GMW																								255
GME																								265
POL																								290
AUS																								305
HUN																								310
CZE																								315
ITA																								325
ALB																								339
YUG																								345
GRC																								350
BUL																								355
RUM																								360
USR																								365
FIN																								375
SWD																								380
NOR																								385
DEN																								390
SEN			A																					433
DAH			A	C																				434
MAU			A					A															A	435
NIR			A																				A	436
IVC																							A	437
GUI																								438
UPP			A																					439

SECTION I

APPENDIX A: NOTES

SECTION I
APPENDIX A: NOTES

ATTRIBUTES OF NATIONS, 1950-1965: NOTES, VARIABLES 424-453

	424	425	426	427	429	430	431	433	434	436	438	439	440	441	442	443	444	445	446	447	448	449	450	451	452	453	
USA																											002
CAN																											020
CUB																											040
HAI																											041
DOM	C																										042
JAM																									A		051
TRI											A					A					A						052
MEX											A																070
GUA										A																	090
HON																											091
ELS	B																										092
NIC																											093
COS																											094
PAN	E	C																									095
COL		C																									100
VEN																											101
ECU																											130
PER																											135
BRA																											140
BOL																											145
PAR		C																									150
CHL																											155
ARG																											160
URA																											165
UNK																											200
IRE													B	B	B	B	B	B	B	B	B	B	B	B	B		205
NTH																											210
BEL																											211
FRN																											220
SWZ																											225
SPN																											230
POR																											235
GMW									A																		255
GME									A																		265
POL									A																		290
AUS																											305
HUN									A																		310
CZE									A		A																315
ITA																											325
ALB			A						A																		339
YUG																											345
GRC									A																		350
BUL									A																		355
RUM									A																		360
USR									A																		365
FIN																											375
SWD																											380
NOR																											385
DEN																											390
SRN																											433
DAH										A																	434
MAU										A																	435
NIR										A																	436
IVC																											437
GUI																											438
UPP																											439

SECTION I

APPENDIX A: NOTES

ATTRIBUTES OF NATIONS, 1950-1965: NOTES, VARIABLES 424-453

Nation	1	424	425	426	427	429	430	431	433	434	436	438	439	440	442	443	444	445	446	447	449	450	451	452	453	3
LBR																										450
SIE																										451
GHA															B			B		B			B			452
TOG																										461
CAO																										471
NIG																										475
GAM										A																481
CEN										A																482
MLI																										483
CHA																										484
CON																										490
ZAI																										500
UGA																										516
TAZ										A					A					A			A			517
EUI										A					A					A			A			520
RWA																										530
SOM																										560
ETH															B	B	B	B	B	B	B	B	B	B		580
SAP																										
MAG																										600
MOR															A			A		A			A			615
ALG																										616
TUN																										620
LBY																										625
SUD																										630
IRN																										640
TUR							A																			645
IRQ	E																									651
UAR	E																									652
SYR																										660
LEB																										663
JOR																										666
ISR																										670
SAU																										678
YEM									A	A																700
AFG	A																									710
CHN					A	A		A		A	A															712
MON								A																		713
CHT																										731
KOS	B	A	A		A	A	A	A																		732
KON		A	A																							740
JAP							A																			750
IND							A																			770
PAK																										775
BUR																										780
CEY																										790
NEP																										800
TAI																										811
CAM										A																812
LAO																										816
VTN					A	A																				817
VTS					A																					820
MAL																										840
PHI	E						A																			850
INS																										900
NUL																										920
NEW																										

-141-

SECTION II

BEHAVIOR OF NATION DYADS

BEHAVIOR OF NATION DYADS

TABLE OF CONTENTS

VARIABLES

Variable Number	Variable Name	Page Number
1	Dyad.	151
2	Economic Aid A→B 1950	153
3	Economic Aid A→B 1955	153
4	Economic Aid A→B 1960	153
5	Economic Aid A→B 1963	153
6	Economic Aid A→B 1965	154
7	Relative Economic Aid A→B 1950	154
8	Relative Economic Aid A→B 1955	154
9	Relative Economic Aid A→B 1960	154
10	Relative Economic Aid A→B 1963	154
11	Relative Economic Aid A→B 1965	154
12	Treaties A→B 1950	154
13	Treaties A→B 1955	155
14	Treaties A→B 1960	155
15	Treaties A→B 1963	155
16	Treaties A→B 1965	155
17	Relative Treaties 1950	155
18	Relative Treaties 1955	156
19	Relative Treaties 1960	156
20	Relative Treaties 1963	156
21	Relative Treaties 1965	156
22	Official Visits A→B 1950	156
23	Official Visits A→B 1955	157
24	Official Visits A→B 1960	157
25	Official Visits A→B 1963	157
26	Official Visits A→B 1965	157
27	Co-participation in International Conferences A↔B 1950	157
28	Co-participation in International Conferences A↔B 1955	157
29	Co-participation in International Conferences A↔B 1960	158
30	Co-participation in International Conferences A↔B 1963	158
31	Co-participation in International Conferences A↔B 1965	158
32	Export of Books and Magazines A→B 1950	158
33	Export of Books and Magazines A→B 1955	158
34	Export of Books and Magazines A→B 1960	158
35	Export of Books and Magazines A→B 1963	159
36	Export of Books and Magazines A→B 1965	159
37	Relative Export of Books and Magazines A→B 1950	159
38	Relative Export of Books and Magazines A→B 1955	159
39	Relative Export of Books and Magazines A→B 1960	159
40	Relative Export of Books and Magazines A→B 1963	159
41	Relative Export of Books and Magazines A→B 1965	160
42	Book Translations A of B 1950	160
43	Book Translations A of B 1955	160
44	Book Translations A of B 1960	160
45	Book Translations A of B 1963	160
46	Book Translations A of B 1965	161

Variable Number	Variable Name	Page Number
47	Relative Book Translations A of B 1950	161
48	Relative Book Translations A of B 1955	161
49	Relative Book Translations A of B 1960	161
50	Relative Book Translations A of B 1963	161
51	Relative Book Translations A of B 1965	162
52	Warning or Defensive Acts 1950	162
53	Warning or Defensive Acts 1955	162
54	Warning or Defensive Acts 1960	162
55	Warning or Defensive Acts 1963	163
56	Warning or Defensive Acts 1965	163
57	Number of Wars 1950	163
58	Number of Wars 1955	163
59	Number of Wars 1960	163
60	Number of Wars 1963	164
61	Number of Wars 1965	164
62	Violent Actions 1950	164
63	Violent Actions 1955	164
64	Violent Actions 1960	165
65	Violent Actions 1963	165
66	Violent Actions 1965	165
67	Military Actions 1950	165
68	Military Actions 1955	165
69	Military Actions 1960	165
70	Military Actions 1963	166
71	Military Actions 1965	166
72	Duration 1950	166
73	Duration 1955	166
74	Duration 1960	166
75	Duration 1963	166
76	Duration 1965	167
77	Negative Behavior 1950	167
78	Negative Behavior 1955	167
79	Negative Behavior 1960	167
80	Negative Behavior 1963	167
81	Negative Behavior 1965	167
82	Severance of Diplomatic Relations 1950	167
83	Severance of Diplomatic Relations 1955	168
84	Severance of Diplomatic Relations 1960	168
85	Severance of Diplomatic Relations 1963	168
86	Severance of Diplomatic Relations 1965	168
87	Expulsion or Recall of Diplomats and Lesser Officials 1950	168
88	Expulsion or Recall of Diplomats and Lesser Officials 1955	168
89	Expulsion or Recall of Diplomats and Lesser Officials 1960	168
90	Expulsion or Recall of Diplomats and Lesser Officials 1963	169
91	Expulsion or Recall of Diplomats and Lesser Officials 1965	169
92	Boycott or Embargo 1950	169
93	Boycott or Embargo 1955	169
94	Boycott or Embargo 1960	169
95	Boycott or Embargo 1963	169
96	Boycott or Embargo 1965	169
97	Aid to Subversive Groups or Enemy 1950	170
98	Aid to Subversive Groups or Enemy 1955	170
99	Aid to Subversive Groups or Enemy 1960	170
100	Aid to Subversive Groups or Enemy 1963	170
101	Aid to Subversive Groups or Enemy 1965	170

Variable Number	Variable Name	Page Number
102	Negative Communications 1950	170
103	Negative Communications 1955	171
104	Negative Communications 1960	171
105	Negative Communications 1963	171
106	Negative Communications 1965	171
107	Accusation 1950	171
108	Accusation 1955	171
109	Accusation 1960	171
110	Accusation 1963	172
111	Accusation 1965	172
112	Protests 1950	172
113	Protests 1955	172
114	Protests 1960	172
115	Protests 1963	172
116	Protests 1965	172
117	Unofficial Acts 1950	173
118	Unofficial Acts 1955	173
119	Unofficial Acts 1960	173
120	Unofficial Acts 1963	173
121	Unofficial Acts 1965	173
122	Attack on Embassy 1950	173
123	Attack on Embassy 1955	173
124	Attack on Embassy 1960	174
125	Attack on Embassy 1963	174
126	Attack on Embassy 1965	174
127	Nonviolent Behavior 1950	174
128	Nonviolent Behavior 1955	174
129	Nonviolent Behavior 1960	174
130	Nonviolent Behavior 1963	174
131	Nonviolent Behavior 1965	175
132	Weighted UN Voting Distance 1950	175
133	Weighted UN Voting Distance 1955	175
134	Weighted UN Voting Distance 1960	175
135	Weighted UN Voting Distance 1963	175
136	Weighted UN Voting Distance 1965	175
137	Unweighted UN Voting Distance 1950	176
138	Unweighted UN Voting Distance 1955	176
139	Unweighted UN Voting Distance 1960	176
140	Unweighted UN Voting Distance 1963	176
141	Unweighted UN Voting Distance 1965	176
142	Tourists A→B 1950	177
143	Tourists A→B 1955	177
144	Tourists A→B 1960	177
145	Tourists A→B 1963	177
146	Tourists A→B 1965	177
147	Relative Tourists A→B 1950	178
148	Relative Tourists A→B 1955	178
149	Relative Tourists A→B 1960	178
150	Relative Tourists A→B 1963	178
151	Relative Tourists A→B 1965	178
152	Tourists A→B/A's Population 1950	178
153	Tourists A→B/A's Population 1955	179
154	Tourists A→B/A's Population 1960	179
155	Tourists A→B/A's Population 1963	179
156	Tourists A→B/A's Population 1965	179

Variable Number	Variable Name	Page Number
157	Emigrants A→B 1950	179
158	Emigrants A→B 1955	180
159	Emigrants A→B 1960	180
160	Emigrants A→B 1963	180
161	Emigrants A→B 1965	180
162	Relative Emigrants A→B 1950	180
163	Relative Emigrants A→B 1955	180
164	Relative Emigrants A→B 1960	181
165	Relative Emigrants A→B 1963	181
166	Relative Emigrants A→B 1965	181
167	Emigrants A→B/A's Population 1950	181
168	Emigrants A→B/A's Population 1955	181
169	Emigrants A→B/A's Population 1960	182
170	Emigrants A→B/A's Population 1963	182
171	Emigrants A→B/A's Population 1965	182
172	Students A→B 1950	182
173	Students A→B 1955	182
174	Students A→B 1960	182
175	Students A→B 1963	183
176	Students A→B 1965	183
177	Relative Students A→B 1950	183
178	Relative Students A→B 1955	183
179	Relative Students A→B 1960	183
180	Relative Students A→B 1963	184
181	Relative Students A→B 1965	184
182	Exports A→B 1950	184
183	Exports A→B 1955	184
184	Exports A→B 1960	184
185	Exports A→B 1963	185
186	Exports A→B 1965	185
187	Relative Exports A→B 1950	185
188	Relative Exports A→B 1955	185
189	Relative Exports A→B 1960	185
190	Relative Exports A→B 1963	185
191	Relative Exports A→B 1965	186
192	Exports A→B/A's GNP 1950	186
193	Exports A→B/A's GNP 1955	186
194	Exports A→B/A's GNP 1960	186
195	Exports A→B/A's GNP 1963	186
196	Exports A→B/A's GNP 1965	186
197	Intergovernmental Organizations A↔B 1950	187
198	Intergovernmental Organizations A↔B 1955	187
199	Intergovernmental Organizations A↔B 1960	187
200	Intergovernmental Organizations A↔B 1963	187
201	Intergovernmental Organizations A↔B 1965	187
202	Relative IGO A↔B 1950	187
203	Relative IGO A↔B 1955	188
204	Relative IGO A↔B 1960	188
205	Relative IGO A↔B 1963	188
206	Relative IGO A↔B 1965	188
207	NGO A↔B 1950	188
208	NGO A↔B 1955	188
209	NGO A↔B 1960	188
210	NGO A↔B 1963	189
211	NGO A↔B 1965	189

Variable Number	Variable Name	Page Number
212	Relative NGO A↔B 1950.	189
213	Relative NGO A↔B 1955.	189
214	Relative NGO A↔B 1960.	189
215	Relative NGO A↔B 1963.	189
216	Relative NGO A↔B 1965.	189
217	IGO A↔B/Common Membership of A 1950.	190
218	IGO A↔B/Common Membership of A 1955.	190
219	IGO A↔B/Common Membership of A 1960.	190
220	IGO A↔B/Common Membership of A 1963.	190
221	IGO A↔B/Common Membership of A 1965.	190
222	NGO A↔B/Common Membership of A 1950.	190
223	NGO A↔B/Common Membership of A 1955.	191
224	NGO A↔B/Common Membership of A 1960.	191
225	NGO A↔B/Common Membership of A 1963.	191
226	NGO A↔B/Common Membership of A 1965.	191
227	Embassy or Legation A→B 1950.	191
228	Embassy or Legation A→B 1955.	191
229	Embassy or Legation A→B 1960.	192
230	Embassy or Legation A→B 1963.	192
231	Embassy or Legation A→B 1965.	192
232	Relative Diplomatic Representation A→B 1950	192
233	Relative Diplomatic Representation A→B 1955	192
234	Relative Diplomatic Representation A→B 1960	192
235	Relative Diplomatic Representation A→B 1963	193
236	Relative Diplomatic Representation A→B 1965	193
237	Time Since Opposite Sides of a War A↔B 1950.	193
238	Time Since Opposite Sides of a War A↔B 1955.	193
239	Time Since Opposite Sides of a War A↔B 1960.	193
240	Time Since Opposite Sides of a War A↔B 1963.	194
241	Time Since Opposite Sides of a War A↔B 1965.	194
242	Time Since on Same Sides of a War A↔B 1950	194
243	Time Since on Same Sides of a War A↔B 1955	194
244	Time Since on Same Sides of a War A↔B 1960	194
245	Time Since on Same Sides of a War A↔B 1963	194
246	Time Since on Same Sides of a War A↔B 1965	195
247	Lost Territory A→B 1950	195
248	Lost Territory A→B 1955	195
249	Lost Territory A→B 1960	195
250	Lost Territory A→B 1963	195
251	Lost Territory A→B 1965	196
252	Dependent A of B 1950	196
253	Dependent A of B 1955	196
254	Dependent A of B 1960	196
255	Dependent A of B 1963	196
256	Dependent A of B 1965	196
257	Independence A↔B 1950.	197
258	Independence A↔B 1955.	197
259	Independence A↔B 1960.	197
260	Independence A↔B 1963.	197
261	Independence A↔B 1965.	197
262	Common Bloc Membership 1950	198
263	Common Bloc Membership 1955	198
264	Common Bloc Membership 1960	198
265	Common Bloc Membership 1963	198
266	Common Bloc Membership 1965	198

Variable Number	Variable Name	Page Number
267	Bloc Position Index A↔B 1950	199
268	Bloc Position Index A↔B 1955	199
269	Bloc Position Index A↔B 1960	199
270	Bloc Position Index A↔B 1963	199
271	Bloc Position Index A↔B 1965	199
272	Military Alliance A↔B 1950	200
273	Military Alliance A↔B 1955	200
274	Military Alliance A↔B 1960	200
275	Military Alliance A↔B 1963	200
276	Military Alliance A↔B 1965	200

BEHAVIOR OF NATION DYADS

Deck Number
Deck: all, col. 1-2

Variable 1   **DYAD**

OSIRIS: Location 1 width 3   Card: deck all, col. 3-5
Missing data code: none   Decimal place: none

DEFINITION: A three digit, numeric, dyad identification code used by the DON project in the following cases:

Nations Included in the
Selected Dyadic Sample

Brazil=BRA	Cuba=CUB	Indonesia=INS	Netherlands=NTH	United Kingdom=UNK
Burma=BUR	Egypt=EGP	Israel=ISR	Poland=POL	USA=USA
China=CHN	India=IND	Jordan=JOR	USSR=USR	

Selected Dyadic Sample

Numeric Code	Alpha Code	Dyad	Numeric Code	Alpha Code	Dyad
1	BRA→BUR	Brazil→Burma	31	CHN→IND	China→India
2	BRA→CHN	Brazil→China	32	CHN→INS	China→Indonesia
3	BRA→CUB	Brazil→Cuba	33	CHN→ISR	China→Israel
4	BRA→EGP	Brazil→Egypt	34	CHN→JOR	China→Jordan
5	BRA→IND	Brazil→India	35	CHN→NTH	China→Netherlands
6	BRA→INS	Brazil→Indonesia	36	CHN→POL	China→Poland
7	BRA→ISR	Brazil→Israel	37	CHN→USR	China→USSR
8	BRA→JOR	Brazil→Jordan	38	CHN→UNK	China→United Kingdom
9	BRA→NTH	Brazil→Netherlands	39	CHN→USA	China→USA
10	BRA→POL	Brazil→Poland	40	CUB→BRA	Cuba→Brazil
11	BRA→USR	Brazil→USSR	41	CUB→BUR	Cuba→Burma
12	BRA→UNK	Brazil→United Kingdom	42	CUB→CHN	Cuba→China
13	BRA→USA	Brazil→USA	43	CUB→EGP	Cuba→Egypt
14	BUR→BRA	Burma→Brazil	44	CUB→IND	Cuba→India
15	BUR→CHN	Burma→China	45	CUB→INS	Cuba→Indonesia
16	BUR→CUB	Burma→Cuba	46	CUB→ISR	Cuba→Israel
17	BUR→EGP	Burma→Egypt	47	CUB→JOR	Cuba→Jordan
18	BUR→IND	Burma→India	48	CUB→NTH	Cuba→Netherlands
19	BUR→INS	Burma→Indonesia	49	CUB→POL	Cuba→Poland
20	BUR→ISR	Burma→Israel	50	CUB→USR	Cuba→USSR
21	BUR→JOR	Burma→Jordan	51	CUB→UNK	Cuba→United Kingdom
22	BUR→NTH	Burma→Netherlands	52	CUB→USA	Cuba→USA
23	BUR→POL	Burma→Poland	53	EGP→BRA	Egypt→Brazil
24	BUR→USR	Burma→USSR	54	EGP→BUR	Egypt→Burma
25	BUR→UK	Burma→United Kingdom	55	EGP→CHN	Egypt→China
26	BUR→USA	Burma→USA	56	EGP→CUB	Egypt→Cuba
27	CHN→BRA	China→Brazil	57	EGP→IND	Egypt→India
28	CHN→BUR	China→Burma	58	EGP→INS	Egypt→Indonesia
29	CHN→CUB	China→Cuba	59	EGP→ISR	Egypt→Israel
30	CHN→EGP	China→Egypt	60	EGP→JOR	Egypt→Jordan

Numeric Code	Alpha Code	Dyad	Numeric Code	Alpha Code	Dyad
61	EGP→NTH	Egypt→Netherlands	117	JOR→USA	Jordan→USA
62	EGP→POL	Egypt→Poland	118	NTH→BRA	Netherlands→Brazil
63	EGP→USR	Egypt→USSR	119	NTH→BUR	Netherlands→Burma
64	EGP→UNK	Egypt→United Kingdom	120	NTH→CHN	Netherlands→China
65	EGP→USA	Egypt→USA	121	NTH→CUB	Netherlands→Cuba
66	IND→BRA	India→Brazil	122	NTH→EGP	Netherlands→Egypt
67	IND→BUR	India→Burma	123	NTH→IND	Netherlands→India
68	IND→CHN	India→China	124	NTH→INS	Netherlands→Indonesia
69	IND→CUB	India→Cuba	125	NTH→ISR	Netherlands→Israel
70	IND→EGP	India→Egypt	126	NTH→JOR	Netherlands→Jordan
71	IND→INS	India→Indonesia	127	NTH→POL	Netherlands→Poland
72	IND→ISR	India→Israel	128	NTH→USR	Netherlands→USSR
73	IND→JOR	India→Jordan	129	NTH→UNK	Netherlands→United Kingdom
74	IND→NTH	India→Netherlands	130	NTH→USA	Netherlands→USA
75	IND→POL	India→Poland	131	POL→BRA	Poland→Brazil
76	IND→USR	India→USSR	132	POL→BUR	Poland→Burma
77	IND→UNK	India→United Kingdom	133	POL→CHN	Poland→China
78	IND→USA	India→USA	134	POL→CUB	Poland→Cuba
79	INS→BRA	Indonesia→Brazil	135	POL→EGP	Poland→Egypt
80	INS→BUR	Indonesia→Burma	136	POL→IND	Poland→India
81	INS→CHN	Indonesia→China	137	POL→INS	Poland→Indonesia
82	INS→CUB	Indonesia→Cuba	138	POL→ISR	Poland→Israel
83	INS→EGP	Indonesia→Egypt	139	POL→JOR	Poland→Jordan
84	INS→IND	Indonesia→India	140	POL→NTH	Poland→Netherlands
85	INS→ISR	Indonesia→Israel	141	POL→USR	Poland→USSR
86	IND→JOR	Indonesia→Jordan	142	POL→UNK	Poland→United Kingdom
87	IND→NTH	Indonesia→Netherlands	143	POL→USA	Poland→USA
88	IND→POL	Indonesia→Poland	144	USR→BRA	USSR→Brazil
89	IND→USR	Indonesia→USSR	145	USR→BUR	USSR→Burma
90	IND→UNK	Indonesia→United Kingdom	146	USR→CHN	USSR→China
91	IND→USA	Indonesia→USA	147	USR→CUB	USSR→Cuba
92	ISR→BRA	Israel→Brazil	148	USR→EGP	USSR→Egypt
93	ISR→BUR	Israel→Burma	149	USR→IND	USSR→India
94	ISR→CHN	Israel→China	150	USR→INS	USSR→Indonesia
95	ISR→CUB	Israel→Cuba	151	USR→ISR	USSR→Israel
96	ISR→EGP	Israel→Egypt	152	USR→JOR	USSR→Jordan
97	ISR→IND	Israel→India	153	USR→NTH	USSR→Netherlands
98	ISR→INS	Israel→Indonesia	154	USR→POL	USSR→Poland
99	ISR→JOR	Israel→Jordan	155	USR→UNK	USSR→United Kingdom
100	ISR→NTH	Israel→Netherlands	156	USR→USA	USSR→USA
101	ISR→POL	Israel→Poland	157	UNK→BRA	United Kingdom→Brazil
102	ISR→USR	Israel→USSR	158	UNK→BUR	United Kingdom→Burma
103	ISR→UNK	Israel→United Kingdom	159	UNK→CHN	United Kingdom→China
104	ISR→USA	Israel→USA	160	UNK→CUB	United Kingdom→Cuba
105	JOR→BRA	Jordan→Brazil	161	UNK→EGP	United Kingdom→Egypt
106	JOR→BUR	Jordan→Burma	162	UNK→IND	United Kingdom→India
107	JOR→CHN	Jordan→China	163	UNK→INS	United Kingdom→Indonesia
108	JOR→CUB	Jordan→Cuba	164	UNK→ISR	United Kingdom→Israel
109	JOR→EGP	Jordan→Egypt	165	UNK→JOR	United Kingdom→Jordan
110	JOR→IND	Jordan→India	166	UNK→NTH	United Kingdom→Netherlands
111	JOR→INS	Jordan→Indonesia	167	UNK→POL	United Kingdom→Poland
112	JOR→ISR	Jordan→Israel	168	UNK→USR	United Kingdom→USSR
113	JOR→NTH	Jordan→Netherlands	169	UNK→USA	United Kingdom→USA
114	JOR→POL	Jordan→Poland	170	USA→BRA	USA→Brazil
115	JOR→USR	Jordan→USSR	171	USA→BUR	USA→Burma
116	JOR→UNK	Jordan→United Kingdom	172	USA→CHN	USA→China

Numeric Code	Alpha Code	Dyad	Numeric Code	Alpha Code	Dyad
173	USA→CUB	USA→Cuba	178	USA→JOR	USA→Jordan
174	USA→EGP	USA→Egypt	179	USA→NTH	USA→Netherlands
175	USA→IND	USA→India	180	USA→POL	USA→Poland
176	USA→INS	USA→Indonesia	181	USA→USR	USA→USSR
177	USA→ISR	USA→Israel	182	USA→UNK	USA→United Kingdom

Variable 2   ECONOMIC AID A→B (1950)

OSIRIS: Location 4 width 4   Card: deck 1, col. 6-9
Missing data code: 9999   Decimal place: none   Unit: x 10^5 $, US
N=182   Mean=101.65   Standard Deviation=757.51   Range=0-9210

DEFINITION: The amount of economic aid that A has given to B. Data for economic aid include amounts expended in grants or long term loans in cash and in kind, including within the latter category the provision of services as well as of commodities. A.I.D. Economic Data Book: Near East and South Asia. Background material, Foreign Assistance Programs, Committee on Foreign Affairs, "Economic and Military Assistance Programs: Comparative History of Authorizations and Appropriations for Budgeted Programs." Carter, J. R., The Net Cost of Soviet Foreign Aid, Appendices A and B. Eckstein, Alexander, Communist China's Economic Growth and Foreign Trade, Implications for U.S. Policy, Appendix E, pp. 306-7. Fe-Ch'ing Nien-Pao. Official Records of the United Nations, Economic and Social Council, 32nd Session Annexes Agenda, Item No. 5, Document E/3556, Table I International Economic Assistance to Underdeveloped Areas, 1958-1960. OECD, The Flow of Financial Resources To Less Developed Countries, 1961-1965, p. 46. Staff Memorandum on the Communist Economic Offensive, House Committee on Foreign Affairs, March 4, 1958. U.S. Overseas Loans and Grants and Assistance from International Organizations, July 1, 1945 - June 30, 1963. U.S. Overseas Loans and Grants and Assistance from International Organizations, June 1, 1945 - June 30, 1968. Goldman, M. I., Soviet Foreign Aid.

NOTES:
A. Estimate
B. Taken from U.N. Economic and Social Council Documents (E/3556). Figure is between 0 - $50,000. Exact amount unknown.

Variable 3   ECONOMIC AID A→B (1955)

OSIRIS: Location 8 width 4   CARD: Deck 1, Col. 10-13
Missing data code: 9999   Decimal Place: none   Unit: x 10^5 $, US
N=177   Mean=54.06   Standard Deviation=252.19   Range=0-1701

DEFINITION: See Variable 2 for definition and note codes.

Variable 4   ECONOMIC AID A→B (1960)

OSIRIS: Location 12 width 4   CARD: deck 1, col. 14-17
Missing data code: 9999   Decimal place: none   Unit: x 10^5 $, US
N=181   Mean=126.71   Standard Deviation=692.94   Range= -26-7584

DEFINITION: See Variable 2 for definition and note codes.

Variable 5   ECONOMIC AID A→B (1963)

OSIRIS: Location 16 width 4   CARD: Deck 1, col. 18-21
Missing data code: 9999   Decimal place: none   Unit: x 10^5 $, US
N=182   Mean=79.78   Standard Deviation=543.09   Range=0-6849

DEFINITION: See Variable 2 for definition and note codes.

Variable 6   ECONOMIC AID A→B (1965)

OSIRIS: Location 20 width 4   CARD: Deck 1, col. 22-25
Missing data code: 9999   Decimal place: none Unit: $\times 10^5$ $, US
N=181   Mean=94.02   Standard Deviation=591.73   Range=-31-6971

DEFINITION: See Variable 2 for definition and note codes.

Variable 7   RELATIVE ECONOMIC AID A→B (1950)

OSIRIS: Location 24 width 7   CARD: deck 1, col. 26-32
Missing data code: 9999999   Decimal place: none Unit: % $\times 10^2$ $, US
N=181   Mean=71.51   Standard Deviation=603.51   Range=0-7500

DEFINITION: Total amount of economic aid A has given to B, divided by A's total economic aid. Same sources as Variables 2-6

NOTES: See Variable 2

Variable 8   RELATIVE ECONOMIC AID A→B (1955)

OSIRIS: Location 31 width 7   CARD: deck 1, col. 33-39
Missing data code: 9999999   Decimal place: none Unit: % $\times 10^2$ $, US
N=174   Mean=53.14   Standard Deviation=323.93   Range=0-2765

DEFINITION: See Variable 7 for definition and note codes.

Variable 9   RELATIVE ECONOMIC AID A→B (1960)

OSIRIS: Location 38 width 7   CARD: deck 1, col. 40-46
Missing data code: 9999999   Decimal place: none Unit: % $\times 10^2$ $, US
N=179   Mean=135.88 Standard Deviation=791.53   Range=-7-8938

DEFINITION: See Variable 7 for definition and note codes.

Variable 10   RELATIVE ECONOMIC AID A→B (1963)

OSIRIS: Location 45 width 7   CARD: deck 1, col. 47-53
Missing data code: 9999999   Decimal place: none Unit: % $\times 10^2$ $, US
N=182   Mean=39.24   Standard Deviation=195.53   Range=0-1570

DEFINITION: See Variable 7 for definition and note codes.

Variable 11   RELATIVE ECONOMIC AID A→B (1965)

OSIRIS: Location 52 width 7   CARD: deck 1, col. 54-60
Missing data code: 9999999   Decimal place: none Unit: % $\times 10^2$ $, US
N=181   Mean=79.11   Standard Deviation=441.07   Range=-6-3900

DEFINITION: See Variable 7 for definition and note codes.

Variable 12   TREATIES A→B (1950)

OSIRIS: Location 59 width 7   CARD: deck 1, col. 61-67
Missing data code: 9999999   Decimal place: none
N=182   Mean=1.34   Standard Deviation=2.74   Range=0-22

-155-

DEFINITION: Total number of bilateral and multilateral treaties and agreements signed between A and B and filed with the Secretary-General of the UN. Accessions, supplementary agreements, and exchanges of notes constituting an agreement are counted along with formal treaties and agreements. <u>Statement of Treaties and International Agreements, UN; Treaties and Alliances of the World: An International Survey Covering Treaties in Force and Communities of States</u>.

NOTES: See Variable 2

Variable 13   TREATIES A→B (1955)

OSIRIS: Location 66 width 7   CARD: deck 1, col. 68-74
Missing data code: 9999999   Decimal place: none
N=182   Mean=2.16   Standard deviation=4.21   Range=0-25

DEFINITION: See Variable 12 for definition

NOTES: See Variable 2 for note codes.

Variable 14   TREATIES A→B (1960)

OSIRIS: Location 73 width 7   CARD: deck 2, col. 6-12
Missing data code: 9999999   Decimal place: none
N=182   Mean=2.21   Standard Deviation=2.79   Range=0-15

DEFINITION: See Variable 12 for definition

NOTES: See Variable 2 for note codes.

Variable 15   TREATIES A→B (1963)

OSIRIS: Location 80 width 7   CARD: deck 2, col. 13-19
Missing data code: 9999999   Decimal Place: none
N=182   Mean=1.86   Standard Deviation=2.21   Range=0-12

DEFINITION: See Variable 12 for definition

NOTES: See Variable 2 for note codes.

Variable 16   TREATIES A→B (1965)

OSIRIS: Location 87 width 7   CARD: deck 2, col. 20-26
MIssing data code: 9999999   Decimal place: none
N=182   Mean=1.66   Standard Deviation=2.79   Range=0-20

DEFINITION: See Variable 12 for definition

NOTES: See Variable 2 for note codes.

Variable 17   RELATIVE TREATIES (1950)

OSIRIS: Location 94 width 7   CARD: deck 2, col. 27-33
Missing data code: 9999999   Decimal place: none   Unit: $\% \times 10^2$
N=182   Mean=228.90   Standard Deviation=609.91   Range=0-7094

DEFINITION: Total number of bilateral and multilateral treaties and agreements signed between A and B, divided by total number of treaties and agreements A has with all other nations. Same sources as Variable 12.

NOTES: See Variable 2 for note codes.

Variable 18   RELATIVE TREATIES (1955)

OSIRIS: Location 101 width 7   CARD: deck 2, col. 34-40
Missing data code: 9999999   Decimal place: none   Unit: % x 10^2
N=182   Mean=667.86   Standard Deviation=1390.3   Range=0-8570

DEFINITION: See Variable 17 for definition

NOTES: See Variable 2 for note codes

Variable 19   RELATIVE TREATIES (1960)

OSIRIS: Location 108 width 7   CARD: deck 2, col. 41-47
Missing data code: 9999999   Decimal place: none   Unit: % x 10^2
N=182   Mean=819.57   Standard Deviation=1093.4   Range=0-7500

DEFINITION: See Variable 17 for definition

NOTES: See Variable 2 for note codes

Variable 20   RELATIVE TREATIES (1963)

OSIRIS: Location 115 width 7   CARD: deck 2, col. 48-54
Missing data code: 9999999   Decimal place: none   Unit: % x 10^2
N=182   Mean=754.64   Standard Deviation=967.65   Range=0-6667

DEFINITION: See Variable 17 for definition

NOTES: See Variable 2 for note codes

Variable 21   RELATIVE TREATIES (1965)

OSIRIS: Location 122 width 7   CARD: deck 2, col. 55-61
Missing data code: 9999999   Decimal place: none   Unit: % x 10^2
N=182   Mean=644.00   Standard Deviation=1089.7   Range=0-7000

DEFINITION: See Variable 17 for definition

NOTES: See Variable 2 for note codes

Variable 22   OFFICIAL VISITS A→B (1950)

OSIRIS: Location 129 width 7   CARD: deck 2, col. 62-68
Missing data code: 9999999   Decimal place: none
N=182   Mean=.02   Standard Deviation=.17   Range=0-2

DEFINITION: Total number of official political visits A→B. Data include state visit, official visit, or personal visit (e.g., for reason of health) by chief of state, cabinet members, or personal representative of chief of state. Visits for the purpose of participation in an international conference of three or more nations in B are excluded. THE NEW YORK TIMES.

Variable 23   OFFICIAL VISITS A→B (1955)

OSIRIS: Location 136 width 7   CARD: deck 2, col. 69-75
Missing data code: 9999999   Decimal place: none
N=182   Mean=.12   Standard Deviation=.44   Range=0-4

DEFINITION: See Variable 22 for definition

NOTES: See Variable 2 for note codes

Variable 24   OFFICIAL VISITS A→B (1960)

OSIRIS: Location 143 width 7   CARD: deck 3, col. 6-12
Missing data code: 9999999   Decimal place: none
N=182   Mean=.15   Standard Deviation=.46   Range=0-3

DEFINITION: See Variable 22 for definition

NOTES: See Variable 2 for note codes

Variable 25   OFFICIAL VISITS A→B (1963)

OSIRIS: Location 150 width 7   CARD: deck 3, col. 13-19
Missing data code: 9999999   Decimal place: none
N=182   Mean=.23   Standard Deviation=.63   Range=0-4

DEFINITION: See Variable 22 for definition

NOTES: See Variable 2 for note codes

Variable 26   OFFICIAL VISITS A→B (1965)

OSIRIS: Location 157 width 7   CARD: deck 3, col. 20-26
Missing data code: 9999999   Decimal place: none
N=182   Mean=.25   Standard Deviation=.61   Range=0-3

DEFINITION: See Variable 22 for definition

NOTES: See Variable 2 for note codes

Variable 27   CO-PARTICIPATION IN INTERNATIONAL CONFERENCES A↔B (1950)

OSIRIS: Location 164 width 7   CARD: deck 3, col. 27-33
Missing data code: 9999999   Decimal place: none
N=182   Mean=.21   Standard Deviation=.71   Range=0-5

DEFINITION: Total number of co-participation in international conferences of three
or more nations by officials such as chief of state, cabinet members, or personal
representative of chief of state. The regular or emergency UN Security Council or
General Assembly meetings of the UN are excluded. THE NEW YORK TIMES.

Variable 28   CO-PARTICIPATION IN INTERNATIONAL CONFERENCES A↔B (1955)

OSIRIS: Location 171 width 7   CARD: deck 3, col. 34-40
Missing data code: 9999999   Decimal place: none
N=182   Mean=.74   Standard Deviation=2.28   Range=0-18

DEFINITION: See Variable 27 for definition

Variable 29   CO-PARTICIPATION IN INTERNATIONAL CONFERENCES A↔B (1960)

OSIRIS: Location 178 width 7   CARD: deck 3, col. 41-47
Missing data code: 9999999   Decimal place: none
N=182   Mean=.23   Standard Deviation=.85   Range=0-7

DEFINITION: See Variable 27 for definition

Variable 30   CO-PARTICIPATION IN INTERNATIONAL CONFERENCES A↔B (1963)

OSIRIS: Location 185 width 7   CARD: deck 3, col. 48-54
Missing data code: 9999999   Decimal place: none
N=182   Mean=.5   Standard Deviation=1.18   Range=0-9

DEFINITION: See Variable 27 for definition

Variable 31   CO-PARTICIPATION IN INTERNATIONAL CONFERENCES A↔B (1965)

OSIRIS: Location 192 width 7   CARD: deck 3, col. 55-61
Missing data code: 9999999   Decimal place: none
N=182   Mean=1.99   Standard Deviation=3.30   Range=0-23

DEFINITION: See Variable 27 for definition

Variable 32   EXPORT OF BOOKS AND MAGAZINES A→B (1950)

OSIRIS: Location 199 width 7   CARD: deck 3, col. 62-68
Missing data code: 9999999   Decimal place: none   Unit: x 10^3 $, US
N=161   Mean=161.20   Standard Deviation=713.86   Range=0-6388

DEFINITION: Total value of exports of printed matter A→B. Printed matter is defined according to the UN's Standard International Trade Classification #892. Commodity Trade Statistics, UN; Trade by Commodities: Statistics Bulletin for Foreign Trade; World Trade Annual, UN.

NOTES:
A. Estimate
B. UN Statistical Yearbook
C. Less than $500.
D. Nations A and B have same language.
F. Monthly Statistics of the Foreign Trade of India, Vol. I (1964)
G. Trade by Commodities, OECD: Paris (1963)
H. Index Translationum

Variable 33   EXPORTS OF BOOKS AND MAGAZINES A→B (1955)

OSIRIS: Location 206 width 7   CARD: deck 3, col. 69-75
Missing data code: 9999999   Decimal place: none   Unit: x 10^3 $, US
N=157   Mean=183.2   Standard Deviation=738.77   Range=0-5851

DEFINITION: See Variable 32 for definition and note codes.

Variable 34   EXPORTS OF BOOKS AND MAGAZINES A→B (1960)

OSIRIS: Location 213 width 7   CARD: deck 4, col. 6-12
Missing data code: 9999999   Decimal place: none   Unit: x 10^3 $, US
N=147   Mean=338.0   Standard Deviation=1529.9   Range=0-12981

DEFINITION: See Variable 32 for definition and note codes.

Variable 35   EXPORTS OF BOOKS AND MAGAZINES A→B (1963)

OSIRIS: Location 220 width 7   CARD: deck 4, col. 13-19
Missing data code: 9999999   Decimal place: none   Unit: x 10^3 $, US
N=173   Mean=406.84   Standard Deviation=2080.6   Range=0-19150

DEFINITION: See Variable 32 for definition and note codes.

Variable 36   EXPORTS OF BOOKS AND MAGAZINES A→B (1965)

OSIRIS: Location 227 width 7   CARD: deck 4, col. 20-26
Missing data code: 9999999   Decimal place: none   Unit: x 10^3 $, US
N=168   Mean=556.1   Standard Deviation=2860.7   Range=0-26219

DEFINITION: See Variable 32 for definition and note codes.

Variable 37   RELATIVE EXPORT OF BOOKS AND MAGAZINES A→B (1950)

OSIRIS: Location 234 width 7   CARD: deck 4, col. 27-33
Missing data code: 9999999   Decimal place: none   Unit: % x 10^2
N=161   Mean=59.78   Standard Deviation=374.04   Range=0-4408

DEFINITION: Total exports of printed matter A→B, divided by total exports of printed matter by A to all nations. Sources same as Variables 32-36.

NOTES: See Variable 32 for note codes.

Variable 38   RELATIVE EXPORT OF BOOKS AND MAGAZINES A→B (1955)

OSIRIS: Location 241 width 7   CARD: deck 4, col. 34-40
Missing data code: 9999999   Decimal place: none   Unit: % x 10^2
N=151   Mean=42.5   Standard Deviation=186.02   Range=0-1417

DEFINITION: See Variable 37 for definition

NOTES: See Variable 32 for note codes

Variable 39   RELATIVE EXPORT OF BOOKS AND MAGAZINES A→B (1960)

OSIRIS: Location 248 width 7   CARD: deck 4, col. 41-47
Missing data code: 9999999   Decimal place: none   Unit: % x 10^2
N=146   Mean=88.10   Standard Deviation=531.33   Range=0-5995

DEFINITION: See Variable 37 for definition

NOTES: See Variable 32 for note codes

Variable 40   RELATIVE EXPORT OF BOOKS AND MAGAZINES A→B (1963)

OSIRIS: Location 255 width 7   CARD: deck 4, col. 48-54
Missing data code: 9999999   Decimal place: none   Unit: % x 10^2
N=162   Mean=110.36   Standard Deviation=556.39   Range=0-5982

DEFINITION: See Variable 37 for definition

NOTES: See Variable 32 for note codes

Variable 41   RELATIVE EXPORT OF BOOKS AND MAGAZINES A→B (1965)

OSIRIS: Location 262   width 7   CARD: deck 4, col. 55-61
Missing data code: 9999999   Decimal place: none   Unit: % x 10²
N=150   Mean=159.82   Standard Deviation=755.53   Range=0-5822

DEFINITION: See Variable 37 for definition

NOTES: See Variable 32 for note codes

Variable 42   BOOK TRANSLATIONS A of B (1950)

OSIRIS: Location 269   width 7   CARD: deck 4, col. 62-68
Missing data code: 9999999   Decimal place: none
N=161   Mean=10.41   Standard Deviation=49.94   Range=0-400

DEFINITION: The number of translations by A from a language that is the major spoken language of B. When the language from which a work was translated differed from the original language of the work, the original language was used in all data counts. Index Translationum, UNESCO; and UNESCO Statistical Yearbook, UN.

NOTES: See Variable 32 for note codes

Variable 43   BOOK TRANSLATIONS A of B (1955)

OSIRIS: Location 276   width 7   CARD: deck 4, col. 69-75
Missing data code: 9999999   Decimal place: none
N=179   Mean=18.17   Standard Deviation=69.87   Range=0-620

DEFINITION: See Variable 42 for definition

NOTES: See Variable 32 for note codes

Variable 44   BOOK TRANSLATIONS A of B (1960)

OSIRIS: Location 283   width 7   CARD: deck 5, col. 6-12
Missing data code: 9999999   Decimal place: none
N=177   Mean=34.37   Standard Deviation=116.46   Range=0-750

DEFINITION: See Variable 42 for definition

NOTES: See Variable 32 for note codes

Variable 45   BOOK TRANSLATIONS A of B (1963)

OSIRIS: Location 290   width 7   CARD: deck 5, col. 13-19
Missing data code: 9999999   Decimal place: none
N=177   Mean=41.27   Standard Deviation=152.45   Range=0-1214

DEFINITION: See Variable 42 for definition

NOTES: See Variable 32 for note codes

-161-

Variable 46   BOOK TRANSLATIONS A of B (1965)

OSIRIS: Location 297   width 7   CARD: deck 5, col. 20-26
Missing data code: 9999999   Decimal place: none
N=179   Mean=43.36   Standard Deviation=139.85   Range=0-1055

DEFINITION: See Variable 42 for definition

NOTES: See Variable 32 for note codes

Variable 47   RELATIVE BOOK TRANSLATIONS A of B (1950)

OSIRIS: Location 304   width 7   CARD: deck 5, col. 27-33
Missing data code: 9999999   Decimal place: none   Unit: % x 10^2
N=161   Mean=246.71   Standard Deviation=853.56   Range=0-5229

DEFINITION: The number of translations by A from a language that is the major spoken language of B, divided by all A's translations from foreign languages. Same sources as Variables 42-46.

NOTES: See Variable 32 for note codes

Variable 48   RELATIVE BOOK TRANSLATIONS A of B (1955)

OSIRIS: Location 311   width 7   CARD: deck 5, col. 34-40
Missing data code: 9999999   Decimal place: none   Unit: % x 10^2
N=172   Mean=359.72   Standard Deviation=1091.3   Range=0-5840

DEFINITION: See Variable 47 for definition

NOTES: See Variable 32 for note codes

Variable 49   RELATIVE BOOK TRANSLATIONS A of B (1960)

OSIRIS: Location 318   width 7   CARD: deck 5, col. 41-47
Missing data code: 9999999   Decimal place: none   Unit: % x 10^2
N=176   Mean=553.28   Standard Deviation=1552.7   Range=0-7714

DEFINITION: See Variable 47 for definition

NOTES: See Variable 32 for note codes

Variable 50   RELATIVE BOOK TRANSLATIONS A of B (1963)

OSIRIS: Location 325   width 7   CARD: deck 5, col. 48-54
Missing data code: 9999999   Decimal place: none   Unit: % x 10^2
N=177   Mean=569.99   Standard Deviation=1569.7   Range=0-8266

DEFINITION: See Variable 47 for definition

NOTES: See Variable 32 for note codes

Variable 51   RELATIVE BOOK TRANSLATIONS A of B (1965)

OSIRIS: Location 332   width 7   CARD: deck 5, col. 55-61
Missing data code: 9999999   Decimal place: none   Unit: % x 10^2
N=179   Mean=776.22   Standard Deviation=2029.9   Range=0-1000

DEFINITION: See Variable 47 for definition

NOTES: See Variable 32 for note codes

NOTE: The data for the foreign conflict behavior variables, #52-131, were collected from the New York Times Index and recorded on the DON Project's foreign conflict behavior code sheets. Supplemental information was also taken from Keesing's Contemporary Archives and Facts on File. For a more extensive elaboration of the data collection methods and definitions, see R. J. Rummel, "A Foreign Conflict Behavior Code Sheet," World Politics, Vol. XVIII, No. 2, January, 1966; or DON Reprint No. 8.

Variable 52   WARNING OR DEFENSIVE ACTS (1950)

OSIRIS: Location 339   width 4   CARD: deck 5, col. 62-65
Missing data code: 9999   Decimal place: none
N=182   Mean=.066   Standard Deviation=.51   Range=0-6

DEFINITION: These are distinctively military in nature, but are nonviolent. The acts are related to a developing conflict situation, thus excluding military acts purely contingent on changes in domestic policy or regimes, such as the strengthening of conventional U.S. forces with the change from a Republican to a Democratic administration in 1961.

Variable 53   WARNING OR DEFENSIVE ACTS (1955)

OSIRIS: Location 343   width 4   CARD: deck 5, col. 66-69
Missing data code: 9999   Decimal place: none
N=182   Mean=.044   Standard Deviation=.36   Range=0-4

DEFINITION: See Variable 52 for definition

NOTES:
A. Estimate
B. Supplemental information taken from Keesing's Contemporary Archives.
C. Supplemental information taken from Facts on File.

Variable 54   WARNING OR DEFENSIVE ACTS (1960)

OSIRIS: Location 347   width 4   CARD: deck 5, col. 70-73
Missing data code: 9999   Decimal place: none
N=182   Mean=.088   Standard Deviation=.40   Range=0-3

DEFINITION: See Variable 52 for definition

NOTES: See Variable 53 for note codes

Variable 55   WARNING OR DEFENSIVE ACTS (1963)

OSIRIS: Location 351   width 4   CARD: deck 5, col. 74-77
Missing data code: 9999   Decimal place: none
N=182   Mean=.016   Standard Deviation=.13   Range=0-1

DEFINITION: See Variable 52 for definition

NOTES: See Variable 53 for note codes

Variable 56   WARNING OR DEFENSIVE ACTS (1965)

OSIRIS: Location 355   width 4   CARD: deck 6, col. 6-9
Missing data code: 9999   Decimal place: none
N=182   Mean=.06   Standard Deviation=.46   Range=0-5

DEFINITION: See Variable 52 for definition

NOTES: See Variable 53 for note codes

Variable 57   NUMBER OF WARS (1950)

OSIRIS: Location 359   width 7   CARD: deck 6, col. 10-16
Missing data code: 9999999   Decimal place: none
N=182   Mean=.027   Standard Deviation=.16   Range=0-1

DEFINITION: Any military action for a particular country in which the number of its soldiers involved equal or exceed .02 percent of its population. This number need not be actually involved in the shooting, but must be involved at the front logistically or as reserves.

NOTES: See Variable 53 for note codes

Variable 58   NUMBER OF WARS (1955)

OSIRIS: Location 366   width 7   CARD: deck 6, Col. 17-23
Missing data code: 9999999   Decimal place: none
N=182   Mean=0.0   Standard Deviation=0.0   Range=0-0

DEFINITION: See Variable 57 for definition

NOTES: See Variable 53 for note codes

Variable 59   NUMBER OF WARS (1960)

OSIRIS: Location 373   width 7   CARD: deck 6, col. 24-30
Missing data code: 9999999   Decimal place: none
N=182   Mean=0.0   Standard Deviation=0.0   Range=0-0

DEFINITION: See Variable 57 for definition

NOTES: See Variable 53 for note codes

-164-

Variable 60   NUMBER OF WARS (1963)

OSIRIS: Location 380   width 7   CARD: deck 6, col. 31-37
Missing data code: 9999999   Decimal place: none
N=182   Mean=0.0   Standard Deviation=0.0   Range=0-0

DEFINITION: See Variable 57 for definition

NOTES: See Variable 53 for note codes

Variable 61   NUMBER OF WARS (1965)

OSIRIS: Location 387   width 7   CARD: deck 6, col. 38-44
Missing data code: 9999999   Decimal place: none
N=0   Mean=0.0   Standard Deviation=0.0   Range=0-0

DEFINITION: See Variable 57 for definition

NOTES: See Variable 53 for note codes

Variable 62   VIOLENT ACTIONS (1950)

OSIRIS: Location 394   width 4   CARD: deck 6, col. 45-51
Missing data code: 9999999   Decimal place: none
N=182   Mean=.071   Standard Deviation=.26   Range=0-1

DEFINITION: Coding: 0 - no, 1 - yes. Violent actions comprise war, continuous military action, discrete military action, or clash. War is any continuous military hostilities in which the number of soldiers of a nation involved equals or exceeds .02 percent of the population. Continuous military action refers to any military engagement involving violence that continues for more than twenty-four hours, but that the number of soldiers is less than the percentage that defines war. Discrete military action refers to any action completed within twenty-four hours, such as any firing upon another country's plane or ship which is no part of war or continuous military action or clash. Clash refers to a violent action between opposing forces involving ships, planes, or troops, which is not part of a war or continuous military action, and is completed in less than twenty-four hours. By definition, war, continuous military action, and clash are symmetric, and discrete military action is asymmetric.

NOTES: See Variable 53 for note codes

Variable 63   VIOLENT ACTIONS (1955)

OSIRIS: Location 401   width 7   CARD: deck 6, col. 52-58
Missing data code: 9999999   Decimal place: none
N=182   Mean=.049   Standard Deviation=.22   Range=0-1

DEFINITION: See Variable 62 for definition

NOTES: See Variable 53 for note codes

Variable 64   VIOLENT ACTIONS (1960)

OSIRIS: Location 408   width 7   CARD: deck 6, col. 59-65
Missing data code: 9999999   Decimal place: none
N=182   Mean=.044   Standard Deviation=.21   Range=0-2

DEFINITION: See Variable 62 for definition

NOTES: See Variable 53 for note codes

Variable 65   VIOLENT ACTIONS (1963)

OSIRIS: Location 415   width 7   CARD: deck 6, col. 66-72
Missing data code: 9999999   Decimal place: none
N=182   Mean=.044   Standard Deviation=.23   Range=0-2

DEFINITION: See Variable 62 for definition

NOTES: See Variable 53 for note codes

Variable 66   VIOLENT ACTIONS (1965)

OSIRIS: Location 422   width 7   CARD: deck 6, col. 73-79
Missing data code: 9999999   Decimal place: none
N=182   Mean=.050   Standard Deviation=.22   Range=0-1

DEFINITION: See Variable 62 for definition

Variable 67   MILITARY ACTIONS (1950)

OSIRIS: Location 429   width 7   CARD: deck 7, col. 6-12
Missing data code: 9999999   Decimal place: none
N=182   Mean=.077   Standard Deviation=.48   Range=0-5

DEFINITION: Total number of continuous military action, discrete military action, and clash.

NOTES: See Variable 53 for note codes

Variable 68   MILITARY ACTIONS (1955)

OSIRIS: Location 436   width 7   CARD: deck 7, col. 13-19
Missing data code: 9999999   Decimal place: none
N=182   Mean=1.24   Standard Deviation=9.52   Range=0-98

DEFINITION: See Variable 67 for definition

NOTES: See Variable 53 for note codes

Variable 69   MILITARY ACTIONS (1960)

OSIRIS: Location 443   width 7   CARD: deck 7, col. 20-26
Missing data code: 9999999   Decimal place: none
N=182   Mean=.11   Standard Deviation=.60   Range=0-5

DEFINITION: See Variable 67 for definition

NOTES: See Variable 53 for note codes

Variable 70   MILITARY ACTIONS (1963)

OSIRIS: Location 450   width 7   CARD: deck 7, col. 27-33
Missing data code: 9999999   Decimal place: none
N=182   Mean=.082   Standard Deviation=.44   Range=0-3

DEFINITION: See Variable 67 for definition

NOTES: See Variable 53 for note codes

Variable 71   MILITARY ACTIONS (1965)

OSIRIS: Location 457   width 7   CARD: deck 7, col. 34-40
Missing data code: 9999999   Decimal place: none
N=182   Mean=.46   Standard Deviation=2.30   Range=0-16

DEFINITION: See Variable 67 for definition

NOTES: See Variable 53 for note codes

Variable 72   DURATION (1950)

OSIRIS: Location 464   width 7   CARD: deck 7, col. 41-47
Missing data code: 9999999   Decimal place: none
N=182   Mean=2.1   Standard Deviation=10.92   Range=0-61

DEFINITION: Total duration of war, continuous military action, discrete military action and clash.

NOTES: See Variable 53 for note codes

Variable 73   DURATION (1955)

OSIRIS: Location 471   width 7   CARD: deck 7, col. 48-54
Missing data code: 9999999   Decimal place: none
N=182   Mean=4.23   Standard Deviation=37.17   Range=0-355

DEFINITION: See Variable 72 for definition

NOTES: See Variable 53 for note codes

Variable 74   DURATION (1960)

OSIRIS: Location 478   width 7   CARD: deck 7, col. 55-61
Missing data code: 9999999   Decimal place: none
N=182   Mean=.13   Standard Deviation=.72   Range=0-5

DEFINITION: See Variable 72 for definition

NOTES: See Variable 53 for note codes

Variable 75   DURATION (1963)

OSIRIS: Location 485   width 7   CARD: deck 7, col. 62-68
Missing data code: 9999999   Decimal place: none
N=182   Mean=.48   Standard Deviation=5.29   Range=0-71

DEFINITION: See Variable 72 for definition

NOTES: See Variable 53 for note codes

Variable 76   DURATION (1965)

OSIRIS: Location 492   width 7   CARD: deck 7, col. 69-75
Missing data code: 9999999   Decimal place: none
N=182   Mean=.48   Standard Deviation=2.43   Range=0-18

DEFINITION: See Variable 72 for definition

NOTES: See Variable 53 for note codes

Variable 77   NEGATIVE BEHAVIOR (1950)

OSIRIS: Location 499   width 7   CARD: deck 8, col. 6-12
Missing data code: 9999999   Decimal place: none
N=182   Mean=.62   Standard Deviation=2.56   Range=0-23

DEFINITION: Any acts or actions that reflect strained, tense, unfriendly, or hostile feelings or relations between nations A and B.

Variable 78   NEGATIVE BEHAVIOR (1955)

OSIRIS: Location 506   width 7   CARD: deck 8, col. 13-19
Missing data code: 9999999   Decimal place: none
N=182   Mean=.41   Standard Deviation=1.49   Range=0-11

DEFINITION: See Variable 77 for definition

Variable 79   NEGATIVE BEHAVIOR (1960)

OSIRIS: Location 513   width 7   CARD: deck 8, col. 20-26
Missing data code: 9999999   Decimal place: none
N=182   Mean=.56   Standard Deviation=2.82   Range=0-30

DEFINITION: See Variable 77 for definition

Variable 80   NEGATIVE BEHAVIOR (1963)

OSIRIS: Location 520   width 7   CARD: deck 8, col. 27-33
Missing data code: 9999999   Decimal place: none
N=182   Mean=.13   Standard Deviation=.49   Range=0-4

DEFINITION: See Variable 77 for definition.

Variable 81   NEGATIVE BEHAVIOR (1965)

OSIRIS: Location 527   width 7   CARD: deck 8, col. 34-40
Missing data code: 9999999   Decimal place: none
N=182   Mean=5.0   Standard Deviation=1.70   Range=0-14

DEFINITION: See Variable 77 for definition

Variable 82   SEVERANCE OF DIPLOMATIC RELATIONS (1950)

OSIRIS: Location 534   width 7   CARD: deck 8, col. 41-47
Missing data code: 9999999   Decimal place: none
N=182   Mean=0.0   Standard Deviation=0.0   Range=0-0

DEFINITION: The interruption of formal diplomatic relations by A with B

Variable 83   SEVERANCE OF DIPLOMATIC RELATIONS (1955)

OSIRIS: Location 541   width 7   CARD: deck 8, col. 48-54
Missing data code: 9999999   Decimal place: none
N=182   Mean=0.0   Standard Deviation=0.0   Range=0-0

DEFINITION: See Variable 82 for definition

Variable 84   SEVERANCE OF DIPLOMATIC RELATIONS (1960)

OSIRIS: Location 548   width 7   CARD: deck 8, col. 55-61
Missing data code: 9999999   Decimal place: none
N=182   Mean=.005   Standard Deviation=.074   Range=0-1

DEFINITION: See Variable 82 for definition

Variable 85   SEVERANCE OF DIPLOMATIC RELATIONS (1963)

OSIRIS: Location 555   width 7   CARD: deck 8, col. 62-68
Missing data code: 9999999   Decimal place: none
N=182   Mean=0.0   Standard Deviation=0.0   Range=0-0

DEFINITION: See Variable 82 for definition

Variable 86   SEVERANCE OF DIPLOMATIC RELATIONS (1965)

OSIRIS: Location 562   width 7   CARD: deck 8, col. 69-75
Missing data code: 9999999   Decimal place: none
N=182   Mean=.011   Standard Deviation=.10   Range=0-1

DEFINITION: See Variable 82 for definition

Variable 87   EXPULSION OR RECALL OF DIPLOMATS AND LESSER OFFICIALS (1950)

OSIRIS: Location 569   width 4   CARD: deck 9, col. 6-9
Missing Data code: 9999   Decimal place: none
N=182   Mean=.022   Standard Deviation=.15   Range=0-1

DEFINITION: The number of any expulsion of ambassadors and other diplomatic officials from another country, or any recalling of such officials for other than administrative reasons. This does not include any expulsion or recall involved in the severance of diplomatic relations.

Variable 88   EXPULSION OR RECALL OF DIPLOMATS AND LESSER OFFICIALS (1955)

OSIRIS: Location 573   width 4   CARD: deck 9, col. 10-13
Missing data code: 9999   Decimal place: none
N=182   Mean=.005   Standard Deviation=.074   Range=0-1

DEFINITION: See Variable 87 for definition

Variable 89   EXPULSION OR RECALL OF DIPLOMATS AND LESSER OFFICIALS (1960)

OSIRIS: Location 577   width 4   CARD: deck 9, col. 14-17
Missing data code: 9999   Decimal place: none
N=182   Mean=.060   Standard Deviation=.37   Range=0-3

DEFINITION: See Variable 87 for definition

Variable 90   EXPULSION OR RECALL OF DIPLOMATS AND LESSER OFFICIALS (1963)

OSIRIS: Location 581   width 4   CARD: deck 9, col. 18-21
Missing data code: 9999   Decimal place: none
N=182   Mean=.016   Standard Deviation=.13   Range=0-1

DEFINITION: See Variable 87 for definition

Variable 91   EXPULSION OR RECALL OF DIPLOMATS AND LESSER OFFICIALS (1965)

OSIRIS: Location 585   width 4   CARD: deck 9, col. 22-25
Missing data code: 9999   Decimal place: none
N=182   Mean=.038   Standard Deviation=.27   Range=0-3

DEFINITION: See Variable 87 for definition

Variable 92   BOYCOTT OR EMBARGO (1950)

OSIRIS: Location 589   width 7   CARD: deck 9, col. 26-32
Missing data code: 9999999   Decimal place: none
N=182   Mean=.049   Standard Deviation=.28   Range=0-2

DEFINITION: The number of boycotts or embargoes. Boycott is an act that constitutes refusal to deal (e.g., communicate, buy, negotiate, and so on) with another country. Embargo is either a general or a particular restriction on commerce with another country.

Variable 93   BOYCOTT OR EMBARGO (1955)

OSIRIS: Location 596   width 7   CARD: deck 9, col. 33-39
Missing data code: 9999999   Decimal place: none
N=182   Mean=.005   Standard Deviation=.074   Range=0-1

DEFINITION: See Variable 92 for definition

Variable 94   BOYCOTT OR EMBARGO (1960)

OSIRIS: Location 603   width 7   CARD: deck 9, col. 40-46
Missing data code: 9999999   Decimal place: none
N=182   Mean=.022   Standard Deviation=.18   Range=0-2

DEFINITION: See Variable 92 for definition

Variable 95   BOYCOTT OR EMBARGO (1963)

OSIRIS: Location 610   width 7   CARD: deck 9, col. 47-53
Missing data code: 9999999   Decimal place: none
N=182   Mean=.016   Standard Deviation=.17   Range=0-2

DEFINITION: See Variable 92 for definition

Variable 96   BOYCOTT OR EMBARGO (1965)

OSIRIS: Location 617   width 7   CARD: deck 9, col. 54-60
Missing data code: 9999999   Decimal place: none
N=182   Mean=.071   Standard Deviation=.43   Range=0-5

DEFINITION: See Variable 92 for definition

Variable 97   AID TO SUBVERSIVE GROUPS OR ENEMY (1950)

OSIRIS: Location 624   width 7   CARD: deck 9, col. 61-67
Missing data code: 9999999   Decimal place: none
N=182   Mean=.010   Standard Deviation=.10   Range=0-1

DEFINITION: Total frequency of aid to subversive groups or enemy. The aid comprises training rebels or subversive nationals of another country, giving them economic or military aid to another country's violent enemy.

Variable 98   AID TO SUBVERSIVE GROUPS OR ENEMY (1955)

OSIRIS: Location 631   width 7   CARD: deck 9, col. 68-74
Missing data code: 9999999   Decimal place: none
N=182   Mean=.005   Standard Deviation=.074   Range=0-1

DEFINITION: See Variable 97 for definition

Variable 99   AID TO SUBVERSIVE GROUPS OR ENEMY (1960)

OSIRIS: Location 638   width 7   CARD: deck 10, col. 6-12
Missing data code: 9999999   Decimal place: none
N=182   Mean=.011   Standard Deviation=.10   Range=0-1

DEFINITION: See Variable 97 for definition

Variable 100   AID TO SUBVERSIVE GROUPS OR ENEMY (1963)

OSIRIS: Location 645   width 7   CARD: deck 10, col. 13-19
Missing data code: 9999999   Decimal place: none
N=182   Mean=.016   Standard Deviation=.13   Range=0-1

DEFINITION: See Variable 97 for definition

Variable 101   AID TO SUBVERSIVE GROUPS OR ENEMY (1965)

OSIRIS: Location 652   width 7   CARD: deck 10, col. 20-26
Missing data code: 9999999   Decimal place: none
N=182   Mean=.016   Standard Deviation=.17   Range=0-2

Variable 102   NEGATIVE COMMUNICATIONS (1950)

OSIRIS: Location 659   width 7   CARD: deck 10, col. 27-33
Missing data code: 9999999   Decimal place: none
N=182   Mean=2.01   Standard Deviation=10.2   Range-0-102

DEFINITION: Total frequency of written or oral communication by officials of a political unit such as accusation, representative protest, warning, threat, ultimatum and denunciation. Accusation is a negative charge or allegation directed at another country. Representative protest consists of any official communication or government statement labeled a protest or representation by the actor. Warning raises the possibility that certain negative sanctions may occur as a result of specified actions or lack of actions by the object. Threat involves stating explicitly that certain negative sanctions may occur as a result of actions by the object. Ultimatum adds to a threat a specific time in which the specified action must occur. Denunciation consists of highly derogatory statements about the character or policies of the object, its leaders, or its people.

Variable 103   NEGATIVE COMMUNICATIONS (1955)

   OSIRIS: Location 666   width 7   CARD: deck 10, col. 34-40
   Missing data code: 9999999   Decimal place: none
   N=182   Mean=2.55   Standard Deviation=10.47   Range=0-90

   DEFINITION: See variable 102 for definition

Variable 104   NEGATIVE COMMUNICATIONS (1960)

   OSIRIS: Location 673   width 7   CARD: deck 10, col. 41-47
   Missing data code: 9999999   Decimal place: none
   N=182   Mean=2.11   Standard Deviation=9.83   Range=0-82

   DEFINITION: See Variable 102 for definition

Variable 105   NEGATIVE COMMUNICATIONS (1963)

   OSIRIS: Location 680   width 7   CARD: deck 10, col. 48-54
   Missing data code: 9999999   Decimal place: none
   N=182   Mean=.96   Standard Deviation=3.87   Range=0-26

   DEFINITION: See Variable 102 for definition

Variable 106   NEGATIVE COMMUNICATIONS (1965)

   OSIRIS: Location 687   width 7   CARD: deck 10, col. 55-61
   Missing data code: 9999999   Decimal place: none
   N=182   Mean=1.99   Standard Deviation=8.84   Range=0-84

   DEFINITION: See Variable 102 for definition

Variable 107   ACCUSATION (1950)

   OSIRIS: Location 694   width 7   CARD: deck 10, col. 62-68
   Missing data code: 9999999   Decimal place: none
   N=182   Mean=1.20   Standard Deviation=6.71   Range=0-71

   DEFINITION: A negative charge or allegation directed at B

Variable 108   ACCUSATION (1955)

   OSIRIS: Location 701   width 7   CARD: deck 10, col. 69-75
   Missing data code: 9999999   Decimal place: none
   N=182   Mean=1.80   Standard Deviation=8.31   Range=0-74

Variable 109   ACCUSATION (1960)

   OSIRIS: Location 708   width 7   CARD: deck 11, col. 6-12
   Missing data code: 9999999   Decimal place: none
   N=182   Mean=1.27   Standard Deviation=6.12   Range=0-50

   DEFINITION: See Variable 107 for definition

Variable 110   ACCUSATION (1963)

OSIRIS: Location 715   width 7   CARD: deck 11, col. 13-19
Missing data code: 9999999   Decimal place: none
N=182   Mean=.56   Standard Deviation=2.77   Range=0-20

DEFINITION: See Variable 107 for definition

Variable 111   ACCUSATION (1965)

OSIRIS: Location 722   width 7   CARD: deck 11, col. 20-26
Missing data code: 9999999   Decimal place: none
N=182   Mean=.96   Standard Deviation=4.65   Range=0-42

DEFINITION: See Variable 107 for definition

Variable 112   PROTESTS (1950)

OSIRIS: Location 729   width 7   CARD: deck 11, col. 27-33
Missing data code: 9999999   Decimal place: none
N=182   Mean=.16   Standard Deviation=.75   Range=0-8

DEFINITION: The number of any official diplomatic communication or governmental statement by the executive leaders by a country which has as its primary purpose to protest against the actions of another nation.

Variable 113   PROTESTS (1955)

OSIRIS: Location 736   width 7   CARD: deck 11, col. 34-40
Missing data code: 9999999   Decimal place: none
N=182   Mean=.26   Standard Deviation=.87   Range=0-5

DEFINITION: See Variable 112 for definition

Variable 114   PROTESTS (1960)

OSIRIS: Location 743   width 7   CARD: deck 11, col. 41-47
Missing data code: 9999999   Decimal place: none
N=182   Mean=.14   Standard Deviation=.70   Range=0-7

DEFINITION: See Variable 112 for definition

Variable 115   PROTESTS (1963)

OSIRIS: Location 750   width 7   CARD: deck 11, col. 48-54
Missing data code: 9999999   Decimal place: none
N=182   Mean=.25   Standard Deviation=1.12   Range=0-10

DEFINITION: See Variable 112 for definition

Variable 116   PROTESTS (1965)

OSIRIS: Location 757   width 7   CARD: deck 11, col. 55-61
Missing data code: 9999999   Decimal place: none
N=182   Mean=.34   Standard Deviation=1.46   Range=0-13

DEFINITION: See Variable 112 for definition

Variable 117   UNOFFICIAL ACTS (1950)

OSIRIS: Location 764   width 7   CARD: deck 11, col. 62-68
Missing data code: 9999999   Decimal place: none
N=182   Mean=.027   Standard Deviation=.19   Range=0-2

DEFINITION: Total frequency of unofficial violence. Violence refers to any action or engagement in which the intent is to destroy or damage the property of the object, or injure, wound, or kill any of its members.

Variable 118   UNOFFICIAL ACTS (1955)

OSIRIS: Location 771   width 7   CARD: deck 11, col. 69-75
Missing data code: 9999999   Decimal place: none
N=182   Mean=.033   Standard Deviation=.21   Range=0-2

DEFINITION: See Variable 117 for definition

Variable 119   UNOFFICIAL ACTS (1960)

OSIRIS: Location 778   width 7   CARD: deck 12, col. 6-12
Missing data code: 9999999   Decimal place: none
N=182   Mean=.022   Standard Deviation=.18   Range=0-2

DEFINITION: See Variable 117 for definition

Variable 120   UNOFFICIAL ACTS (1963)

OSIRIS: Location 785   width 7   CARD: deck 12, col. 13-19
Missing data code: 9999999   Decimal place: none
N=182   Mean=.027   Standard Deviation=.19   Range=0-2

DEFINITION: See Variable 117 for definition

Variable 121   UNOFFICIAL ACTS (1965)

OSIRIS: Location 792   width 7   CARD: deck 12, col. 20-26
Missing data code: 9999999   Decimal place: none
N=182   Mean=.082   Standard Deviation=.57   Range=0-6

DEFINITION: See Variable 117 for definition

Variable 122   ATTACK ON EMBASSY (1950)

OSIRIS: Location 799   width 4   CARD: deck 12, col. 27-30
Missing data code: 9999   Decimal place: none
N=182   Mean=.011   Standard Deviation=.15   Range=0-2

DEFINITION: Any public demonstration by the actor's citizens directed at the object's foreign mission.

Variable 123   ATTACK ON EMBASSY (1955)

OSIRIS: Location 803   width 4   CARD: deck 12, col. 31-34
Missing data code: 9999   Decimal place: none
N=182   Mean=.011   Standard Deviation=.10   Range=0-1

DEFINITION: See Variable 122 for definition

-174-

Variable 124   ATTACK ON EMBASSY (1960)

OSIRIS: Location 807   width 4   CARD: deck 12, col. 35-38
Missing data code: 9999   Decimal place: none
N=182   Mean=.005   Standard Deviation=.074   Range=0-1

DEFINITION: See Variable 122 for definition

Variable 125   ATTACK ON EMBASSY (1963)

OSIRIS: Location 811   width 4   CARD: deck 12, col. 39-42
Missing data code: 9999   Decimal place: none
N=182   Mean=.016   Standard Deviation=.17   Range=0-2

DEFINITION: See Variable 122 for definition

Variable 126   ATTACK ON EMBASSY (1965)

OSIRIS: Location 815   width 4   CARD: deck 12, col. 43-46
Missing data code: 9999   Decimal place: none
N=182   Mean=.005   Standard Deviation=.074   Range=0-1

DEFINITION: See Variable 122 for definition

Variable 127   NONVIOLENT BEHAVIOR (1950)

OSIRIS: Location 819   width 7   CARD: deck 12, col. 47-53
Missing data code: 9999999   Decimal place: none
N=182   Mean=.033   Standard Deviation=.18   Range=0-1

DEFINITION: Negative acts that reflect strained, unfriendly, or hostile feelings of some of the actor's citizens against an object of its policies.

Variable 128   NONVIOLENT BEHAVIOR (1955)

OSIRIS: Location 826   width 7   CARD: deck 12, col. 54-60
Missing data code: 9999999   Decimal place: none
N=182   Mean=.055   Standard Deviation=.42   Range=0-5

DEFINITION: See Variable 127 for definition

Variable 129   NONVIOLENT BEHAVIOR (1960)

OSIRIS: Location 833   width 7   CARD: deck 12, col. 61-67
Missing data code: 9999999   Decimal place: none
N=182   Mean=.082   Standard Deviation=.42   Range=0-3

DEFINITION: See Variable 127 for definition

Variable 130   NONVIOLENT BEHAVIOR (1963)

OSIRIS: Location 840   width 7   CARD: deck 12, col. 68-74
Missing data code: 9999999   Decimal place: none
N=182   Mean=.016   Standard Deviation=.17   Range=0-2

DEFINITION: See Variable 127 for definition

Variable 131   NONVIOLENT BEHAVIOR (1965)

OSIRIS: Location 847   width 7   CARD: deck 13, col. 6-12
Missing data code: 9999999   Decimal place: none
N=182   Mean=.27   Standard Deviation=1.43   Range=0-16

DEFINITION: See Variable 127 for definition

Variable 132   WEIGHTED UN VOTING DISTANCE (1950)

OSIRIS: Location 854   width 7   CARD: deck 13, col. 13-19
Missing data code: 9999999   Decimal place: none
N=132   Mean=434.85   Standard Deviation=1147.3   Range=-2361-2455

DEFINITION: The only difference from Variable 32 is that here the distances on issue dimensions are weighted by their percentage contribution to the total variance. The formula for computation is

$$d_{A \to B} [\sum_{j=1}^{\rho} (S_{jA} - S_{jB})^2 W_j]^{1/2}$$

where W_j is the percentage of the total variance accounted for by the jth dimension.

Variable 133   WEIGHTED UN VOTING DISTANCE (1955)

OSIRIS: Location 861   width 7   CARD: deck 13, col. 20-26
Missing data code: 9999999   Decimal place: none
N=132   Mean=209.91   Standard Deviation=940.98   Range=-2630-1749

DEFINITION: See Variable 132 for definition

Variable 134   WEIGHTED UN VOTING DISTANCE (1960)

OSIRIS: Location 868   width 7   CARD: deck 13, col. 27-33
Missing data code: 9999999   Decimal place: none
N=156   Mean=111.42   Standard Deviation=908.93   Range=-2267-1692

DEFINITION: See Variable 132 for definition

Variable 135   WEIGHTED UN VOTING DISTANCE (1963)

OSIRIS: Location 875   width 7   CARD: deck 13, col. 34-40
Missing data code: 9999999   Decimal place: none
N=156   Mean=606.92   Standard Deviation=908.64   Range=-1619-2186

DEFINITION: See Variable 132 for definition

Variable 136   WEIGHTED UN VOTING DISTANCE (1965)

OSIRIS: Location 882   width 7   CARD: deck 13, col. 41-47
Missing data code: 9999999   Decimal place: none
N=131   Mean=499.48   Standard Deviation=957.30   Range=-1884-2927

DEFINITION: See Variable 132 for definition

Variable 137   UNWEIGHTED UN VOTING DISTANCE (1950)

   OSIRIS: Location 889   width 7   CARD: deck 13, col. 48-54
   Missing data code: 9999999   Decimal place: none
   N=132   Mean=118.38   Standard Deviation=813.04   Range=-2446-1452

   DEFINITION: Factor score distance between A↔B on major rotated dimensions
   extracted from roll call voting statistics in the UN General Assembly Plenary
   Sessions. Distances are computed by the formula

$$d_{A \to B} = [\sum_{j=1}^{\rho} (S_{jA} - S_{jB})^2]^{1/2}$$

   where $d_{A \to B}$ is the voting distance between A and B, S_j is the jth issue dimension of
   the ρ issue dimensions extracted.

Variable 138   UNWEIGHTED UN VOTING DISTANCE (1955)

   OSIRIS: Location 896   width 7   CARD: deck 13, col. 55-61
   Missing data code: 9999999   Decimal place: none
   N=132   Mean=217.23   Standard Deviation=965.79   Range=-2738-2158

   DEFINITION: See Variable 137 for definition

Variable 139   UNWEIGHTED UN VOTING DISTANCE (1960)

   OSIRIS: Location 903   width 7   CARD: deck 13, col. 62-68
   Missing data code: 9999999   Decimal place: none
   N=156   Mean=145.07   Standard Deviation=936.49   Range=-2264-2210

   DEFINITION: See Variable 137 for definition

Variable 140   UNWEIGHTED UN VOTING DISTANCE (1963)

   OSIRIS: Location 910   width 7   CARD: deck 13, col. 69-75
   Missing data code: 9999999   Decimal place: none
   N=156   Mean=596.90   Standard Deviation=903.86   Range=-1993-1815

   DEFINITION: See Variable 137 for definition

Variable 141   UNWEIGHTED UN VOTING DISTANCE (1965)

   OSIRIS: Location 917   width 7   CARD: deck 14, col. 6-12
   Missing data code: 9999999   Decimal place: none
   N=132   Mean=582.58   Standard Deviation=1097.5   Range=-1557-4082

   DEFINITION: See Variable 137 for definition

-177-

Variable 142   TOURISTS A→B (1950)

OSIRIS: Location 924   width 7   CARD: deck 14, col. 13-19
Missing data code: 9999999   Decimal place: none   Unit: $\times 10^2$
N=120   Mean=439.11   Standard Deviation=1779.4   Range=0-12758

DEFINITION: Total number of tourists A→B. Tourist is defined as any person travelling for a period of twenty-four hours or more in a country other than that in which he usually resides. International Travel Statistics, International Union of Official Travel Organization; and UN Statistical Yearbook, UN.

NOTES:
A. Estimate
B. Statistical Abstract of the U.S. (1952)
C. Data for Federation of Malaysia are included in data for India.
D. Statistical Abstract of Israel (1966)
E. Great Britain Central Office Annual Abstract of Statistics, 1965.
F. The International Migration Digest, Vol. I. No. 2, (Fall 1964)
G. International Migration, 1945-1957, Geneva, (1959)

Variable 143   TOURISTS A→B (1955)

OSIRIS: Location 931   width 7   CARD: deck 14, col. 20-26
Missing data code: 9999999   Decimal place: none   Unit: $\times 10^2$
N=141   Mean=67.98   Standard Deviation=278.80   Range=0-2391

DEFINITION: See Variable 142 for definition and note codes.

Variable 144   TOURISTS A→B (1960)

OSIRIS: Location 938   width 7   CARD: deck 14, col. 27-33
Missing data code: 9999999   Decimal place: none   Unit: $\times 10^2$
N=149   Mean=123.77   Standard Deviation=497.96   Range=0-4265

DEFINITION: See Variable 142 for definition and note codes.

Variable 145   TOURISTS A→B (1963)

OSIRIS: Location 945   width 7   CARD: deck 14, col. 34-40
Missing data code: 9999999   Decimal place: none   Unit: $\times 10^2$
N=171   Mean=111.37   Standard Deviation=488.19   Range=0-5091

DEFINITION: See Variable 142 for definition and note codes.

Variable 146   TOURISTS A→B (1965)

OSIRIS: Location 952   width 7   CARD: deck 14, col. 41-47
Missing data code: 9999999   Decimal place: none   Unit: $\times 10^2$
N=153   Mean=165.73   Standard Deviation=679.04   Range=0-6743

DEFINITION: See Variable 142 for definition and note codes.

Variable 147   RELATIVE TOURISTS A→B (1950)

OSIRIS: Location 959   width 7   CARD: deck 14, col. 48-54
Missing data code: 9999999   Decimal place: none   Unit: $\% \times 10^2$
N=123   Mean=140.09   Standard Deviation=501.89   Range=0-3071

DEFINITION: Total number of tourists A→B, divided by total number of tourists to B from foreign countries. Same sources as Variables 142-146.

NOTES: See Variable 142 for note codes.

Variable 148   RELATIVE TOURISTS A→B (1955)

OSIRIS: Location 966   width 7   CARD: deck 14, col. 55-61
Missing data code: 9999999   Decimal place: none   Unit: $\% \times 10^2$
N=144   Mean=144.79   Standard Deviation=505.46   Range=0-3800

DEFINITION: See Variable 147 for definition.

NOTES: See Variable 142 for note codes.

Variable 149   RELATIVE TOURISTS A→B (1960)

OSIRIS: Location 973   width 7   CARD: deck 14, col. 62-68
Missing data code: 9999999   Decimal place: none   Unit: $\% \times 10^2$
N=151   Mean=280.40   Standard Deviation=1407.2   Range=0-16180

DEFINITION: See Variable 147 for definition.

NOTES: See Variable 142 for note codes.

Variable 150   RELATIVE TOURISTS A→B (1963)

OSIRIS: Location 980   width 7   CARD: deck 14, col. 69-75
Missing data code: 9999999   Decimal place: none   Unit: $\% \times 10^2$
N=168   Mean=152.42   Standard Deviation=477.81   Range=0-3444

DEFINITION: See Variable 147 for definition.

NOTES: See Variable 142 for note codes.

Variable 151   RELATIVE TOURISTS A→B (1965)

OSIRIS: Location 987   width 7   CARD: deck 15, col. 6-12
Missing data code: 9999999   Decimal place: none   Unit: $\% \times 10^2$
N=156   Mean=159.97   Standard Deviation=476.98   Range=0-2801

Variable 152   TOURISTS (A→B)/A's POPULATION (1950)

OSIRIS: Location 994   width 7   CARD: deck 15, col. 13-19
Missing data code: 9999999   Decimal place: none   Unit: $\% \times 10^3$
N=123   Mean=255.78   Standard Deviation=1473.0   Range=0-14640

DEFINITION: Total number of tourists A→B, divided by A's population. Sources same as Variables 147-151.

NOTES: See Variable 142 for note codes.

-179-

Variable 153   TOURISTS (A→B)/A's POPULATION (1955)

OSIRIS: Location 1001   width 7   CARD: deck 15, col. 20-26
Missing data code: 9999999   Decimal place: none   Unit: % x 10^3
N=144   Mean=2.84   Standard Deviation=15.32   Range=0-166

DEFINITION: See Variable 152 for definition.

NOTES: See Variable 142 for note codes.

Variable 154   TOURISTS (A→B)/A's POPULATION (1960)

OSIRIS: Location 1008   width 7   CARD: deck 15, col. 27-33
Missing data code: 9999999   Decimal place: none   Unit: % x 10^3
N=151   Mean=31.79   Standard Deviation=115.9   Range=0-880

DEFINITION: See Variable 152 for definition.

NOTES: See Variable 142 for note codes.

Variable 155   TOURISTS (A→B)/A's POPULATION (1963)

OSIRIS: Location 1015   width 7   CARD: deck 15, col. 34-40
Missing data code: 9999999   Decimal place: none   Unit: % x 10^3
N=170   Mean=22.71   Standard Deviation=88.21   Range=0-676

DEFINITION: See Variable 152 for definition.

NOTES: See Variable 142 for note codes.

Variable 156   TOURISTS (A→B)/A's POPULATION (1965)

OSIRIS: Location 1022   width 7   CARD: deck 15, col. 41-47
Missing data code: 9999999   Decimal place: none   Unit: % x 10^3
N=156   Mean=43.97   Standard Deviation=173.57   Range=0-1373

DEFINITION: See Variable 152 for definition.

NOTES: See Variable 142 for note codes.

Variable 157   EMIGRANTS A→B (1950)

OSIRIS: Location 1029   width 7   CARD: deck 15, col. 48-54
Missing data code: 9999999   Decimal place: none
N=160   Mean=101.24   Standard Deviation=516.94   Range=0-5612

DEFINITION: Total number of emigrants A→B. Emigrants are defined as nationals leaving their country with the intention of staying abroad for a period exceeding one year. Anuario Estatistico Do Brasil--1971, Instituto Brasileiro de Estatistica, Rio de Janeiro, Vol. 32; Concise Statistical Yearbook of Poland 1970, Central Statistical Office of the Polish People's Republic, Vol. Xii; Cuba 1968: Supplement to the Statistical Abstract of Latin America, Latin American Center, p. 82; Demographic Yearbook 1952, 1957, 1959, 1970, UN Department of Justice, Immigration and Naturalization Service, Annual Report, and releases, Table 6A; Statistical Abstract of Israel, Central Bureau of Statistics, 1967, No. 18; Statistical Yearbook of the Netherlands, 1971, the Hague, Staatsutgeverij, Netherlands Central Bureau of Statistics; Taft, D. R., and Robbins, R., International Migrations: The Immigrant in the Modern World, 1955; U.S. Bureau of the Census, Statistical Abstract of the United States 1965, 86th edition.

NOTES: See Variable 142 for note codes.

Variable 158   EMIGRANTS A→B (1955)

   OSIRIS: Location 1036   width 7   CARD: deck 15, col. 55-61
   Missing data code: 9999999   Decimal place: none
   N=162   Mean=57.85   Standard Deviation=285.11   Range=0-2405

   DEFINITION: See Variable 157 for definition.

   NOTES: See Variable 142 for note codes.

Variable 159   EMIGRANTS A→B (1960)

   OSIRIS: Location 1043   width 7   CARD: deck 15, col. 62-68
   Missing data code: 9999999   Decimal place: none
   N=162   Mean=50.27   Standard Deviation=220.1   Range=0-2087

   DEFINITION: See Variable 157 for definition.

   NOTES: See Variable 142 for note codes.

Variable 160   EMIGRANTS A→B (1963)

   OSIRIS: Location 1050   width 7   CARD: deck 15, col. 69-75
   Missing data code: 9999999   Decimal place: none
   N=154   Mean=40.31   Standard Deviation=216.5   Range=0-2366

   DEFINITION: See Variable 157 for definition.

   NOTES: See Variable 142 for note codes.

Variable 161   EMIGRANTS A→B (1965)

   OSIRIS: Location 1057   width 7   CARD: deck 16, col. 6-12
   Missing data code: 9999999   Decimal place: none
   N=149   Mean=43.42   Standard Deviation=243.9   Range=0-2428

   DEFINITION: See Variable 157 for definition

   NOTES: See Variable 142 for note codes.

Variable 162   RELATIVE EMIGRANTS A→B (1950)

   OSIRIS: Location 1064   width 7   CARD: deck 16, col. 13-19
   Missing data code: 9999999   Decimal place: none   Unit: % x 10^2
   N=143   Mean=22.78   Standard Deviation=109.6   Range=0-948

   DEFINITION: Total number of emigrants A→B, divided by total number of emigrants of A. Same sources as Variables 157-161.

   NOTES: See Variable 142 for note codes.

Variable 163   RELATIVE EMIGRANTS A→B (1955)

   OSIRIS: Location 1071   width 7   CARD: deck 16, col. 20-26
   Missing data code: 9999999   Decimal place: none   Unit: % x 10^2
   N=152   Mean=110.1   Standard Deviation=459.8   Range=0-5869

   DEFINITION: See Variable 162 for definition.

   NOTES: See Variable 142 for note codes.

Variable 164   RELATIVE EMIGRANTS A→B (1960)

OSIRIS: Location 1078   width 7   CARD: deck 16, col. 27-33
Missing data code: 9999999   Decimal place: none   Unit: % x 10^2
N=147   Mean=112.4   Standard Deviation=583.1   Range=0-5091

DEFINITION: See Variable 162 for definition.

NOTES: See Variable 142 for note codes.

Variable 165   RELATIVE EMIGRANTS A→B (1963)

OSIRIS: Location 1085   width 7   CARD: deck 16, col. 34-40
Missing data code: 9999999   Decimal place: none   Unit: % x 10^2
N=149   Mean=93.88   Standard Deviation=625.8   Range=0-6263

DEFINITION: See Variable 162 for definition.

NOTES: See Variable 142 for note codes.

Variable 166   RELATIVE EMIGRANTS A→B (1965)

OSIRIS: Location 1092   width 7   CARD: deck 16, col. 41-47
Missing data code: 9999999   Decimal place: none   Unit: % x 10^2
N=141   Mean=52.0   Standard Deviation=499.3   Range=0-5839

DEFINITION: See Variable 162 for definition.

NOTES: See Variable 142 for note codes.

Variable 167   EMIGRANTS (A→B)/A's POPULATION (1950)

OSIRIS: 1099   width 4   CARD: deck 16, col. 48-51
Missing data code: 9999   Decimal place: none   Unit: x 10^6
N=153   Mean=29.28   Standard Deviation=119.0   Range=0-953

DEFINITION: Total number of emigrants of A toward B, divided by A's population.
See Variable 41 for definition of emigrants. Same sources as Variables 157-161.

NOTES:
A. Estimate
B. No indication in primary source whether emigration data refers to CHT or CHN.
C. Concise Statistical Yearbook of Poland, Vol. Xii (1970)
D. EGP and SYR are combined.
E. CHN, KON, VTN, and OUT are combined.
F. Derived from trade returns of the importing country.
G. Economic Bulletin for Asia and the Far East, Vol. XVII, no. 2 (Sept., 1966).
H. Monthly Statistics of the Foreign Trade of India, Vol. I (March, 1964)

Variable 168   EMIGRANTS (A→B)/A's POPULATION (1955)

OSIRIS: Location 1103   width 4   CARD: deck 16, col. 52-55
Missing data code: 9999   Decimal place: none   Unit: x 10^6
N=166   Mean=18.34   Standard Deviation=87.26   Range=0-874

DEFINITION: See Variable 167 for definition.

NOTES: See Variable 167 for note codes.

Variable 169   EMIGRANTS (A→B)/A's POPULATION (1960)

OSIRIS: Location 1107   width 4   CARD: deck 16, col. 56-59
Missing data code: 9999   Decimal place: none   Unit: $\times 10^6$
N=163   Mean=112.1   Standard Deviation=539.8   Range=0-5034

DEFINITION: See Variable 167 for definition and note codes.

Variable 170   EMIGRANTS (A→B)/A's POPULATION (1963)

OSIRIS: Location 1111   width 4   CARD: deck 16, col. 60-63
Missing data code: 9999   Decimal place: none   Unit: $\times 10^6$
N=167   Mean=38.02   Standard Deviation=278.0   Range=0-3450

DEFINITION: See Variable 167 for definition and note codes.

Variable 171   EMIGRANTS (A→B)/A's POPULATION (1965)

OSIRIS: Location 1115   width 4   CARD: deck 16, col. 64-67
Missing data code: 9999   Decimal place: none   Unit: $\times 10^6$
N=161   Mean=23.44   Standard Deviation=155.3   Range=0-1725

DEFINITION: See Variable 167 for definition and note codes.

Variable 172   STUDENTS A→B (1950)

OSIRIS: Location 1119   width 7   CARD: deck 16, col. 68-74
Missing data code: 9999999   Decimal place: none
N=137   Mean=41.65   Standard Deviation=170.19   Range=0-1099

DEFINITION: A's total number of students in country B. Student is defined as any person who received all or part of their academic training. *Basic Facts and Figures*, UNESCO; and *Study Abroad*, UNESCO.

NOTES: See Variable 167 for note codes.

Variable 173   STUDENTS A→B (1955)

OSIRIS: Location 1126   width 7   CARD: deck 17, col. 6-12
Missing data code: 9999999   Decimal place: none
N=170   Mean=84.91   Standard Deviation=452.0   Range=0-4964

DEFINITION: See Variable 172 for definition.

NOTES: See Variable 167 for note codes.

Variable 174   STUDENTS A→B (1960)

OSIRIS: Location 1133   width 7   CARD: deck 17, col. 13-19
Missing data code: 9999999   Decimal place: none
N=178   Mean=141.9   Standard Deviation=741.6   Range=0-7500

DEFINITION: See Variable 172 for definition.

NOTES: See Variable 167 for note codes.

Variable 175   STUDENTS A→B (1963)

   OSIRIS: Location 1140   width 7   CARD: deck 17, col. 20-26
   Missing data code: 9999999   Decimal place: none
   N=182   Mean=131.1   Standard Deviation=548.9   Range=0-6387

   DEFINITION: See Variable 172 for definition.

   NOTES: See Variable 167 for note codes.

Variable 176   STUDENTS A→B (1965)

   OSIRIS: Location 1147   width 7   CARD: deck 17, col. 27-33
   Missing data code: 9999999   Decimal place: none
   N=148   Mean=180.7   Standard Deviation=818.4   Range=0-7518

   DEFINITION: See Variable 172 for definition.

   NOTES: See Variable 167 for note codes.

Variable 177   RELATIVE STUDENTS A→B (1950)

   OSIRIS: Location 1154   width 7   CARD: deck 17, col. 34-40
   Missing data code: 9999999   Decimal place: none   Unit: % x 10^2
   N=135   Mean=12.67   Standard Deviation=54.78   Range=0-361

   DEFINITION: A's total number of students in country B, divided by total foreign students in B. Same sources as Variables 172-176.

   NOTES: See Variable 167 for note codes.

Variable 178   RELATIVE STUDENTS A→B (1955)

   OSIRIS: 1161   width 7   CARD: deck 17, col. 41-47
   Missing data code: 9999999   Decimal place: none   Unit: % x 10^2
   N=170   Mean=101.4   Standard Deviation=518.6   Range=0-4611

   DEFINITION: See Variable 177 for definition.

   NOTES: See Variable 167 for note codes.

Variable 179   RELATIVE STUDENTS A→B (1960)

   OSIRIS: Location 1168   width 7   CARD: deck 17, col. 48-54
   Missing data code: 9999999   Decimal place: none   Unit: % x 10^2
   N=177   Mean=38.51   Standard Deviation=198.4   Range=0-1932

   DEFINITION: See Variable 177 for definition.

   NOTES: See Variable 167 for note codes.

Variable 180 RELATIVE STUDENTS A→B (1963)

OSIRIS: Location 1175   width 7   CARD: deck 17, col. 55-61
Missing data code: 9999999   Decimal place: none   Unit: % x 10^2
N=182   Mean=59.71   Standard Deviation=257.0   Range=0-2038

DEFINITION: See Variable 177 for definition.

NOTES: See Variable 167 for note codes.

Variable 181 RELATIVE STUDENTS A→B (1965)

OSIRIS: Location 1182   width 7   CARD: deck 17, col. 62-68
Missing data code: 9999999   Decimal place: none   Unit: % x 10^2
N=145   Mean=252.34   Standard Deviation=1348.72   Range=0-13638

DEFINITION: See Variable 177 for definition.

NOTES: See Variable 167 for note codes.

Variable 182 EXPORTS A→B (1950)

OSIRIS: Location 1189   width 7   CARD: deck 17, col. 69-75
Missing data code: 9999999   Decimal place: none   Unit: x 10^5, $ US
N=180   Mean=396.6   Standard Deviation=1010.3   Range=0-7145

DEFINITION: Total value of exports f.o.b. A→B. Goods passing through a country only for the purposes of transport are excluded. Statistical Yearbook, UN; Yearbook of International Trade Statistics; UNESCO Statistical Yearbook: Exports; and Direction of International Trade, UN.

NOTES: See Variable 167 for note codes.

Variable 183 EXPORTS A→B (1955)

OSIRIS: Location 1196   width 7   CARD: deck 18, col. 6-12
Missing data code: 9999999   Decimal place: none   Unit: x 10^5, $ US
N=182   Mean=552.7   Standard Deviation=1415.6   Range=0-9304

DEFINITION: See Variable 182 for definition.

Variable 184 EXPORTS A→B (1960)

OSIRIS: Location 1203   width 7   CARD: deck 18, col. 13-19
Missing data code: 9999999   Decimal place: none   Unit: x 10^5, $ US
N=182   Mean=712.0   Standard Deviation=1744.1   Range=0-11386

DEFINITION: See Variable 182 for definition.

NOTES: See Variable 167 for note codes.

Variable 185   EXPORTS A→B (1963)

OSIRIS: Location 1210   width 7   CARD: deck 18, col. 20-26
Missing data code: 9999999   Decimal place: none   Unit: $\times 10^5$, $ US
N=182   Mean=730.84   Standard Deviation=1759.4   Range=0-11729

DEFINITION: See Variable 182 for definition.

NOTES: See Variable 167 for note codes.

Variable 186   EXPORTS A→B (1965)

OSIRIS: Location 1217   width 7   CARD: deck 18, col. 27-33
Missing data code: 9999999   Decimal place: none   Unit: $\times 10^5$, $ US
N=171   Mean=883.7   Standard Deviation=2246.9   Range=0-16150

DEFINITION: See Variable 182 for definition.

NOTES: See Variable 167 for note codes.

Variable 187   RELATIVE EXPORTS A→B (1950)

OSIRIS: Location 1224   width 7   CARD: deck 18, col. 34-40
Missing data code: 9999999   Decimal place: none   Unit: % $\times 10^2$
N=155   Mean=309.5   Standard Deviation=858.0   Range=0-6316

DEFINITION: The total value of exports of A to B, divided by total value of exports of A to all other countries. Direction of International Trade, UN; UNESCO Statistical Yearbook; Yearbook of International Trade Statistics; and Eckstein (for China) Communist China's Economic Growth and Foreign Trade: Implications for U.S. Policy.

NOTES: See Variable 167 for note codes.

Variable 188   RELATIVE EXPORTS A→B (1955)

OSIRIS: Location 1231   width 7   CARD: deck 18, col. 41-47
Missing data code: 9999999   Decimal place: none   Unit: % $\times 10^2$
N=182   Mean=312.2   Standard Deviation=828.7   Range=0-6754

DEFINITION: See Variable 187 for definition.

Variable 189   RELATIVE EXPORTS A→B (1960)

OSIRIS: Location 1238   width 7   CARD: deck 18, col. 48-54
Missing data code: 9999999   Decimal place: none   Unit: % $\times 10^2$
N=182   Mean=316.4   Standard Deviation=744.4   Range=0-5322

DEFINITION: See Variable 187 for definition.

Variable 190   RELATIVE EXPORTS A→B (1963)

OSIRIS: Location 1245   width 7   CARD: deck 18, col. 55-61
Missing data code: 9999999   Decimal place: none   Unit: % $\times 10^2$
N=182   Mean=271.4   Standard Deviation=578.4   Range=0-3773

DEFINITION: See Variable 187 for definition.

Variable 191   RELATIVE EXPORTS A→B (1965)

OSIRIS: Location 1252   width 7   CARD: deck 18, col. 62-68
Missing data code: 9999999   Decimal place: none   Unit: % x 10^2
N=171   Mean=288.6   Standard Deviation=635.9   Range=0-4699

DEFINITION: See Variable 187 for definition.

NOTES: See Variable 167 for note codes.

Variable 192   EXPORTS (A→B)/A's GNP (1950)

OSIRIS: Location 1259   width 7   CARD: deck 18, col. 69-75
Missing data code: 9999999   Decimal place: none   Unit: % x 10^2
N=163   Mean=43.83   Standard Deviation=178.1   Range=0-2028

DEFINITION: Principal export of A to B, divided by A's GNP. Direction of International Trade, UN; Statistical Yearbook, UN; UNESCO Statistical Yearbook; Yearbook of International Trade Statistics; and Council on Foreign Relations, Trade, Aid and Development.

NOTES: See Variable 167 for note codes.

Variable 193   EXPORTS (A→B)/A's GNP (1955)

OSIRIS: Location 1266   width 7   CARD: deck 19, col. 6-12
Missing data code: 9999999   Decimal place: none   Unit: % x 10^2
N=182   Mean=40.12   Standard Deviation=151.7   Range=0-1824

DEFINITION: See Variable 192 for definition.

Variable 194   EXPORTS (A→B)/A's GNP (1960)

OSIRIS: Location 1273   width 7   CARD: deck 19, col. 13-19
Missing data code: 9999999   Decimal place: none   Unit: % x 10^2
N=182   Mean=36.26   Standard Deviation=111.3   Range=0-1197

DEFINITION: See Variable 192 for definition.

Variable 195   EXPORTS (A→B)/A's GNP (1963)

OSIRIS: Location 1280   width 7   CARD: deck 19, col. 20-26
Missing data code: 9999999   Decimal place: none   Unit: % x 10^2
N=182   Mean=27.69   Standard Deviation=65.03   Range=0-432

DEFINITION: See Variable 192 for definition.

Variable 196   EXPORTS (A→B)/A's GNP (1965)

OSIRIS: Location 1287   width 7   CARD: deck 19, col. 27-33
Missing data code: 9999999   Decimal place: none   Unit: % x 10^2
N=171   Mean=31.01   Standard Deviation=93.86   Range=0-1007

DEFINITION: See Variable 192 for definition.

NOTES: See Variable 167 for note codes.

Variable 197   INTERGOVERNMENTAL ORGANIZATIONS A↔B (1950)

OSIRIS: Location 1294   width 4   CARD: deck 19, col. 34-37
Missing data code: 9999   Decimal place: none
N=182   Mean=12.50   Standard Deviation=10.22   Range=0-48

DEFINITION: The number of intergovernmental organizations in which both countries (A↔B) have common membership. J. J. Lador-Lederer, International Non-Governmental Organizations; Yearbook of International Organizations; and Moshe Y. Sachs, Worldmark Encyclopedia of the Nations.

NOTES: Estimate

Variable 198   INTERGOVERNMENTAL ORGANIZATIONS A↔B (1955)

OSIRIS: Location 1298   width 4   CARD: deck 19, col. 38-41
Missing data code: 9999   Decimal place: none
N=182   Mean=16.93   Standard Deviation=10.04   Range=0-48

DEFINITION: See Variable 197 for definition.

Variable 199   INTERGOVERNMENTAL ORGANIZATIONS A↔B (1960)

OSIRIS: Location 1302   width 4   CARD: deck 19, col. 42-45
Missing data code: 9999   Decimal place: none
N=182   Mean=18.23   Standard Deviation=10.43   Range=0-57

DEFINITION: See Variable 197 for definition and note codes.

Variable 200   INTERGOVERNMENTAL ORGANIZATIONS A↔B (1963)

OSIRIS: Location 1306   width 4   CARD: deck 19, col. 46-49
Missing data code: 9999   Decimal place: none
N=182   Mean=19.53   Standard Deviation=11.11   Range=0-57

DEFINITION: See Variable 197 for definition and note codes.

Variable 201   INTERGOVERNMENTAL ORGANIZATIONS A↔B (1965)

OSIRIS: Location 1310   width 4   CARD: deck 19, col. 50-53
Missing data code: 9999   Decimal place: none
N=182   Mean=23.10   Standard Deviation=11.33   Range=2-65

DEFINITION: See Variable 197 for definition.

Variable 202   RELATIVE IGO A↔B (1950)

OSIRIS: Location 1314   width 7   CARD: deck 19, col. 54-60
Missing data code: 9999999   Decimal place: none   Unit: % x 10^2
N=182   Mean=4325.2   Standard Deviation=2868.6   Range=0-9999

DEFINITION: The proportion of A's total IGO membership which is accounted for by the (A↔B) relationship. Same sources as Variables 197-201.

NOTES: Estimate

Variable 203   RELATIVE IGO A↔B (1955)

OSIRIS: Location 1321   width 7   CARD: deck 19, col. 61-67
Missing data code: 9999999   Decimal place: none   Unit: $\% \times 10^2$
N=182   Mean=5167.4   Standard Deviation=2840.8   Range=0-1000

DEFINITION: See Variable 202 for definition and note codes.

Variable 204   RELATIVE IGO A↔B (1960)

OSIRIS: Location 1328   width 7   CARD: deck 19, col. 68-74
Missing data code: 9999999   Decimal place: none   Unit: $\% \times 10^2$
N=181   Mean=5183.0   Standard Deviation=2718.8   Range=0-1000

DEFINITION: See Variable 202 for definition and note codes.

Variable 205   RELATIVE IGO A↔B (1963)

OSIRIS: Location 1335   width 7   CARD: deck 20, col. 6-12
Missing data code: 9999999   Decimal place: none   Unit: $\% \times 10^2$
N=182   Mean=4856.7   Standard Deviation=2440.9   Range=0-1000

DEFINITION: See Variable 202 for definition.

Variable 206   RELATIVE IGO A↔B (1965)

OSIRIS: Location 1342   width 7   CARD: deck 20, col. 13-19
Missing data code: 9999999   Decimal place: none   Unit: $\% \times 10^2$
N=182   Mean=5413.8   Standard Deviation=2117.8   Range=833-1000

DEFINITION: See Variable 202 for definition.

Variable 207   NGO A↔B (1950)

OSIRIS: Location 1349   width 7   CARD: deck 20, col. 20-26
Missing data code: 9999999   Decimal place: none
N=182   Mean=85.56   Standard Deviation=81.98   Range=3-426

DEFINITION: The number of non-governmental organizations in which both countries (A↔B) have common membership. Same sources as Variables 197-201.

Variable 208   NGO A↔B (1955)

OSIRIS: Location 1356   width 7   CARD: deck 20, col. 27-33
Missing data code: 9999999   Decimal place: none
N=182   Mean=108.8   Standard Deviation=114.2   Range=2-579

DEFINITION: See Variable 207 for definition.

Variable 209   NGO A↔B (1960)

OSIRIS: Location 1363   width 7   CARD: deck 20, col. 34-40
Missing data code: 9999999   Decimal place: none
N=182   Mean=140.6   Standard Deviation=127.1   Range=8-654

DEFINITION: See Variable 207 for definition.

Variable 210   NGO A↔B (1963)

OSIRIS: Location 1370 width 7   CARD: deck 20, col. 41-47
Missing data code: 9999999   Decimal place: none
N=182   Mean=169.6   Standard Deviation=150.9   Range=5-784

DEFINITION: See Variable 207 for definition.

Variable 211   NGO A↔B (1965)

OSIRIS: Location 1377 width 7   CARD: deck 20, col. 48-54
Missing data code: 9999999   Decimal place: none
N=182   Mean=187.2   Standard Deviation=151.3   Range=25-811

DEFINITION: See Variable 207 for definition.

Variable 212   RELATIVE NGO A↔B (1950)

OSIRIS: Location 1384 width 7   CARD: deck 20, col. 55-61
Missing data code: 9999999   Decimal place: none   Unit: $\% \times 10^2$
N=182   Mean=4864.5   Standard Deviation=2758.4   Range=194-9999

DEFINITION: The proportion of A's total NGO membership which is accounted for by the (A↔B) relationship. Same sources as Variables 197-201.

Variable 213   RELATIVE NGO A↔B (1955)

OSIRIS: Location 1391 width 7   CARD: deck 20, col. 62-68
Missing data code: 9999999   Decimal place: none   Unit: $\% \times 10^2$
N=182   Mean=4712.0   Standard Deviation=2926.4   Range=77-9730

DEFINITION: See Variable 212 for definition.

Variable 214   RELATIVE NGO A↔B (1960)

OSIRIS: Location 1398 width 7   CARD: deck 20, col. 69-75
Missing data code: 9999999   Decimal place: none   Unit: $\% \times 10^2$
N=182   Mean=4972.3   Standard Deviation=2799.2   Range=293-9509

DEFINITION: See Variable 212 for definition.

Variable 215   RELATIVE NGO A↔B (1963)

OSIRIS: Location 1405 width 7   CARD: deck 21, col. 6-12
Missing data code: 9999999   Decimal place: none   Unit: $\% \times 10^2$
N=182   Mean=5016.2   Standard Deviation=2807.5   Range=208-9545

DEFINITION: See Variable 212 for definition.

Variable 216   RELATIVE NGO A↔B (1965)

OSIRIS: Location 1412 width 7   CARD: deck 21, col. 13-19
Missing data code: 9999999   Decimal place: none   Unit: $\% \times 10^2$
N=182   Mean=5208.8   Standard Deviation=2641.1   Range=499-9455

DEFINITION: See Variable 212 for definition.

Variable 217   IGO A↔B/COMMON MEMBERSHIP OF A (1950)

OSIRIS: Location 1419   width 7   CARD: deck 21, col. 20-26
Missing data code: 9999999   Decimal place: none   Unit: % x 10^2
N=182   Mean=135.4   Standard Deviation=86.37   Range=0-367

DEFINITION: This variable is a measure of the interaction of dyads in the smaller, more specific orientated intergovernmental organizations, as opposed to co-membership in only the larger IGO's. Specifically, the variable is the total membership (i.e., the number of nations in each) of the IGO's to which both nations A and B belong, divided by the total membership of all the IGO's to which nation A belongs. Same sources as Variables 197-201.

NOTES: Estimate

Variable 218   IGO A↔B/COMMON MEMBERSHIP OF A (1955)

OSIRIS: Location 1426   width 7   CARD: deck 21, col. 27-33
Missing data code: 9999999   Decimal place: none   Unit: % x 10^2
N=182   Mean=122.4   Standard Deviation=62.72   Range=0-293

DEFINITION: See Variable 217 for definition.

Variable 219   IGO A↔B/COMMON MEMBERSHIP OF A (1960)

OSIRIS: Location 1433   width 7   CARD: deck 21, col. 34-40
Missing data code: 9999999   Decimal place: none   Unit: % x 10^2
N=178   Mean=118.4   Standard Deviation=56.83   Range=0-269

DEFINITION: See Variable 217 for definition and note codes.

Variable 220   IGO A↔B/COMMON MEMBERSHIP OF A (1963)

OSIRIS: Location 1440   width 7   CARD: deck 21, col. 41-47
Missing data code: 9999999   Decimal place: none   Unit: % x 10^2
N=182   Mean=109.9   Standard Deviation=64.31   Range=0-576

DEFINITION: See Variable 217 for definition and note codes.

Variable 221   IGO A↔B/COMMON MEMBERSHIP OF A (1965)

OSIRIS: Location 1447   width 7   CARD: deck 21, col. 48-54
Missing data code: 9999999   Decimal place: none   Unit: % x 10^2
N=182   Mean=105.2   Standard Deviation=38.98   Range=11-211

DEFINITION: See Variable 217 for definition.

Variable 222   NGO A↔B/COMMON MEMBERSHIP OF A (1950)

OSIRIS: Location 1454   width 7   CARD: deck 21, col. 55-61
Missing data code: 9999999   Decimal place: none   Unit: % x 10^2
N=182   Mean=176.6   Standard Deviation=99.54   Range=10-457

DEFINITION: The total membership (i.e., the number of nations in each) of the NGO's to which both nations A and B belong, divided by the total membership of all the NGO's to which nation A belongs. Same sources as Variables 197-201.

-191-

Variable 223   NGO A↔B/COMMON MEMBERSHIP OF A (1955)

OSIRIS: Location 1461   width 7   CARD: deck 21, col. 62-68
Missing data code: 9999999   Decimal place: none   Unit: % x 10^2
N=182   Mean=154.8   Standard Deviation=95.49   Range=4-414

DEFINITION: See Variable 222 for definition.

Variable 224   NGO A↔B/COMMON MEMBERSHIP OF A (1960)

OSIRIS: Location 1468   width 7   CARD: deck 21, col. 69-75
Missing data code: 9999999   Decimal place: none   Unit: % x 10^2
N=182   Mean=147.7   Standard Deviation=82.33   Range=13-374

DEFINITION: See Variable 222 for definition.

Variable 225   NGO A↔B/COMMON MEMBERSHIP OF A (1963)

OSIRIS: Location 1475   width 7   CARD: deck 22, col. 6-12
Missing data code: 9999999   Decimal place: none   Unit: % x 10^2
N=182   Mean=139.0   Standard Deviation=76.47   Range=10-354

DEFINITION: See Variable 222 for definition.

Variable 226   NGO A↔B/COMMON MEMBERSHIP OF A (1965)

OSIRIS: Location 1482   width 7   CARD: deck 22, col. 13-19
Missing data code: 9999999   Decimal place: none   Unit: % x 10^2
N=182   Mean=134.8   Standard Deviation=67.50   Range=22-336

Variable 227   EMBASSY OR LEGATION A→B (1950)

OSIRIS: Location 1489   width 7   CARD: deck 22, col. 20-26
Missing data code: 9999999   Decimal place: none
N=179   Mean=.56   Standard Deviation=.50   Range=0-1

DEFINITION: Rating: embassy or legation A→B - 1, none - 0. Embassy is defined as a diplomatic mission of the first class, headed by an Ambassador Extraordinary and Plenipotentiary. The term refers to the entire mission and staff. Legation is a diplomatic mission headed by an Envoy Extraordinary and Minister Plenipotentiary (second class), a minister-resident (intermediate class), or, in the diplomatic relations between smaller nations. Diplomatic Yearbook, UN.

NOTES:
A. Estimate
B. Refers to mainland China
G. Europa Yearbook, Vols. I and II
H. The Foreign Office List and Diplomatic and Consular Yearbook for 1964.

Variable 228   EMBASSY OR LEGATION A→B (1955)

OSIRIS: Location 1496   width 7   CARD: deck 22, col. 27-33
Missing data code: 9999999   Decimal place: none
N=182   Mean=.76   Standard Deviation=.43   Range=0-1

DEFINITION: See Variable 227 for definition and note codes.

Variable 229   EMBASSY OR LEGATION A→B (1960)

OSIRIS: Location 1503   width 7   CARD: deck 22, col. 34-40
Missing data code: 9999999   Decimal place: none
N=182   Mean=.75   Standard Deviation=.43   Range=0-1

DEFINITION: See Variable 227 for definition and note codes.

Variable 230   EMBASSY OR LEGATION A→B (1963)

OSIRIS: Location 1510   width 7   CARD: deck 22, col. 41-47
Missing data code: 9999999   Decimal place: none
N=182   Mean=.78   Standard Deviation=.42   Range=0-1

DEFINITION: See Variable 227 for definition and note codes.

Variable 231   EMBASSY OR LEGATION A→B (1965)

OSIRIS: Location 1517   width 7   CARD: deck 22, col. 48-54
Missing data code: 9999999   Decimal place: none
N=182   Mean=.77   Standard Deviation=.42   Range=0-1

DEFINITION: See Variable 227 for definition and note codes.

Variable 232   RELATIVE DIPLOMATIC REPRESENTATION A→B (1950)

OSIRIS: Location 1524   width 7   CARD: deck 22, col. 55-61
Missing data code: 9999999   Decimal place: none   Unit: $\% \times 10^2$
N=172   Mean=189.6   Standard Deviation=281.5   Range=0-1667

DEFINITION: The number of embassies or legations that A has in B, divided by total number of embassies or legations that A has in all other countries. See Variable 58 for definitions of embassy and legation. Same source as Variables 227-231.

NOTES: See Variable 227 for note codes.

Variable 233   RELATIVE DIPLOMATIC REPRESENTATION A→B (1955)

OSIRIS: Location 1531   width 7   CARD: deck 22, col. 62-68
Missing data code: 9999999   Decimal place: none   Unit: $\% \times 10^2$
N=182   Mean=153.2   Standard Deviation=123.7   Range=0-560

DEFINITION: See Variable 232 for definition.

NOTES: See Variable 227 for note codes.

Variable 234   RELATIVE DIPLOMATIC REPRESENTATION A→B (1960)

OSIRIS: Location 1538   width 7   CARD: deck 22, col. 69-75
Missing data code: 9999999   Decimal place: none   Unit: $\% \times 10^2$
N=182   Mean=149.3   Standard Deviation=118.2   Range=0-625

DEFINITION: See Variable 232 for definition.

NOTES: See Variable 227 for note codes.

Variable 235   RELATIVE DIPLOMATIC REPRESENTATION A→B (1963)

OSIRIS: Location 1545   width 7   CARD: deck 23, col. 6-12
Missing data code: 9999999   Decimal place: none   Unit: % x 10^2
N=182   Mean=154.8   Standard Deviation=117.7   Range=0-555

DEFINITION: See Variable 232 for definition.

NOTES: See Variable 227 for note codes.

Variable 236   RELATIVE DIPLOMATIC REPRESENTATION A→B (1965)

OSIRIS: Location 1552   width 7   CARD: deck 23, col. 13-19
Missing data code: 9999999   Decimal place: none   Unit: % x 10^2
N=182   Mean=131.7   Standard Deviation=101.1   Range=0-416

DEFINITION: See Variable 232 for definition.

NOTES: See Variable 227 for note codes.

Variable 237   TIME SINCE OPPOSITE SIDES OF A WAR A↔B (1950)

OSIRIS: Location 1559   width 7   CARD: deck 23, col. 20-26
Missing data code: 9999999   Decimal place: none
N=182   Mean=1.29   Standard Deviation=4.51   Range=0-32

DEFINITION: Rating: pre-1900 or never - 0, 1901-1910 - 1, 1911-1920 - 2,
1921-1930 - 4, 1931-1940 - 8, 1941-1950 - 16, 1951-1960 - 32, 1961- - 64.
For the purpose of data collection, hostilities which were recognized as legal
states of war or which involved over 50,000 troops were classified as war. In
some cases hostilities of lesser magnitude which led to important legal or
political results were included. Quincy Wright, A Study of War; World Almanac,
1964; and Worldmark Encyclopedia of the Nations.

NOTES:
A. Estimate
B. Snell, John L., Illusion and Necessity, Boston (1963), p. 96.
C. World Almanac (1964), "Memorial Dates", p. 144.

Variable 238   TIME SINCE OPPOSITE SIDES OF A WAR A↔B (1955)

OSIRIS: Location 1566   width 7   CARD: deck 23, col. 27-33
Missing data code: 9999999   Decimal place: none
N=182   Mean=1.73   Standard Deviation=6.12   Range=0-32

DEFINITION: See Variable 237 for definition and note codes.

Variable 239   TIME SINCE OPPOSITE SIDES OF A WAR A↔B (1960)

OSIRIS: Location 1573   width 7   CARD: deck 23, col. 34-40
Missing data code: 9999999   Decimal place: none
N=182   Mean=2.25   Standard Deviation=7.42   Range=0-32

DEFINITION: See Variable 237 for definition and note codes.

Variable 240   TIME SINCE OPPOSITE SIDES OF A WAR A↔B (1963)

OSIRIS: Location 1580   width 7   CARD: deck 23, col. 41-47
Missing data code: 9999999   Decimal place: none
N=182   Mean=3.65   Standard Deviation=11.72   Range=0-64

DEFINITION: See Variable 237 for definition and note codes.

Variable 241   TIME SINCE OPPOSITE SIDES OF A WAR A↔B (1965)

OSIRIS: Location 1587   width 7   CARD: deck 23, col. 48-54
Missing data code: 9999999   Decimal place: none
N=182   Mean=3.65   Standard Deviation=11.72   Range=0-64

DEFINITION: See Variable 237 for definition and note codes.

Variable 242   TIME SINCE ON SAME SIDES OF WAR A↔B (1950)

OSIRIS: Location 1594   width 7   CARD: deck 23, col. 55-61
Missing data code: 9999999   Decimal place: none
N=182   Mean=8.26   Standard Deviation=8.19   Range=0-32

DEFINITION: Rating: pre-1900 or never - 0, 1901-1910 - 1, 1911-1920 - 2, 1921-1930 - 4, 1931-1940 - 8, 1941-1950 - 16, 1951-1960 - 32, 1961-   - 64. Same sources as Variables 237-241.

NOTES: See Variable 237 for note codes.

Variable 243   TIME SINCE ON SAME SIDES OF WAR A↔B (1955)

OSIRIS: Location 1601   width 7   CARD: deck 23, col. 62-68
Missing data code: 9999999   Decimal place: none
N=182   Mean=8.44   Standard Deviation=8.52   Range=0-32

DEFINITION: See Variable 242 for definition.

NOTES: See Variable 237 for note codes.

Variable 244   TIME SINCE ON SAME SIDES OF WAR A↔B (1960)

OSIRIS: Location 1608   width 7   CARD: deck 23, col. 69-75
Missing data code: 9999999   Decimal place: none
N=182   Mean=8.70   Standard Deviation=8.83   Range=0-32

DEFINITION: See Variable 242 for definition.

NOTES: See Variable 237 for note codes.

Variable 245   TIME SINCE ON SAME SIDES OF WAR A↔B (1963)

OSIRIS: Location 1615   width 7   CARD: deck 24, col. 6-12
Missing data code: 9999999   Decimal place: none
N=182   Mean=8.88   Standard Deviation=8.97   Range=0-32

DEFINITION: See Variable 242 for definition.

NOTES: See Variable 237 for note codes.

Variable 246   TIME SINCE ON SAME SIDES OF WAR A↔B (1965)

OSIRIS: Location 1622   width 7   CARD: deck 24, col. 13-19
Missing data code: 9999999   Decimal place: none
N=182   Mean=8.88   Standard Deviation=8.97   Range=0-32

DEFINITION: See Variable 242 for definition.

NOTES: See Variable 237 for note codes.

Variable 247   LOST TERRITORY A→B (1950)

OSIRIS: Location 1629   width 7   CARD: deck 24, col. 20-26
Missing data code: 9999999   Decimal place: none
N=182   Mean=.016   Standard Deviation=.128   Range=0-1

DEFINITION: A has lost, and not regained, territory to B since 1900 or not. Rating: yes - 1, no - 0. Occupation of a territory by another country during wartime is disregarded. However, if the territorial change becomes permanent after the war has ended then it is counted. Territorial changes for new nations are recorded only after the country has gained independence. Encyclopedia Britannica; and Worldmark Encyclopedia of the Nations.

NOTES: See Variable 237 for note codes.

Variable 248   LOST TERRITORY A→B (1955)

OSIRIS: Location 1636   width 7   CARD: deck 24, col. 27-33
Missing data code: 9999999   Decimal place: none
N=182   Mean=.016   Standard Deviation=.128   Range=0-1

DEFINITION: See Variable 247 for definition.

NOTES: See Variable 237 for note codes.

Variable 249   LOST TERRITORY A→B (1960)

OSIRIS: Location 1643   width 7   CARD: deck 24, col. 34-40
Missing data code: 9999999   Decimal place: none
N=182   Mean=.016   Standard Deviation=.128   Range=0-1

DEFINITION: See Variable 247 for definition.

NOTES: See Variable 237 for note codes.

Variable 250   LOST TERRITORY A→B (1963)

OSIRIS: Location 1650   width 7   CARD: deck 24, col. 41-47
Missing data code: 9999999   Decimal place: none
N=182   Mean=.016   Standard Deviation=.128   Range=0-1

DEFINITION: See Variable 247 for definition.

NOTES: See Variable 237 for note codes.

Variable 251   LOST TERRITORY A→B (1965)

OSIRIS: Location 1657   width 7   CARD: deck 24, col. 48-54
Missing data code: 9999999   Decimal place: none
N=182   Mean=.016   Standard Deviation=.128   Range=0-1

DEFINITION: See Variable 247 for definition.

NOTES: See Variable 237 for note codes.

Variable 252   DEPENDENT A of B (1950)

OSIRIS: Location 1664   width 4   CARD: deck 24, col. 55-58
Missing data code: 9999   Decimal place: none
N=182   Mean=.5   Standard Deviation=2.68   Range=0-16

DEFINITION: A once a colony, territory or part of homeland of B. Rating: pre-1900 or never - 0, 1901-1910 - 1, 1911-1920 - 2, 1921-1930 - 4, 1931-1940 - 8, 1941-1950 - 16, 1951-1960 - 32, after 1961 - 64. Information Please Almanac; Stateman's Yearbook; and The World Almanac.

NOTES:
A. Estimate
B. Information Please Almanac (1964).
C. Military occupation during World War II ignored.

Variable 253   DEPENDENT A of B (1955)

OSIRIS: Location 1668   width 4   CARD: deck 24, col. 59-62
Missing data code: 9999   Decimal place: none
N=182   Mean=.50   Standard Deviation=2.68   Range=0-16

DEFINITION: See Variable 252 for definition and note codes.

Variable 254   DEPENDENT A of B (1960)

OSIRIS: Location 1672   width 4   CARD: deck 24, col. 63-66
Missing data code: 9999   Decimal place: none
N=182   Mean=.50   Standard Deviation=2.68   Range=0-16

DEFINITION: See Variable 252 for definition.

Variable 255   DEPENDENT A of B (1963)

OSIRIS: Location 1676   width 4   CARD: deck 24, col. 67-70
Missing data code: 9999   Decimal place: none
N=182   Mean=.50   Standard Deviation=2.68   Range=0-16

DEFINITION: See Variable 252 for definition and note codes.

Variable 256   DEPENDENT A of B (1965)

OSIRIS: Location 1680   width 4   CARD: deck 24, col. 71-74
Missing data code: 9999   Decimal place: none
N=182   Mean=.41   Standard Deviation=2.42   Range=0-16

DEFINITION: See Variable 252 for definition and note codes.

Variable 257   INDEPENDENCE A↔B (1950)

OSIRIS: Location 1684   width 7   CARD: deck 25, col. 6-12
Missing data code: 9999999   Decimal place: none
N=182   Mean=.40   Standard Deviation=.49   Range=0-1

DEFINITION: Independence of A and B predates 1946 or not. Rating: independence of A and B predates 1946 - 1, no - 0. An entity was classed as independent if it enjoyed some measure of diplomatic recognition as well as effective control over its own foreign affairs and armed forces. Russett, "National Political Units in thd 20th Century," APSR, Vol. 62, No. 3, 932-951; and Worldmark Encyclopedia of Nations.

Variable 258   INDEPENDENCE A↔B (1955)

OSIRIS: Location 1691   width 7   CARD: deck 25, col. 13-19
Missing data code: 9999999   Decimal place: none
N=182   Mean=.40   Standard Deviation=.49   Range=0-1

DEFINITION: See Variable 257 for definition.

NOTES: See Variable 252 for note codes.

Variable 259   INDEPENDENCE A↔B (1960)

OSIRIS: Location 1698   width 7   CARD: deck 25, col. 20-26
Missing data code: 9999999   Decimal place: none
N=182   Mean=.40   Standard Deviation=.49   Range=0-1

DEFINITION: See Variable 257 for definition.

Variable 260   INDEPENDENCE A↔B (1963)

OSIRIS: Location 1705   width 7   CARD: deck 25, col. 27-33
Missing data code: 9999999   Decimal place: none
N=182   Mean=.43   Standard Deviation=.50   Range=0-1

DEFINITION: See Variable 257 for definition.

NOTES: See Variable 252 for note codes.

Variable 261   INDEPENDENCE A↔B (1965)

OSIRIS: Location 1712   width 7   CARD: deck 25, col. 34-40
Missing data code: 9999999   Decimal place: none
N=182   Mean=.43   Standard Deviation=.50   Range=0-1

DEFINITION: See Variable 257 for definition.

NOTES: See Variable 252 for note codes.

Variable 262   COMMON BLOC MEMBERSHIP (1950)

OSIRIS: Location 1719   width 7   CARD: deck 25, col. 41-47
Missing data code: 9999999   Decimal place: none
N=182   Mean=1.14   Standard Deviation=.67   Range=0-2

DEFINITION: Rating: A and B have common bloc membership - 2, different - 1, opposing - 0. Blocs are Communist, Western and neutral. Communist and Western bloc membership is determined by military treaties or alliances with the Soviet Union or the United States. The neutral bloc is a residual category in which nations are categorized if they have no military treaties or alliances with either of the aforementioned bloc leaders. T. N. Dupuy, The Almanac of World Military Power; and Treaties and Alliances of the World.

NOTES: See Variable 252 for note codes.

Variable 263   COMMON BLOC MEMBERSHIP (1955)

OSIRIS: Location 1726   width 7   CARD: deck 25, col. 48-54
Missing data code: 9999999   Decimal place: none
N=182   Mean=1.14   Standard Deviation=.67   Range=0-2

DEFINITION: See Variable 262 for definition.

Variable 264   COMMON BLOC MEMBERSHIP (1960)

OSIRIS: Location 1733   width 7   CARD: deck 25, col. 55-61
Missing data code: 9999999   Decimal place: none
N=182   Mean=1.14   Standard Deviation=.67   Range=0-2

DEFINITION: See Variable 262 for definition.

Variable 265   COMMON BLOC MEMBERSHIP (1963)

OSIRIS: Location 1740   width 7   CARD: deck 25, col. 62-68
Missing data code: 9999999   Decimal place: none
N=182   Mean=1.12   Standard Deviation=.68   Range=0-2

DEFINITION: See Variable 262 for definition.

Variable 266   COMMON BLOC MEMBERSHIP (1965)

OSIRIS: Location 1747   width 7   CARD: deck 25, col. 69-75
Missing data code: 9999999   Decimal place: none
N=182   Mean=1.13   Standard Deviation=.67   Range=0-2

DEFINITION: See Variable 262 for definition.

NOTES: See Variable 252 for note codes.

Variable 267   BLOC POSITION INDEX A↔B (1950)

OSIRIS: Location 1754   width 7   CARD: deck 26, col. 6-12
Missing data code: 9999999   Decimal place: none
N=182   Mean=2.00   Standard Deviation=1.52   Range=0-6

DEFINITION: Bloc position A↔B measured as absolute difference of position on following scale:

1	2	4	6	7
USA	Non-USA Western bloc member	Neutral bloc member	Non-USSR Communist bloc member	USSR

T. N. Dupuy, The Almanac of World Military Power; Treaties and Alliances of the World; and Worldmark Encyclopedia of the Nations.

Variable 268   BLOC POSITION INDEX A↔B (1955)

OSIRIS: Location 1761   width 7   CARD: deck 26, col. 13-19
Missing data code: 9999999   Decimal place: none
N=182   Mean=2.00   Standard Deviation=1.52   Range=0-6

DEFINITION: See Variable 267 for definition.

Variable 269   BLOC POSITION INDEX A↔B (1960)

OSIRIS: Location 1768   width 7   CARD: deck 26, col. 20-26
Missing data code: 9999999   Decimal place: none
N=182   Mean=2.00   Standard Deviation=1.52   Range=0-6

DEFINITION: See Variable 267 for definition.

Variable 270   BLOC POSITION INDEX A↔B (1963)

OSIRIS: Location 1775   width 7   CARD: deck 26, col. 27-33
Missing data code: 9999999   Decimal place: none
N=182   Mean=2.04   Standard Deviation=1.52   Range=0-6

DEFINITION: See Variable 267 for definition.

Variable 271   BLOC POSITION A↔B (1965)

OSIRIS: Location 1782   width 7   CARD: deck 26, col. 34-40
Missing data code: 9999999   Decimal place: none
N=182   Mean=2.04   Standard Deviation=1.52   Range=0-6

DEFINITION: See Variable 267 for definition.

Variable 272   MILITARY ALLIANCE A↔B (1950)

OSIRIS: Location 1789   width 7   CARD: deck 26, col. 41-47
Missing data code: 9999999   Decimal place: none
N=182   Mean=.099   Standard Deviation=.300   Range=0-1

DEFINITION: Two countries are in alliance if a mutual defense treaty exists between them. Rating: mutual defense treaty yes - 1, no - 0. Information Please Almanac; Treaties and Alliances of the World; World Almanac; and The Worldmark Encyclopedia of the Nations.

Variable 273   MILITARY ALLIANCE A↔B (1955)

OSIRIS: Location 1796   width 7   CARD: deck 26, col. 48-54
Missing data code: 9999999   Decimal place: none
N=182   Mean=.121   Standard Deviation=.327   Range=0-1

DEFINITION: See Variable 272 for definition.

Variable 274   MILITARY ALLIANCE A↔B (1960)

OSIRIS: Location 1803   width 7   CARD: deck 26, col. 55-61
Missing data code: 9999999   Decimal place: none
N=182   Mean=.093   Standard Deviation=.292   Range=0-1

DEFINITION: See Variable 272 for definition.

Variable 275   MILITARY ALLIANCE A↔B (1963)

OSIRIS: Location 1810   width 7   CARD: deck 26, col. 62-68
Missing data code: 9999999   Decimal place: none
N=182   Mean=.093   Standard Deviation=.292   Range=0-1

DEFINITION: See Variable 272 for definition.

Variable 276   MILITARY ALLIANCE A↔B (1965)

OSIRIS: Location 1817   width 7   CARD: deck 26, col. 69-75
Missing data code: 9999999   Decimal place: none
N=182   Mean=.115   Standard Deviation=.320   Range=0-1

DEFINITION: See Variable 272 for definition.

SECTION II

APPENDICES: A & B

SECTION II
APPENDIX A: DATA FORMAT AND SUMMARY STATISTICS

APPENDIX A: DATA FORMAT AND SUMMARY STATISTICS

Variable Number	Variable Name	OSIRIS Location	Width	Deck	Card-Image Col.	Missing Data Code	N	Mean	Standard Deviation	Range
1	DYAD	1	3	all	3-5	none	182	101.65	757.51	0-9210
2	AID50	4	4	1	6-9	9999	177	54.06	252.19	0-1701
3	AID55	8	4	1	10-13	9999	181	126.71	692.94	-26-7584
4	AID60	12	4	1	14-17	9999	182	79.78	543.09	0-6849
5	AID63	16	4	1	18-21	9999	181	94.02	591.73	-31-6971
6	AID65	20	4	1	22-25	9999	181	71.51	603.51	0-7500
7	R-AID50	24	7	1	26-32	9999999	181	53.14	323.92	0-2765
8	R-AID55	31	7	1	33-39	9999999	174	135.88	791.53	-7-8938
9	R-AID60	38	7	1	40-46	9999999	179	39.24	195.53	0-1570
10	R-AID63	45	7	1	47-53	9999999	182	79.11	441.07	-6-3900
11	R-AID65	52	7	1	54-60	9999999	181	1.34	2.74	0-22
12	TREATY50	59	7	1	61-67	9999999	182	2.16	4.21	0-25
13	TREATY55	66	7	1	68-74	9999999	182	2.21	2.79	0-15
14	TREATY60	73	7	2	6-12	9999999	182	1.86	2.21	0-12
15	TREATY63	80	7	2	13-19	9999999	182	1.66	2.79	0-20
16	TREATY65	87	7	2	20-26	9999999	182	228.90	609.91	0-7094
17	R-TRTY50	94	7	2	27-33	9999999	182	667.86	1390.3	0-8570
18	R-TRTY55	101	7	2	34-40	9999999	182	819.57	1093.4	0-7500
19	R-TRTY60	108	7	2	41-47	9999999	182	754.64	967.65	0-6667
20	R-TRTY63	115	7	2	48-54	9999999	182	644.00	1089.7	0-7000
21	R-TRTY65	122	7	2	55-61	9999999	182	.02	.17	0-2
22	VISITS50	129	7	2	62-68	9999999	182	.12	.44	0-4
23	VISITS55	136	7	2	69-75	9999999	182	.15	.46	0-3
24	VISITS60	143	7	3	6-12	9999999	182	.23	.63	0-4
25	VISITS63	150	7	3	13-19	9999999	182	.25	.61	0-3
26	VISITS65	157	7	3	20-26	9999999	182	.21	.71	0-5
27	CONFER50	164	7	3	27-33	9999999	182	.74	2.28	0-18
28	CONFER55	171	7	3	34-40	9999999	182	.23	.85	0-7
29	CONFER60	178	7	3	41-47	9999999	182	.5	1.18	0-9
30	CONFER63	185	7	3	48-54	9999999	182	1.99	3.30	0-23
31	CONFER65	192	7	3	55-61	9999999	182	161.20	713.86	0-6388
32	BOOKS50	199	7	3	62-68	9999999	161	183.2	738.77	0-5851
33	BOOKS55	206	7	3	69-75	9999999	157	338.0	1529.9	0-12981
34	BOOKS60	213	7	4	6-12	9999999	147	406.84	2080.6	0-19150
35	BOOKS63	220	7	4	13-19	9999999	173	556.1	2860.7	0-26219
36	BOOKS65	227	7	4	20-26	9999999	168			

-202-

SECTION II

APPENDIX A: DATA FORMAT AND SUMMARY STATISTICS

Variable Number	Variable Name	OSIRIS Location	Width	Deck	Card-Image Col.	Missing Data Code	N	Mean	Standard Deviation	Range
37	R-BOOK50	234	7	4	27-33	9999999	161	59.78	374.04	0-4408
38	R-BOOK55	241	7	4	34-40	9999999	151	42.5	186.02	0-1417
39	R-BOOK60	248	7	4	41-47	9999999	146	88.10	531.33	0-5995
40	R-BOOK63	255	7	4	48-54	9999999	162	110.36	556.39	0-5982
41	R-BOOK65	262	7	4	55-61	9999999	150	159.82	755.53	0-5822
42	TRANSL50	269	7	4	62-68	9999999	161	10.41	49.94	0-400
43	TRANSL55	276	7	4	69-75	9999999	179	18.17	69.87	0-620
44	TRANSL60	283	7	5	6-12	9999999	177	34.37	116.46	0-750
45	TRANSL63	290	7	5	13-19	9999999	177	41.27	152.45	0-1214
46	TRANSL65	297	7	5	20-26	9999999	179	43.36	139.85	0-1055
47	R-TRAN50	304	7	5	27-33	9999999	161	246.71	853.56	0-5229
48	R-TRAN55	311	7	5	34-40	9999999	172	359.72	1091.3	0-5840
49	R-TRAN60	318	7	5	41-47	9999999	176	553.28	1552.7	0-7714
50	R-TRAN63	325	7	5	48-54	9999999	177	569.99	1569.7	0-8266
51	R-TRAN65	332	7	5	55-61	9999999	179	776.22	2029.9	0-1000
52	WARNDF50	339	4	5	62-65	9999	182	.066	.51	0-6
53	WARNDF55	343	4	5	66-69	9999	182	.044	.36	0-4
54	WARNDF60	347	4	5	70-73	9999	182	.088	.40	0-3
55	WARNDF63	351	4	5	74-77	9999	182	.016	.13	0-1
56	WARNDF65	355	4	6	6-9	9999	182	.06	.46	0-5
57	WARTOT50	359	7	6	10-16	9999999	182	.027	.16	0-1
58	WARTOT55	366	7	6	17-23	9999999	182	0.0	0.0	0-0
59	WARTOT60	373	7	6	24-30	9999999	182	0.0	0.0	0-0
60	WARTOT63	380	7	6	31-37	9999999	182	0.0	0.0	0-0
61	WARTOT65	387	7	6	38-44	9999999	0	0.0	0.0	0-0
62	VIOLAC50	394	7	6	45-51	9999999	182	.071	.26	0-1
63	VIOLAC55	401	7	6	52-58	9999999	182	.049	.22	0-1
64	VIOLAC60	408	7	6	59-65	9999999	182	.044	.21	0-1
65	VIOLAC63	415	7	6	66-72	9999999	182	.044	.23	0-2
66	VIOLAC65	422	7	6	73-79	9999999	182	.050	.22	0-1
67	MILACT50	429	7	7	6-12	9999999	182	.077	.48	0-5
68	MILACT55	436	7	7	13-19	9999999	182	1.24	9.52	0-98
69	MILACT60	443	7	7	20-26	9999999	182	.11	.60	0-5
70	MILACT63	450	7	7	27-33	9999999	182	.082	.44	0-3
71	MILACT65	457	7	7	34-40	9999999	182	.46	2.30	0-16
72	DAYSVL50	464	7	7	41-47	9999999	182	2.1	10.92	0-61
73	DAYSVL55	471	7	7	48-54	9999999	182	4.23	37.17	0-355
74	DAYSVL60	478	7	7	55-61	9999999	182	.13	.72	0-5

-203-

SECTION II

APPENDIX A: DATA FORMAT AND SUMMARY STATISTICS

Variable Number	Variable Name	OSIRIS Location	Width	Deck	Card-Image Col.	Missing Data Code	N	Mean	Standard Deviation	Range
75	DAYSVL63	485	7	7	62-68	9999999	182	.48	5.29	0-71
76	DAYSVL65	492	7	7	69-75	9999999	182	.48	2.43	0-18
77	NEGBEH50	499	7	8	6-12	9999999	182	.62	2.56	0-23
78	NEGBEH55	506	7	8	13-19	9999999	182	.41	1.49	0-11
79	NEGBEH60	513	7	8	20-26	9999999	182	.56	2.82	0-30
80	NEGBEH63	520	7	8	27-33	9999999	182	.13	.49	0-4
81	NEGBEH65	527	7	8	34-40	9999999	182	5.0	1.70	0-14
82	SEVDIP50	534	7	8	41-47	9999999	182	0.0	0.0	0-0
83	SEVDIP55	541	7	8	48-54	9999999	182	0.0	0.0	0-0
84	SEVDIP60	548	7	8	55-61	9999999	182	.005	.074	0-1
85	SEVDIP63	555	7	8	62-68	9999999	182	0.0	0.0	0-0
86	SEVDIP65	562	7	8	69-75	9999999	182	.011	.10	0-1
87	EXPREC50	569	4	9	6-9	9999	182	.022	.15	0-1
88	EXPREC55	573	4	9	10-13	9999	182	.005	.074	0-1
89	EXPREC60	577	4	9	14-17	9999	182	.060	.37	0-3
90	EXPREC63	581	4	9	18-21	9999	182	.016	.13	0-1
91	EXPREC65	585	4	9	22-25	9999	182	.038	.27	0-3
92	BCTEMB50	589	7	9	26-32	9999999	182	.049	.28	0-2
93	BCTEMB55	596	7	9	33-39	9999999	182	.005	.074	0-1
94	BCTEMB60	603	7	9	40-46	9999999	182	.022	.18	0-2
95	BCTEMB63	610	7	9	47-53	9999999	182	.016	.17	0-2
96	BCTEMB65	617	7	9	54-60	9999999	182	.071	.43	0-5
97	AIDREB50	624	7	9	61-67	9999999	182	.010	.10	0-1
98	AIDREB55	631	7	9	68-74	9999999	182	.005	.074	0-1
99	AIDREB60	638	7	10	6-12	9999999	182	.011	.10	0-1
100	AIDREB63	645	7	10	13-19	9999999	182	.016	.13	0-1
101	AIDREB65	652	7	10	20-26	9999999	182	.016	.17	0-2
102	NEGCOM50	659	7	10	27-33	9999999	182	2.01	10.2	0-102
103	NEGCOM55	666	7	10	34-40	9999999	182	2.55	10.47	0-90
104	NEGCOM60	673	7	10	41-47	9999999	182	2.11	9.83	0-82
105	NEGCOM63	680	7	10	48-54	9999999	182	.96	3.87	0-26
106	NEGCOM65	687	7	10	55-61	9999999	182	1.99	8.84	0-84
107	ACCUSN50	694	7	10	62-68	9999999	182	1.20	6.71	0-71
108	ACCUSN55	701	7	10	69-75	9999999	182	1.80	8.31	0-74
109	ACCUSN60	708	7	11	6-12	9999999	182	1.27	6.12	0-50
110	ACCUSN63	715	7	11	13-19	9999999	182	.56	2.77	0-20
111	ACCUSN65	722	7	11	20-26	9999999	182	.96	4.65	0-42

-205-

SECTION II

APPENDIX A: DATA FORMAT AND SUMMARY STATISTICS

Variable Number	Variable Name	OSIRIS Location	Width	Deck	Card-Image Col.	Missing Data Code	N	Mean	Standard Deviation	Range
112	PROTST50	729	7	11	27-33	9999999	182	.16	.75	0-8
113	PROTST55	736	7	11	34-40	9999999	182	.26	.87	0-5
114	PROTST60	743	7	11	41-47	9999999	182	.14	.70	0-7
115	PROTST63	750	7	11	48-54	9999999	182	.25	1.12	0-10
116	PROTST65	757	7	11	55-61	9999999	182	.34	1.46	0-13
117	UNOFAC50	764	7	11	62-68	9999999	182	.027	.19	0-2
118	UNOFAC55	771	7	11	69-75	9999999	182	.033	.21	0-2
119	UNOFAC60	778	7	12	6-12	9999999	182	.022	.18	0-2
120	UNOFAC63	785	7	12	13-19	9999999	182	.027	.19	0-2
121	UNOFAC65	792	7	12	20-26	9999999	182	.082	.57	0-6
122	ATTACK50	799	4	12	27-30	9999	182	.011	.15	0-2
123	ATTACK55	803	4	12	31-34	9999	182	.011	.10	0-1
124	ATTACK60	807	4	12	35-38	9999	182	.005	.074	0-1
125	ATTACK63	811	4	12	39-42	9999	182	.016	.17	0-2
126	ATTACK65	815	4	12	43-46	9999	182	.005	.074	0-1
127	NVBEH50	819	7	12	47-53	9999999	182	.033	.18	0-1
128	NVBEH55	826	7	12	54-60	9999999	182	.055	.42	0-5
129	NVBEH60	833	7	12	61-67	9999999	182	.082	.42	0-3
130	NVBEH63	840	7	12	68-74	9999999	182	.016	.17	0-2
131	NVBEH65	847	7	13	6-12	9999999	182	.27	1.43	0-16
132	WD-UN50	854	7	13	13-19	9999999	132	434.85	1147.3	-2361-2455
133	WD-UN55	861	7	13	20-26	9999999	132	209.91	940.98	-2630-1749
134	WD-UN60	868	7	13	27-33	9999999	156	111.42	908.93	-2267-1692
135	WD-UN63	875	7	13	34-40	9999999	156	606.92	908.64	-1619-2186
136	WD-UN65	882	7	13	41-47	9999999	131	499.48	957.30	-1884-2927
137	D-UN50	889	7	13	48-54	9999999	132	118.38	813.04	-2446-1452
138	D-UN55	896	7	13	55-61	9999999	132	217.23	965.79	-2738-2158
139	D-UN60	903	7	13	62-68	9999999	156	145.07	936.49	-2264-2210
140	D-UN63	910	7	13	69-75	9999999	156	596.90	903.86	-1993-1815
141	D-UN65	917	7	14	6-12	9999999	132	582.58	1097.5	-1557-4082
142	TOURIS50	924	7	14	13-19	9999999	120	439.11	1779.4	0-12758
143	TOURIS55	931	7	14	20-26	9999999	141	67.98	278.80	0-2391
144	TOURIS60	938	7	14	27-33	9999999	149	123.77	497.96	0-4265
145	TOURIS63	945	7	14	34-40	9999999	171	111.37	488.19	0-5091
146	TOURIS65	952	7	14	41-47	9999999	153	165.73	679.04	0-6743
147	R-TOUR50	959	7	14	48-54	9999999	123	140.09	501.89	0-3071
148	R-TOUR55	966	7	14	55-61	9999999	144	144.79	505.46	0-3800
149	R-TOUR60	973	7	14	62-68	9999999	151	280.40	1407.2	0-16180
150	R-TOUR63	980	7	14	69-75	9999999	168	152.42	477.81	0-3444
151	R-TOUR65	987	7	15	6-12	9999999	156	159.97	476.98	0-2801

SECTION II

APPENDIX A: DATA FORMAT AND SUMMARY STATISTICS

Variable Number	Variable Name	OSIRIS Location	Width	Deck	Card-Image Col.	Missing Data Code	N	Mean	Standard Deviation	Range
152	T/POPU50	994	7	15	13-19	9999999	123	255.78	1473.0	0-14640
153	T/POPU55	1001	7	15	20-26	9999999	144	2.84	15.32	0-166
154	T/POPU60	1008	7	15	27-33	9999999	151	31.79	115.9	0-880
155	T/POPU63	1015	7	15	34-40	9999999	170	22.71	88.21	0-676
156	T/POPU65	1022	7	15	41-47	9999999	156	43.97	173.57	0-1373
157	EMIGRA50	1029	7	15	48-54	9999999	160	101.24	516.94	0-5612
158	EMIGRA55	1036	7	15	55-61	9999999	162	57.85	285.11	0-2405
159	EMIGRA60	1043	7	15	62-68	9999999	162	50.27	220.1	0-2087
160	EMIGRA63	1050	7	15	69-75	9999999	154	40.31	216.5	0-2366
161	EMIGRA65	1057	7	16	6-12	9999999	149	43.42	243.9	0-2428
162	R-EMIG50	1064	7	16	13-19	9999999	143	22.78	109.6	0-948
163	R-EMIG55	1071	7	16	20-26	9999999	152	110.1	459.8	0-5869
164	R-EMIG60	1078	7	16	27-33	9999999	147	112.4	583.1	0-5091
165	R-EMIG63	1085	7	16	34-40	9999999	149	93.88	625.8	0-6263
166	R-EMIG65	1092	7	16	41-47	9999999	141	52.0	499.3	0-5839
167	E/POPU50	1099	4	16	48-51	9999	153	29.28	119.0	0-953
168	E/POPU55	1103	4	16	52-55	9999	166	18.34	87.26	0-874
169	E/POPU60	1107	4	16	56-59	9999	163	112.1	539.8	0-5034
170	E/POPU63	1111	4	16	60-63	9999	167	38.02	278.0	0-3450
171	E/POPU65	1115	4	16	64-67	9999	161	23.44	155.3	0-1725
172	STUDNT50	1119	7	16	68-74	9999999	137	41.65	170.19	0-1099
173	STUDNT55	1126	7	17	6-12	9999999	170	84.91	452.0	0-4964
174	STUDNT60	1133	7	17	13-19	9999999	178	141.9	741.6	0-7500
175	STUDNT63	1140	7	17	20-26	9999999	182	131.1	548.9	0-6387
176	STUDNT65	1147	7	17	27-33	9999999	148	180.7	818.4	0-7518
177	R-STUD50	1154	7	17	34-40	9999999	135	12.67	54.78	0-361
178	R-STUD55	1161	7	17	41-47	9999999	170	101.4	518.6	0-4611
179	R-STUD60	1168	7	17	48-54	9999999	177	38.51	198.4	0-1932
180	R-STUD63	1175	7	17	55-61	9999999	182	59.71	257.0	0-2038
181	R-STUD65	1182	7	17	62-68	9999999	145	252.34	1348.72	0-13638
182	EXPORT50	1189	7	17	69-75	9999999	180	396.6	1010.3	0-7145
183	EXPORT55	1196	7	18	6-12	9999999	182	552.7	1415.6	0-9304
184	EXPORT60	1203	7	18	13-19	9999999	182	712.0	1744.1	0-11386
185	EXPORT63	1210	7	18	20-26	9999999	182	730.84	1759.4	0-11729
186	EXPORT65	1217	7	18	27-33	9999999	171	883.7	2246.9	0-16150
187	R-EXPT50	1224	7	18	34-40	9999999	155	309.5	858.0	0-6316
188	R-EXPT55	1231	7	18	41-47	9999999	182	312.2	828.7	0-6754
189	R-EXPT60	1238	7	18	48-54	9999999	182	316.4	744.4	0-5322

SECTION II
APPENDIX A: DATA FORMAT AND SUMMARY STATISTICS

Variable Number	Variable Name	OSIRIS Location	Width	Deck	Card-Image Col.	Missing Data Code	N	Mean	Standard Deviation	Range
190	R-EXPT63	1245	7	18	55-61	9999999	182	271.4	578.4	0-3773
191	R-EXPT65	1252	7	18	62-68	9999999	171	288.6	635.9	0-4699
192	E/GNP50	1259	7	18	69-75	9999999	163	43.83	178.1	0-2028
193	E/GNP55	1266	7	19	6-12	9999999	182	40.12	151.7	0-1824
194	E/GNP60	1273	7	19	13-19	9999999	182	36.26	111.3	0-1197
195	E/GNP63	1280	7	19	20-26	9999999	182	27.69	65.03	0-432
196	E/GNP65	1287	7	19	27-33	9999999	171	31.01	93.86	0-1007
197	IG050	1294	4	19	34-37	9999	182	12.50	10.22	0-48
198	IG055	1298	4	19	38-41	9999	182	16.93	10.04	0-48
199	IG060	1302	4	19	42-45	9999	182	18.23	10.43	0-57
200	IG063	1306	4	19	46-49	9999	182	19.53	11.11	0-57
201	IG065	1310	4	19	50-53	9999	182	23.10	11.33	2-65
202	R-IG050	1314	7	19	54-60	9999999	182	4325.2	2868.6	0-9999
203	R-IG055	1321	7	19	61-67	9999999	182	5167.4	2840.8	0-1000
204	R-IG060	1328	7	19	68-74	9999999	181	5183.0	2718.8	0-1000
205	R-IG063	1335	7	20	6-12	9999999	182	4856.7	2440.9	0-1000
206	R-IG065	1342	7	20	13-19	9999999	182	5413.8	2117.8	833-1000
207	NG050	1349	7	20	20-26	9999999	182	85.56	81.98	3-426
208	NG055	1356	7	20	27-33	9999999	182	108.8	114.2	2-579
209	NG060	1363	7	20	34-40	9999999	182	140.6	127.1	8-654
210	NG063	1370	7	20	41-47	9999999	182	169.6	150.9	5-784
211	NG065	1377	7	20	48-54	9999999	182	187.2	151.3	25-811
212	R-NG050	1384	7	20	55-61	9999999	182	4864.5	2758.4	194-9999
213	R-NG055	1391	7	20	62-68	9999999	182	4712.8	2926.4	77-9730
214	R-NG060	1398	7	20	69-75	9999999	182	4972.3	2799.2	293-9509
215	R-NG063	1405	7	21	6-12	9999999	182	5016.2	2807.5	208-9545
216	R-NG065	1412	7	21	13-19	9999999	182	5208.8	2641.1	499-9455
217	N-IG050	1419	7	21	20-26	9999999	182	135.4	86.37	0-367
218	N-IG055	1426	7	21	27-33	9999999	182	122.4	62.72	0-293
219	N-IG060	1433	7	21	34-40	9999999	182	118.4	56.83	0-269
220	N-IG063	1440	7	21	41-47	9999999	178	109.9	64.31	0-576
221	N-IG065	1447	7	21	48-54	9999999	182	105.2	38.98	11-211
222	N-NG050	1454	7	21	55-61	9999999	182	176.6	99.54	10-457
223	N-NG055	1461	7	21	62-68	9999999	182	154.8	95.49	4-414
224	N-NG060	1468	7	21	69-75	9999999	182	147.7	82.33	13-374
225	N-NG063	1475	7	22	6-12	9999999	182	139.0	76.47	10-354
226	N-NG065	1482	7	22	13-19	9999999	182	134.8	67.50	22-336
227	EMBLEG50	1489	7	22	20-26	9999999	179	.56	.50	0-1
228	EMBLEG55	1496	7	22	27-33	9999999	182	.76	.43	0-1

-207-

SECTION II

APPENDIX A: DATA FORMAT AND SUMMARY STATISTICS

Variable Number	Variable Name	OSIRIS Location	Width	Deck	Card-Image Col.	Missing Data Code	N	Mean	Standard Deviation	Range
229	EMBLEG60	1503	7	22	34-40	9999999	182	.75	.43	0-1
230	EMBLEG63	1510	7	22	41-47	9999999	182	.78	.42	0-1
231	EMBLEG65	1517	7	22	48-54	99999-9	182	.77	.42	0-1
232	R-EMB50	1524	7	22	55-61	9999999	172	189.6	281.5	0-1667
233	R-EMB55	1531	7	22	62-68	9999999	182	153.2	123.7	0-560
234	R-EMB60	1538	7	22	69-75	9999999	182	149.3	118.2	0-625
235	R-EMB63	1545	7	23	6-12	9999999	182	154.8	117.7	0-555
236	R-EMB65	1552	7	23	13-19	9999999	182	131.7	101.1	0-416
237	WAROPP50	1559	7	23	20-26	9999999	182	1.29	4.51	0-32
238	WAROPP55	1566	7	23	27-33	9999999	182	1.73	6.12	0-32
239	WAROPP60	1573	7	23	34-40	9999999	182	2.25	7.42	0-32
240	WAROPP63	1580	7	23	41-47	9999999	182	3.65	11.72	0-64
241	WAROPP65	1587	7	23	48-54	9999999	182	3.65	11.72	0-64
242	WARSAM50	1594	7	23	55-61	9999999	182	8.26	8.19	0-32
243	WARSAM55	1601	7	23	62-68	9999999	182	8.44	8.52	0-32
244	WARSAM60	1608	7	23	69-75	9999999	182	8.70	8.83	0-32
245	WARSAM63	1615	7	24	6-12	9999999	182	8.88	8.97	0-32
246	WARSAM65	1622	7	24	13-19	9999999	182	8.88	8.97	0-32
247	LOSTER50	1629	7	24	20-26	9999999	182	.016	.128	0-1
248	LOSTER55	1636	7	24	27-33	9999999	182	.016	.128	0-1
249	LOSTER60	1643	7	24	34-40	9999999	182	.016	.128	0-1
250	LOSTER63	1650	7	24	41-47	9999999	182	.016	.128	0-1
251	LOSTER65	1657	7	24	48-54	9999999	182	.016	.128	0-1
252	DEPEND50	1664	4	24	55-58	9999	182	.50	2.68	0-16
253	DEPEND55	1668	4	24	59-62	9999	182	.50	2.68	0-16
254	DEPEND60	1672	4	24	63-66	9999	182	.50	2.68	0-16
255	DEPEND63	1676	4	24	67-70	9999	182	.50	2.68	0-16
256	DEPEND65	1680	4	24	71-74	9999	182	.41	2.42	0-16
257	INDEP50	1684	7	25	6-12	9999999	182	.40	.49	0-1
258	INDEP55	1691	7	25	13-19	9999999	182	.40	.49	0-1
259	INDEP60	1698	7	25	20-26	9999999	182	.40	.49	0-1
260	INDEP63	1705	7	25	27-33	9999999	182	.43	.50	0-1
261	INDEP65	1712	7	25	34-40	9999999	182	.43	.50	0-1
262	COMBLC50	1719	7	25	41-47	9999999	182	1.14	.67	0-2
263	COMBLC55	1726	7	25	48-54	9999999	182	1.14	.67	0-2
264	COMBLC60	1733	7	25	55-61	9999999	182	1.14	.67	0-2
265	COMBLC63	1740	7	25	62-68	9999999	182	1.12	.68	0-2
266	COMBLC65	1747	7	25	69-75	9999999	182	1.13	.67	0-2

SECTION II

APPENDIX A: DATA FORMAT AND SUMMARY STATISTICS

Variable Number	Variable Name	OSIRIS Location	Width	Deck	Card-Image Col.	Missing Data Code	N	Mean	Standard Deviation	Range
267	COMPOS50	1754	7	26	6-12	9999999	182	2.00	1.52	0-6
268	COMPOS55	1761	7	26	13-19	9999999	182	2.00	1.52	0-6
269	COMPOS60	1768	7	26	20-26	9999999	182	2.00	1.52	0-6
270	COMPOS63	1775	7	26	27-33	9999999	182	2.04	1.52	0-6
271	COMPOS65	1782	7	26	34-40	9999999	182	2.04	1.52	0-6
272	ALLIAN50	1789	7	26	41-47	9999999	182	.099	.300	0-1
273	ALLIAN55	1796	7	26	48-54	9999999	182	.121	.327	0-1
274	ALLIAN60	1803	7	26	55-61	9999999	182	.093	.292	0-1
275	ALLIAN63	1810	7	26	62-68	9999999	182	.093	.292	0-1
276	ALLIAN65	1817	7	26	69-75	9999999	182	.115	.320	0-1

SECTION II

APPENDIX B: NOTES

SECTION II

APPENDIX B: NOTES

SECTION II

APPENDIX B: NOTES

SECTION II
APPENDIX B: NOTES

BEHAVIOR OF NATION DYADS, 1950-1965: NOTES, VARIABLES 2-21

KEY: Variable 1, the numbers on the extreme left and right of each page, represent the dyad number.

Nations Included in the Selected Dyadic Sample

Brazil=BRA	Cuba=CUB	Indonesia=INS	Netherlands=NTH	United Kingdom=UNK
Burma=BUR	Egypt=EGP	Israel=ISR	Poland=POL	USA=USA
China=CHN	India=IND	Jordan=JOR	USSR=USR	

#	Dyad	#	Dyad	#	Dyad	#	Dyad	#	Dyad	#	Dyad
1	BRA-BUR	27	CHN-BRA	53	EGP-BRA	79	INS-BRA	105	JOR-BRA	131	POL-BRA	157	UNK-BRA
2	BRA-CHN	28	CHN-BUR	54	EGP-BUR	80	INS-BUR	106	JOR-BUR	132	POL-BUR	158	UNK-BUR
3	BRA-CUB	29	CHN-CUB	55	EGP-CHN	81	INS-CHN	107	JOR-CHN	133	POL-CHN	159	UNK-CHN
4	BRA-EGP	30	CHN-EGP	56	EGP-CUB	82	INS-CUB	108	JOR-CUB	134	POL-CUB	160	UNK-CUB
5	BRA-IND	31	CHN-IND	57	EGP-IND	83	INS-EGP	109	JOR-EGP	135	POL-EGP	161	UNK-EGP
6	BRA-INS	32	CHN-INS	58	EGP-INS	84	INS-IND	110	JOR-IND	136	POL-IND	162	UNK-IND
7	BRA-ISR	33	CHN-ISR	59	EGP-ISR	85	INS-ISR	111	JOR-INS	137	POL-INS	163	UNK-INS
8	BRA-JOR	34	CHN-JOR	60	EGP-JOR	86	INS-JOR	112	JOR-ISR	138	POL-ISR	164	UNK-ISR
9	BRA-NTH	35	CHN-NTH	61	EGP-NTH	87	IND-NTH	113	JOR-NTH	139	POL-NTH	165	UNK-JOR
10	BRA-POL	36	CHN-POL	62	EGP-POL	88	IND-POL	114	JOR-POL	140	POL-NTH	166	UNK-NTH
11	BRA-USR	37	CHN-USR	63	EGP-USR	89	IND-USR	115	JOR-USR	141	POL-POL	167	UNK-POL
12	BRA-UNK	38	CHN-UNK	64	EGP-UNK	90	IND-UNK	116	JOR-UNK	142	POL-UNK	168	UNK-USR
13	BRA-USA	39	CHN-USA	65	EGP-USA	91	IND-USA	117	JOR-USA	143	POL-USA	169	UNK-USA
14	BUR-BRA	40	CUB-BRA	66	ISR-BRA	92	IND-BRA	118	NTH-BRA	144	USR-BRA	170	USA-BRA
15	BUR-CHN	41	CUB-BUR	67	ISR-BUR	93	IND-BUR	119	NTH-BUR	145	USR-BUR	171	USA-BUR
16	BUR-CUB	42	CUB-CHN	68	ISR-CHN	94	IND-CHN	120	NTH-CHN	146	USR-CHN	172	USA-CHN
17	BUR-EGP	43	CUB-EGP	69	ISR-CUB	95	IND-CUB	121	NTH-CUB	147	USR-CUB	173	USA-CUB
18	BUR-IND	44	CUB-IND	70	ISR-EGP	96	IND-EGP	122	NTH-EGP	148	USR-EGP	174	USA-EGP
19	BUR-INS	45	CUB-INS	71	ISR-IND	97	IND-INS	123	NTH-IND	149	USR-IND	175	USA-IND
20	BUR-ISR	46	CUB-ISR	72	ISR-INS	98	IND-INS	124	NTH-INS	150	USR-INS	176	USA-INS
21	BUR-JOR	47	CUB-JOR	73	ISR-JOR	99	IND-JOR	125	NTH-ISR	151	USR-ISR	177	USA-ISR
22	BUR-NTH	48	CUB-NTH	74	ISR-NTH	100	IND-NTH	126	NTH-JOR	152	USR-JOR	178	USA-JOR
23	BUR-POL	49	CUB-POL	75	ISR-POL	101	IND-POL	127	NTH-POL	153	USR-NTH	179	USA-NTH
24	BUR-USR	50	CUB-USR	76	ISR-USR	102	IND-USR	128	NTH-USR	154	USR-POL	180	USA-POL
25	BUR-UK	51	CUB-UNK	77	ISR-UNK	103	IND-UNK	129	NTH-UNK	155	USR-UNK	181	USA-USR
26	BUR-USA	52	CUB-USA	78	ISR-USA	104	IND-USA	130	NTH-USA	156	USR-USA	182	USA-UNK

-213-

-214-

SECTION II

APPENDIX B: NOTES

-215-

SECTION II

APPENDIX B: NOTES

SECTION II

APPENDIX B: NOTES

BEHAVIOR OF NATION DYADS, 1950-1965: NOTES, VARIABLES 23-46

1	23	24	25	26	32	33	34	35	36	37	38	39	40	41	42	43	44	45	46	1
113					A	A	A	G	A	A	A	A	G	A	A				H	113
114					A	A	A	A	A	A	A	A	A	A	A				H	114
115					A	A	A	A	A	A	A	A	A	A	A				H	115
116					A	A	A	G	A	A	A	A	A	A	A				H	116
117					A	A	A	G	A	A	A	A	A	A	A				H	117
118																				118
119					B															119
120					B												B	B		120
121																				121
122					B															122
123																				123
124					B	A	A			B	A									124
125					B	A				B	A	A								125
126					B					B										126
127																	B	B		127
128					A	A	A	A	A	A	A	A	A	A	A		B	B		128
129					A	A	A	A	A	A	A	A	A	A	A		B			129
130					A	A	A	A	A	A	A	A	A	A	A					130
131					A	A	A	F	A	A	A	A	A	A	A			B		131
132					A	A	A	A	A	A	A	A	A	A	A					132
133					A	A	A	A	A	A	A	A	A	A	A		B			133
134					A	A	A	A	A	A	A	A	A	A	A					134
135					A	A	A	A	A	A	A	A	A	A	A					135
136					A	A	A	G	A	A	A	A	A	A	A					136
137					A	A	A	A	A	A	A	A	A	A	A	A				137
138					A	A	A	G	A	A	A	A	A	A	A		B	B		138
139					A	A	A	G	A	A	A	A	A	A	A		B	B		139
140																	B			140
141								G												141
142					A	A	A	G	A	A	A	A	A	A	A		A	B		142
143					A	A	A	A	A	A	A	A	A	A	A					143
144																				144
145					A			F	A	A	A									145
146					A				A	A	A			A						146
147					A	A	A	A	A	A	A	A	A	A						147
148					A	A	A	G	A	A	A	G	A							148
149																				149
150																				150
151								G												151
152								G												152
153																	B	B		153
154																	B			154
155																				155
156																				156
157																				157
158																				158
159																A	B	B		159
160																				160
161																				161
162																				162
163																				163
164					B					B										164
165																				165
166																				166
167																				167
168					B					B							B	B		168

-216-

SECTION II
APPENDIX B: NOTES

BEHAVIOR OF NATION DYADS, 1950-1965: NOTES, VARIABLES 23-46

	23	24	25	26	32	33	34	35	36	37	38	39	40	41	42	43	44	45	46	1
169																				169
170																				170
171																D	D		D	171
172					B															172
173																				173
174																	A			174
175																	A			175
176																A	B			176
177																				177
178										B								B		178
179										B										179
180					B												B	B		180
181					B					B					D	D	D	D	D	181
182																				182

KEY: Variable 1, the numbers on the extreme left and right of each page, represent the dyad number.

Brazil=BRA	Cuba=CUB	Indonesia=INS	Netherlands=NTH	United Kingdom=UNK
Burma=BUR	Egypt=EGP	Israel=ISR	Poland=POL	USA=USA
China=CHN	India=IND	Jordan=JOR	USSR=USR	

Nations Included in the Selected Dyadic Sample

1	BRA→BUR	27	CHN→BRA	53	EGP→BRA	79	INS→BRA	105	JOR→BRA	131	NTH→BRA	157	POL→BRA
2	BRA→CHN	28	CHN→BUR	54	EGP→BUR	80	INS→BUR	106	JOR→BUR	132	NTH→BUR	158	POL→BUR
3	BRA→CUB	29	CHN→CUB	55	EGP→CHN	81	INS→CHN	107	JOR→CHN	133	NTH→CHN	159	POL→CHN
4	BRA→EGP	30	CHN→EGP	56	EGP→CUB	82	INS→CUB	108	JOR→CUB	134	NTH→CUB	160	POL→CUB
5	BRA→IND	31	CHN→IND	57	EGP→IND	83	INS→EGP	109	JOR→EGP	135	NTH→EGP	161	POL→EGP
6	BRA→INS	32	CHN→INS	58	EGP→INS	84	INS→IND	110	JOR→IND	136	NTH→IND	162	POL→IND
7	BRA→ISR	33	CHN→ISR	59	EGP→ISR	85	INS→ISR	111	JOR→INS	137	NTH→INS	163	POL→INS
8	BRA→JOR	34	CHN→JOR	60	EGP→JOR	86	INS→JOR	112	JOR→ISR	138	NTH→ISR	164	POL→ISR
9	BRA→NTH	35	CHN→NTH	61	EGP→NTH	87	IND→NTH	113	JOR→NTH	139	NTH→JOR	165	POL→JOR
10	BRA→POL	36	CHN→POL	62	EGP→POL	88	IND→POL	114	JOR→POL	140	NTH→IND	166	POL→NTH
11	BRA→USR	37	CHN→USR	63	EGP→USR	89	IND→USR	115	JOR→USR	141	NTH→INS	167	POL→USR
12	BRA→UNK	38	CHN→UNK	64	EGP→UNK	90	IND→UNK	116	JOR→UNK	142	NTH→ISR	168	POL→UNK
13	BRA→USA	39	CHN→USA	65	EGP→USA	91	IND→USA	117	JOR→USA	143	NTH→JOR	169	POL→USA
14	BUR→BRA	40	CUB→BRA	66	IND→BRA	92	ISR→BRA	118	NTH→BRA	144	NTH→POL	170	USR→BRA
15	BUR→CHN	41	CUB→CHN	67	IND→BUR	93	ISR→BUR	119	NTH→BUR	145	NTH→USR	171	USR→BUR
16	BUR→CUB	42	CUB→CUB	68	IND→CHN	94	ISR→CHN	120	NTH→CHN	146	NTH→UNK	172	USR→CHN
17	BUR→EGP	43	CUB→EGP	69	IND→CUB	95	ISR→CUB	121	NTH→CUB	147	NTH→USA	173	USR→CUB
18	BUR→IND	44	CUB→IND	70	IND→EGP	96	ISR→EGP	122	NTH→EGP	148		174	USR→EGP
19	BUR→INS	45	CUB→INS	71	IND→INS	97	ISR→IND	123	NTH→IND	149		175	USR→IND
20	BUR→ISR	46	CUB→ISR	72	IND→ISR	98	ISR→INS	124	NTH→INS	150		176	USR→INS
21	BUR→JOR	47	CUB→JOR	73	IND→JOR	99	ISR→JOR	125	NTH→ISR	151		177	USR→ISR
22	BUR→NTH	48	CUB→NTH	74	IND→NTH	100	ISR→NTH	126	NTH→JOR	152		178	USR→JOR
23	BUR→POL	49	CUB→POL	75	IND→POL	101	ISR→POL	127	NTH→POL	153		179	USR→NTH
24	BUR→USR	50	CUB→USR	76	IND→USR	102	ISR→USR	128	NTH→USR	154		180	USR→POL
25	BUR→UK	51	CUB→UNK	77	IND→UNK	103	ISR→UNK	129	NTH→UNK	155		181	USR→UNK
26	BUR→USA	52	CUB→USA	78	IND→USA	104	ISR→USA	130	NTH→USA	156		182	USR→USA

-218-

SECTION II

APPENDIX B: NOTES

SECTION II

APPENDIX B: NOTES

SECTION II

APPENDIX B: NOTES

SECTION II
APPENDIX B: NOTES

-221-

BEHAVIOR OF NATION DYADS, 1950-1965: NOTES, VARIABLES 47-146

	1	47	48	49	50	51	67	68	69	70	71	72	73	74	75	76	142	143	144	145	146	1
	169	D		D	D	D																169
	170																					170
	171																A	A	A	A	A	171
	172																A	A	A	A	A	172
	173		A	B		B						C										173
	174																					174
	175			A																		175
	176																					176
	177																					177
	178																	A				178
	179																					179
	180			B		B																180
	181	L		D	D	D																181
	182																					182

KEY: Variable 1, the numbers on the extreme left and right of each page, represent the dyad number.

Nations Included in the Selected Dyadic Sample

Brazil=BRA Cuba=CUB Indonesia=INS Netherlands=NTH United Kingdom=UNK
Burma=BUR Egypt=EGP Israel=ISR Poland=POL USA=USA
China=CHN India=IND Jordan=JOR USSR=USR

1 BRA→BUR	27 CHN→BRA	53 CUB→BRA	79 EGP→BRA	105 INS→BRA	131 JOR→BRA	157 UNK→BRA
2 BRA→CHN	28 CHN→BUR	54 CUB→BUR	80 EGP→BUR	106 INS→BUR	132 JOR→BUR	158 UNK→BUR
3 BRA→CUB	29 CHN→CUB	55 CUB→CHN	81 EGP→CHN	107 INS→CHN	133 JOR→CHN	159 UNK→CHN
4 BRA→EGP	30 CHN→EGP	56 CUB→EGP	82 EGP→CUB	108 INS→CUB	134 JOR→CUB	160 UNK→CUB
5 BRA→IND	31 CHN→IND	57 CUB→IND	83 EGP→IND	109 INS→EGP	135 JOR→EGP	161 UNK→EGP
6 BRA→INS	32 CHN→INS	58 CUB→INS	84 EGP→INS	110 INS→IND	136 JOR→IND	162 UNK→IND
7 BRA→ISR	33 CHN→ISR	59 CUB→ISR	85 EGP→ISR	111 INS→ISR	137 JOR→INS	163 UNK→INS
8 BRA→JOR	34 CHN→JOR	60 CUB→JOR	86 EGP→JOR	112 IND→BRA	138 JOR→ISR	164 UNK→ISR
9 BRA→NTH	35 CHN→NTH	61 CUB→NTH	87 EGP→NTH	113 IND→BUR	139 JOR→NTH	165 UNK→JOR
10 BRA→POL	36 CHN→POL	62 CUB→POL	88 EGP→POL	114 IND→CHN	140 JOR→NTH	166 UNK→NTH
11 BRA→USR	37 CHN→USR	63 CUB→USR	89 EGP→USR	115 IND→CUB	141 JOR→POL	167 UNK→POL
12 BRA→UNK	38 CHN→UNK	64 CUB→UNK	90 EGP→UNK	116 IND→JNK	142 JOR→USR	168 UNK→USR
13 BRA→USA	39 CHN→USA	65 CUB→USA	91 EGP→USA	117 ISR→BRA	143 JOR→USA	169 UNK→USA
14 BUR→BRA	40 CUB→BRA	66 IND→BRA	92 ISR→BRA	118 NTH→BRA	144 NTH→BRA	170 USA→BRA
15 BUR→CHN	41 CUB→BRA	67 IND→BUR	93 ISR→BUR	119 NTH→BUR	145 NTH→BUR	171 USA→BUR
16 BUR→CUB	42 CUB→CHN	68 IND→CHN	94 ISR→CHN	120 NTH→CHN	146 NTH→CHN	172 USA→CHN
17 BUR→EGP	43 CUB→EGP	69 IND→CUB	95 ISR→CUB	121 NTH→CUB	147 NTH→CUB	173 USA→CUB
18 BUR→IND	44 CUB→IND	70 IND→EGP	96 ISR→EGP	122 NTH→EGP	148 NTH→EGP	174 USA→EGP
19 BUR→INS	45 CUB→INS	71 IND→INS	97 ISR→INS	123 NTH→IND	149 NTH→IND	175 USA→IND
20 BUR→ISR	46 CUB→ISR	72 IND→ISR	98 ISR→JOR	124 NTH→INS	150 NTH→INS	176 USA→INS
21 BUR→JOR	47 CUB→JOR	73 IND→JOR	99 ISR→JOR	125 NTH→ISR	151 NTH→ISR	177 USA→ISR
22 BUR→NTH	48 CUB→NTH	74 IND→NTH	100 ISR→NTH	126 NTH→JOR	152 NTH→JOR	178 USA→JOR
23 BUR→POL	49 CUB→POL	75 IND→POL	101 ISR→POL	127 NTH→POL	153 NTH→POL	179 USA→NTH
24 BUR→USR	50 CUB→USR	76 IND→USR	102 ISR→USR	128 NTH→USR	154 NTH→USR	180 USA→POL
25 BUR→UK	51 CUB→UNK	77 IND→UNK	103 ISR→UNK	129 NTH→UNK	155 NTH→UNK	181 USA→USR
26 BUR→USA	52 CUB→USA	78 IND→USA	104 ISR→USA	130 NTH→USA	156 NTH→USA	182 USA→UNK

-222-

SECTION II

APPENDIX B: NOTES

SECTION II

APPENDIX B: NOTES

SECTION II

APPENDIX B: NOTES

SECTION II -225-
APPENDIX B: NOTES

BEHAVIOR OF NATION DYADS, 1950-1965: NOTES, VARIABLES 147-165

	147	148	149	150	151	152	153	154	155	156	157	158	159	160	161	162	163	164	165	166
169																				
170	A	A	A	A	A	A	A	A	A	A						A				
171	A	A	A	A	A	A	A	A	A	A				B	B		A	A	A	A
172	A	A	A	A	A	A	A	A	A	A	B	B			A	A	A	A	A	A
173															A					
174										B	B	B			A					
175										B					A					
176										B					A					
177															A					
178					A						A	A	A	A	A	A	A	A	A	A
179										B					A	A			A	A
180										B					A	A			A	A
181																				
182																				

KEY: Variable 1, the numbers on the extreme left and right of each page, represent the dyad number.

Nations Included in the Selected Dyadic Sample

Brazil=BRA Cuba=CUB Indonesia=INS Netherlands=NTH United Kingdom=UNK
Burma=BUR Egypt=EGP Israel=ISR Poland=POL USA=USA
China=CHN India=IND Jordan=JOR USSR=USR

1	BRA→BUR	27	CHN→BRA	53	EGP→BRA	79	INS→BRA	105	JOR→BRA	131	POL→BRA	157	UNK→BRA
2	BRA→CHN	28	CHN→BUR	54	EGP→BUR	80	INS→BUR	106	JOR→BUR	132	POL→BUR	158	UNK→BUR
3	BRA→CUB	29	CHN→CUB	55	EGP→CHN	81	INS→CHN	107	JOR→CHN	133	POL→CHN	159	UNK→CHN
4	BRA→EGP	30	CHN→EGP	56	EGP→CUB	82	INS→CUB	108	JOR→CUB	134	POL→CUB	160	UNK→CUB
5	BRA→IND	31	CHN→IND	57	EGP→IND	83	INS→IND	109	JOR→EGP	135	POL→EGP	161	UNK→EGP
6	BRA→INS	32	CHN→INS	58	EGP→INS	84	INS→ISR	110	JOR→IND	136	POL→IND	162	UNK→IND
7	BRA→ISR	33	CHN→ISR	59	EGP→ISR	85	INS→JOR	111	JOR→INS	137	POL→INS	163	UNK→INS
8	BRA→JOR	34	CHN→JOR	60	EGP→JOR	86	INS→NTH	112	JOR→ISR	138	POL→ISR	164	UNK→ISR
9	BRA→NTH	35	CHN→NTH	61	EGP→NTH	87	IND→JOR	113	JOR→NTH	139	POL→NTH	165	UNK→JOR
10	BRA→POL	36	CHN→POL	62	EGP→POL	88	IND→NTH	114	JOR→POL	140	POL→JOR	166	UNK→NTH
11	BRA→USR	37	CHN→USR	63	EGP→USR	89	IND→POL	115	JOR→USR	141	POL→POL	167	UNK→POL
12	BRA→UNK	38	CHN→UNK	64	EGP→UNK	90	IND→USR	116	JOR→UNK	142	POL→USR	168	UNK→USR
13	BRA→USA	39	CHN→USA	65	EGP→USA	91	IND→UNK	117	JOR→USA	143	POL→UNK	169	UNK→USA
14	BUR→BRA	40	CUB→BRA	66	IND→BRA	92	IND→USA	118	NTH→BRA	144	POL→USA	170	USA→BRA
15	BUR→CHN	41	CUB→BUR	67	IND→BUR	93	ISR→BRA	119	NTH→BUR	145	USR→BRA	171	USA→BUR
16	BUR→CUB	42	CUB→CHN	68	IND→CUB	94	ISR→BUR	120	NTH→CHN	146	USR→BUR	172	USA→CHN
17	BUR→EGP	43	CUB→EGP	69	IND→CHN	95	ISR→CHN	121	NTH→CUB	147	USR→CHN	173	USA→CUB
18	BUR→IND	44	CUB→IND	70	IND→EGP	96	ISR→CUB	122	NTH→EGP	148	USR→CUB	174	USA→EGP
19	BUR→INS	45	CUB→INS	71	IND→INS	97	ISR→EGP	123	NTH→IND	149	USR→EGP	175	USA→IND
20	BUR→ISR	46	CUB→ISR	72	IND→ISR	98	ISR→IND	124	NTH→INS	150	USR→IND	176	USA→INS
21	BUR→JOR	47	CUB→JOR	73	IND→JOR	99	ISR→INS	125	NTH→ISR	151	USR→INS	177	USA→ISR
22	BUR→NTH	48	CUB→NTH	74	IND→NTH	100	ISR→JOR	126	NTH→JOR	152	USR→ISR	178	USA→JOR
23	BUR→POL	49	CUB→POL	75	IND→POL	101	ISR→NTH	127	NTH→POL	153	USR→JOR	179	USA→NTH
24	BUR→USR	50	CUB→USR	76	IND→USR	102	ISR→POL	128	NTH→USR	154	USR→NTH	180	USA→POL
25	BUR→UK	51	CUB→UNK	77	IND→UNK	103	ISR→UNK	129	NTH→UNK	155	USR→POL	181	USA→USR
26	BUR→USA	52	CUB→USA	78	IND→USA	104	ISR→USA	130	NTH→USA	156	USR→USA	182	USA→UNK

SECTION II

APPENDIX B: NOTES

SECTION II

APPENDIX B: NOTES

-227-

SECTION II

APPENDIX B: NOTES

SECTION II

APPENDIX B: NOTES

-230-

SECTION II

APPENDIX B: NOTES

SECTION II

APPENDIX B: NOTES

SECTION II
APPENDIX B: NOTES

BEHAVIOR OF NATION DYADS, 1950-1965: NOTES, VARIABLES 192-236

	192	196	197	199	200	202	203	204	217	219	227	228	229	230	231	232	233	234	235	236	
113	A																				113
114	A																				114
115	A																				115
116	A																				116
117	A																				117
118																					**118**
119			A	A		A		A	A												119
120																					120
121																					121
122																					**122**
124																					124
125		A																			125
126	A																				126
127																					**127**
128																					**128**
129																					129
130																					130
131	A																				131
132																					**132**
133	A		A						A												133
134	A																				134
135	A																				135
136																					136
137	A																				137
138																					**138**
139	B																				139
140																					140
141																					141
142																					**142**
144	A																				144
145	A		A	A		A		A	A												145
146																					146
147	F																				**147**
148																					**148**
149	A																				149
150			A																		150
151																					151
152	A																				**152**
153																					153
154														A							154
155																					155
156																					156
157																					157
158						A		A	A	A		A	G	H	G		A	A	A	A	**158**
159													G	H	G			A	A	A	159
160													A	H	G			A	A	A	160
161													G	H	G			A	A	A	161
162													A	H	G			A	A	A	**162**
163													A	H	G	A		A	A	A	163
164													G	H	G			A	A	A	164
165													G	H	G			A	A	A	165
166		A											G	H	G			A	A	A	166
167													G	H	G			A	A	A	**167**
168													A	H	G			A	A	A	**168**

SECTION II
APPENDIX B: NOTES   -233-

BEHAVIOR OF NATION DYADS, 1950-1965: NOTES, VARIABLES 192-236

#	192	196	197	199	200	202	203	204	217	219	227	228	229	230	231	232	233	234	235	236
169																				
170														A	G			A	A	A
171														A	G			A		A
172			A	A					A	A	A				G					
173															G					
174															G			A	A	A
175															G			A		A
176															G			A	A	A
177							A				A				G			A		A
178	A														G	A		A		A
179															G			A		A
180															G			A		A
181															G			A		A
182															G			A	A	A

KEY: Variable 1, the numbers on the extreme left and right of each page, represent the dyad number.

Brazil=BRA Cuba=CUB Indonesia=INS Netherlands=NTH United Kingdom=UNK
Burma=BUR   Egypt=EGP Israel=ISR   Poland=POL   USA=USA
China=CHN   India=IND Jordan=JOR   USSR=USR

Nations Included in the Selected Dyadic Sample

1	BRA→BUR	27	CHN→BRA	53	EGP→BRA	79	INS→BRA	105	JOR→BRA	131	NTH→BRA	157	POL→BRA		UNK→BRA
2	BRA→CHN	28	CHN→BUR	54	EGP→BUR	80	INS→BUR	106	JOR→BUR	132	NTH→BUR	158	POL→BUR		UNK→BUR
3	BRA→CUB	29	CHN→CUB	55	EGP→CHN	81	INS→CHN	107	JOR→CHN	133	NTH→CHN	159	POL→CHN		UNK→CHN
4	BRA→EGP	30	CHN→EGP	56	EGP→CUB	82	INS→CUB	108	JOR→CUB	134	NTH→CUB	160	POL→CUB		UNK→CUB
5	BRA→IND	31	CHN→IND	57	EGP→IND	83	INS→IND	109	JOR→EGP	135	NTH→EGP	161	POL→EGP		UNK→EGP
6	BRA→INS	32	CHN→INS	58	EGP→INS	84	INS→EGP	110	JOR→IND	136	NTH→IND	162	POL→IND		UNK→IND
7	BRA→ISR	33	CHN→ISR	59	EGP→ISR	85	INS→ISR	111	JOR→INS	137	NTH→INS	163	POL→INS		UNK→INS
8	BRA→JOR	34	CHN→JOR	60	EGP→JOR	86	IND→JOR	112	JOR→ISR	138	NTH→ISR	164	POL→ISR		UNK→ISR
9	BRA→NTH	35	CHN→NTH	61	EGP→NTH	87	IND→NTH	113	JOR→NTH	139	NTH→JOR	165	POL→JOR		UNK→JOR
10	BRA→POL	36	CHN→POL	62	EGP→POL	88	IND→POL	114	JOR→POL	140	NTH→POL	166	POL→NTH		UNK→NTH
11	BRA→USR	37	CHN→USR	63	EGP→USR	89	IND→USR	115	JOR→USR	141	NTH→USR	167	POL→USR		UNK→POL
12	BRA→UNK	38	CHN→UNK	64	EGP→UNK	90	IND→UNK	116	JOR→UNK	142	NTH→UNK	168	POL→UNK		UNK→USR
13	BRA→USA	39	CHN→USA	65	EGP→USA	91	IND→USA	117	JOR→USA	143	NTH→USA	169	POL→USA		UNK→USA
14	BUR→BRA	40	CUB→BRA	66	IND→BRA	92	ISR→BRA	118		144		170	USR→BRA		USA→BRA
15	BUR→CHN	41	CUB→BUR	67	IND→BUR	93	ISR→BUR	119		145		171	USR→BUR		USA→BUR
16	BUR→CUB	42	CUB→CHN	68	IND→CHN	94	ISR→CHN	120		146		172	USR→CHN		USA→CHN
17	BUR→EGP	43	CUB→EGP	69	IND→CUB	95	ISR→CUB	121		147		173	USR→CUB		USA→CUB
18	BUR→IND	44	CUB→IND	70	IND→EGP	96	ISR→EGP	122		148		174	USR→EGP		USA→EGP
19	BUR→INS	45	CUB→INS	71	IND→INS	97	ISR→IND	123		149		175	USR→IND		USA→IND
20	BUR→ISR	46	CUB→ISR	72	IND→ISR	98	ISR→INS	124		150		176	USR→INS		USA→INS
21	BUR→JOR	47	CUB→JOR	73	IND→JOR	99	ISR→JOR	125		151		177	USR→ISR		USA→ISR
22	BUR→NTH	48	CUB→NTH	74	IND→NTH	100	ISR→NTH	126		152		178	USR→JOR		USA→JOR
23	BUR→POL	49	CUB→POL	75	IND→POL	101	ISR→POL	127		153		179	USR→NTH		USA→NTH
24	BUR→USR	50	CUB→USR	76	IND→USR	102	ISR→USR	128		154		180	USR→POL		USA→POL
25	BUR→UK	51	CUB→UNK	77	IND→UNK	103	ISR→UNK	129		155		181	USR→UNK		USA→USR
26	BUR→USA	52	CUB→USA	78	IND→USA	104	ISR→USA	130		156		182	USR→USA		USA→UNK

SECTION II

APPENDIX B: NOTES

SECTION II

APPENDIX B: NOTES

SECTION II
APPENDIX B: NOTES

SECTION II
APPENDIX B: NOTES

BEHAVIOR OF NATION DYADS, 1950-1965: NOTES, VARIABLES 237-251

	237	238	239	240	241	242	243	244	245	246	247	248	249	250	251
169									A		A				
170	A		A	A	A			A		A					
171															
172								A		A					
173															
174								A							
175								A							
176															
177								A		A					
178						A		A							
179						A		A							
180															
181			A												
182															

KEY: Variable 1, the numbers on the extreme left and right of each page, represent the dyad number.

Nations Included in the Selected Dyadic Sample

Brazil=BRA Cuba=CUB Indonesia=INS Netherlands=NTH United Kingdom=UNK
Burma=BUR   Egypt=EGP Israel=ISR   Poland=POL   USA=USA
China=CHN   India=IND Jordan=JOR   USSR=USR

1	BRA→BUR	27	CHN→BRA	53	EGP→BRA	79	INS→BRA	105
2	BRA→CHN	28	CHN→BUR	54	EGP→BUR	80	INS→BUR	106
3	BRA→CUB	29	CHN→CUB	55	EGP→CHN	81	INS→CHN	107
4	BRA→EGP	30	CHN→EGP	56	EGP→CUB	82	INS→CUB	108
5	BRA→IND	31	CHN→IND	57	EGP→IND	83	INS→EGP	109
6	BRA→INS	32	CHN→INS	58	EGP→INS	84	INS→IND	110
7	BRA→ISR	33	CHN→ISR	59	EGP→ISR	85	INS→ISR	111
8	BRA→JOR	34	CHN→JOR	60	EGP→JOR	86	INS→JOR	112
9	BRA→NTH	35	CHN→NTH	61	EGP→NTH	87	INS→NTH	113
10	BRA→POL	36	CHN→POL	62	EGP→POL	88	IND→POL	114
11	BRA→USR	37	CHN→USR	63	EGP→USR	89	IND→USR	115
12	BRA→UNK	38	CHN→UNK	64	EGP→UNK	90	IND→UNK	116
13	BRA→USA	39	CHN→USA	65	EGP→USA	91	IND→USA	117
14	BUR→BRA	40	CUB→BRA	66	IND→BRA	92	ISR→BRA	118
15	BUR→CHN	41	CUB→BUR	67	IND→BUR	93	ISR→BUR	119
16	BUR→CUB	42	CUB→CHN	68	IND→CHN	94	ISR→CHN	120
17	BUR→EGP	43	CUB→EGP	69	IND→CUB	95	ISR→CUB	121
18	BUR→IND	44	CUB→IND	70	IND→EGP	96	ISR→EGP	122
19	BUR→INS	45	CUB→INS	71	IND→INS	97	ISR→IND	123
20	BUR→ISR	46	CUB→ISR	72	IND→ISR	98	ISR→INS	124
21	BUR→JOR	47	CUB→JOR	73	IND→JOR	99	ISR→JOR	125
22	BUR→NTH	48	CUB→NTH	74	IND→NTH	100	ISR→NTH	126
23	BUR→POL	49	CUB→POL	75	IND→POL	101	ISR→POL	127
24	BUR→USR	50	CUB→USR	76	IND→USR	102	ISR→USR	128
25	BUR→UK	51	CUB→UNK	77	IND→UNK	103	ISR→UNK	129
26	BUR→USA	52	CUB→USA	78	IND→USA	104	ISR→USA	130

131	JOR→BRA	157	POL→BRA
132	JOR→BUR	158	POL→BUR
133	JOR→CHN	159	POL→CHN
134	JOR→CUB	160	POL→CUB
135	JOR→EGP	161	POL→EGP
136	JOR→IND	162	POL→IND
137	JOR→INS	163	POL→INS
138	JOR→ISR	164	POL→ISR
139	JOR→NTH	165	POL→JOR
140	JOR→POL	166	POL→NTH
141	JOR→USR	167	POL→USR
142	JOR→UNK	168	POL→UNK
143	JOR→USA	169	POL→USA
144	NTH→BRA	170	USR→BRA
145	NTH→BUR	171	USR→CHN
146	NTH→CHN	172	USR→CUB
147	NTH→CUB	173	USR→EGP
148	NTH→EGP	174	USR→IND
149	NTH→IND	175	USR→INS
150	NTH→INS	176	USR→ISR
151	NTH→ISR	177	USR→JOR
152	NTH→JOR	178	USR→NTH
153	NTH→POL	179	USR→POL
154	NTH→USR	180	USR→UNK
155	NTH→UNK	181	USR→USA
156	NTH→USA	182	

UNK→BRA	
UNK→BUR	
UNK→CHN	
UNK→CUB	
UNK→EGP	
UNK→IND	
UNK→INS	
UNK→ISR	
UNK→JOR	
UNK→NTH	
UNK→POL	
UNK→USR	
UNK→USA	
USA→BRA	
USA→BUR	
USA→CHN	
USA→CUB	
USA→EGP	
USA→IND	
USA→INS	
USA→ISR	
USA→JOR	
USA→NTH	
USA→POL	
USA→USR	
USA→UNK	

-237-

SECTION II

APPENDIX B: NOTES

SECTION II

APPENDIX B: NOTES

SECTION II

APPENDIX B: NOTES

SECTION II -241-
APPENDIX B: NOTES

BEHAVIOR OF NATION DYADS, 1950-1965: NOTES, VARIABLES 252-266

1	252	253	255	256	258	260	261	262	266	1
169										169
170										170
171										171
172										172
173										173
174										174
175										175
176										176
177										177
178										178
179										179
180										180
181										181
182										182

KEY: Variable 1, the numbers on the extreme left and right of each page, represent the dyad number.

Nations Included in the Selected Dyadic Sample

Brazil=BRA   Cuba=CUB   Indonesia=INS   Netherlands=NTH   United Kingdom=UNK
Burma=BUR   Egypt=EGP   Israel=ISR   Poland=POL   USA=USA
China=CHN   India=IND   Jordan=JOR   USSR=USR

#	Dyad	#	Dyad	#	Dyad	#	Dyad	#	Dyad	#	Dyad
1	BRA→BUR	27	CHN→BRA	53	EGP→BRA	79	INS→BRA	105	JOR→BRA	131	NTH→BRA
2	BRA→CHN	28	CHN→BUR	54	EGP→BUR	80	INS→BUR	106	JOR→BUR	132	NTH→BUR
3	BRA→CUB	29	CHN→CUB	55	EGP→CHN	81	INS→CHN	107	JOR→CHN	133	NTH→CHN
4	BRA→EGP	30	CHN→EGP	56	EGP→CUB	82	INS→CUB	108	JOR→CUB	134	NTH→CUB
5	BRA→IND	31	CHN→IND	57	EGP→IND	83	INS→EGP	109	JOR→EGP	135	NTH→EGP
6	BRA→INS	32	CHN→INS	58	EGP→INS	84	INS→IND	110	JOR→IND	136	NTH→IND
7	BRA→ISR	33	CHN→ISR	59	EGP→ISR	85	INS→ISR	111	JOR→INS	137	NTH→INS
8	BRA→JOR	34	CHN→JOR	60	EGP→JOR	86	INS→JOR	112	JOR→ISR	138	NTH→ISR
9	BRA→NTH	35	CHN→NTH	61	EGP→NTH	87	IND→JOR	113	JOR→NTH	139	NTH→JOR
10	BRA→POL	36	CHN→POL	62	EGP→POL	88	IND→NTH	114	JOR→POL	140	NTH→NTH
11	BRA→USR	37	CHN→USR	63	EGP→USR	89	IND→POL	115	JOR→USR	141	NTH→POL
12	BRA→UNK	38	CHN→UNK	64	EGP→UNK	90	IND→USR	116	JOR→UNK	142	NTH→USR
13	BRA→USA	39	CHN→USA	65	EGP→USA	91	IND→UNK	117	JOR→USA	143	NTH→UNK
14	BUR→BRA	40	CUB→BRA	66	IND→BRA	92	IND→USA	118	NTH→BRA	144	NTH→USA
15	BUR→CHN	41	CUB→BUR	67	IND→BUR	93	ISR→BRA	119	NTH→BUR	145	USR→BUR
16	BUR→CUB	42	CUB→CHN	68	IND→CHN	94	ISR→BUR	120	NTH→CHN	146	USR→CHN
17	BUR→EGP	43	CUB→EGP	69	IND→CUB	95	ISR→CHN	121	NTH→CUB	147	USR→CUB
18	BUR→IND	44	CUB→IND	70	IND→EGP	96	ISR→CUB	122	NTH→EGP	148	USR→EGP
19	BUR→INS	45	CUB→INS	71	IND→INS	97	ISR→EGP	123	NTH→IND	149	USR→IND
20	BUR→ISR	46	CUB→ISR	72	IND→ISR	98	ISR→IND	124	NTH→INS	150	USR→INS
21	BUR→JOR	47	CUB→JOR	73	IND→JOR	99	ISR→INS	125	NTH→ISR	151	USR→ISR
22	BUR→NTH	48	CUB→NTH	74	IND→NTI	100	ISR→NTH	126	NTH→JOR	152	USR→JOR
23	BUR→POL	49	CUB→POL	75	IND→POL	101	ISR→POL	127	NTH→POL	153	USR→NTH
24	BUR→USR	50	CUB→USR	76	IND→USR	102	ISR→USR	128	NTH→USR	154	USR→POL
25	BUR→UK	51	CUB→UNK	77	IND→UNK	103	ISR→UNK	129	NTH→UNK	155	USR→UNK
26	BUR→USA	52	CUB→USA	78	IND→USA	104	ISR→USA	130	NTH→USA	156	USR→USA

#	Dyad	#	Dyad
157	POL→BRA		UNK→BRA
158	POL→BUR		UNK→BUR
159	POL→CHN		UNK→CHN
160	POL→CUB		UNK→CUB
161	POL→EGP		UNK→EGP
162	POL→IND		UNK→IND
163	POL→INS		UNK→INS
164	POL→ISR		UNK→ISR
165	POL→JOR		UNK→JOR
166	POL→NTH		UNK→NTH
167	POL→USR		UNK→POL
168	POL→UNK		UNK→USR
169	POL→USA		UNK→USA
170	USR→BRA		USA→BRA
171	USR→BUR		USA→BUR
172	USR→CHN		USA→CHN
173	USR→CUB		USA→CUB
174	USR→EGP		USA→EGP
175	USR→IND		USA→IND
176	USR→INS		USA→INS
177	USR→ISR		USA→ISR
178	USR→JOR		USA→JOR
179	USR→NTH		USA→NTH
180	USR→POL		USA→POL
181	USR→UNK		USA→USR
182	USR→USA		USA→UNK